The Brain in a Vat

The scenario of the brain in a vat, first aired thirty-five years ago in Hilary Putnam's classic paper, has been deeply influential in philosophy of mind and language, epistemology, and metaphysics. This collection of new essays examines the scenario and its philosophical ramifications and applications, as well as the challenges which it has faced. The essays review historical applications of the brain-in-a-vat scenario and consider its impact on contemporary debates. They explore a diverse range of philosophical issues, from intentionality, external-world skepticism, and the nature of truth, to the extended mind hypothesis, reference magnetism, and new versions of realism. The volume will be a rich and valuable resource for advanced students in metaphysics, epistemology, and philosophy of mind and language, as well as for anyone interested in the relations between language, thought, and the world.

Sanford C. Goldberg is Professor of Philosophy and Chair of the Department of Philosophy at Northwestern University, Illinois, and for 2012–15 he was Professorial Fellow in the Department of Philosophy and Eidyn Research Centre at the University of Edinburgh, Scotland. He is the author of *Anti-Individualism: Mind and Language, Knowledge and Justification* (Cambridge, 2007), *Relying on Others: An Essay in Epistemology* (2010) and *Assertion: A Philosophical Essay on Assertoric Speech* (2015). He is also the editor of *Internalism and Externalism in Semantics and Epistemology* (2007) and *Externalism, Self-Knowledge, and Skepticism: New Essays* (Cambridge, 2015).

Classic Philosophical Arguments

Over the centuries, a number of individual arguments have formed a crucial part of philosophical enquiry. The volumes in this series examine these arguments, looking at the ramifications and applications which they have come to have, the challenges which they have encountered, and the ways in which they have stood the test of time.

Titles in the series

The Prisoner's Dilemma
Edited by Martin Peterson

The Original Position
Edited by Timothy Hinton

The Brain in a Vat
Edited by Sanford C. Goldberg

The Brain in a Vat

Edited by
Sanford C. Goldberg

CAMBRIDGE
UNIVERSITY PRESS

Shaftesbury Road, Cambridge CB2 8EA, United Kingdom

One Liberty Plaza, 20th Floor, New York, NY 10006, USA

477 Williamstown Road, Port Melbourne, VIC 3207, Australia

314–321, 3rd Floor, Plot 3, Splendor Forum, Jasola District Centre, New Delhi – 110025, India

103 Penang Road, #05–06/07, Visioncrest Commercial, Singapore 238467

Cambridge University Press is part of Cambridge University Press & Assessment, a department of the University of Cambridge.

We share the University's mission to contribute to society through the pursuit of education, learning and research at the highest international levels of excellence.

www.cambridge.org
Information on this title: www.cambridge.org/9781107643383

© Cambridge University Press & Assessment 2016

This publication is in copyright. Subject to statutory exception and to the provisions of relevant collective licensing agreements, no reproduction of any part may take place without the written permission of Cambridge University Press & Assessment.

First published 2016

A catalogue record for this publication is available from the British Library

Library of Congress Cataloging-in-Publication data
The brain in a vat / edited by Sanford C. Goldberg.
    pages   cm. – (Classic philosophical arguments)
ISBN 978-1-107-64338-3
1. Philosophy of mind.   2. Metaphysics.   3. Knowledge, Theory of.   I. Goldberg, Sanford, 1967– editor.
BD418.3.B723   2016
128′.2–dc23   2015026793

ISBN   978-1-107-06967-1   Hardback
ISBN   978-1-107-64338-3   Paperback

Cambridge University Press & Assessment has no responsibility for the persistence or accuracy of URLs for external or third-party internet websites referred to in this publication and does not guarantee that any content on such websites is, or will remain, accurate or appropriate.

Contents

List of contributors		*page* vii
Acknowledgments		ix
1.	Introduction: Putnam's reflections on the brain in a vat Sanford C. Goldberg	1
Part I:	**Intentionality and the philosophy of mind and language**	**17**
2.	Putnam on brains in a vat Tony Brueckner	19
3.	How to think about whether we are brains in vats Gary Ebbs	27
4.	Brains in vats, causal constraints on reference and semantic externalism Jesper Kallestrup	37
5.	Extended minds in vats Sven Bernecker	54
Part II:	**Epistemology**	**73**
6.	Putnam on BIVs and radical skepticism Duncan Pritchard and Chris Ranalli	75
7.	New lessons from old demons: the case for reliabilism Thomas Grundmann	90
8.	BIVs, sensitivity, discrimination, and relevant alternatives Kelly Becker	111
Part III:	**Metaphysics**	**129**
9.	Brains in vats and model theory Tim Button	131

10. Realism, skepticism, and the brain in a vat 155
    Janet Folina

11. Rethinking semantic naturalism 174
    Igor Douven

12. Internal to what? Contemporary naturalism and Putnam's
    model-theoretic argument 190
    Patricia Marino

13. The model-theoretic argument: from skepticism to
    a new understanding 208
    Gila Sher

14. Eligibility and ideology in the vat 226
    Tim Sundell

    Bibliography 251
    Index 265

Contributors

Kelly Becker is Professor of Philosophy at the University of New Mexico. He has published many articles on epistemology and the philosophy of mind and language, and is the author of *Epistemology Modalized* (2007) and co-editor of *The Sensitivity Principle in Epistemology* (with Tim Black, Cambridge, 2012).

Sven Bernecker is Professor of Philosophy at the University of California at Irvine. He is the co-editor of several volumes and the author of *Memory: A Philosophical Study* (2010), *The Metaphysics of Memory* (2008), and *Reading Epistemology* (2006).

Tony Brueckner was Professor of Philosophy at the University of California at Santa Barbara. He published more than 150 articles in leading journals and was author of *Essays on Skepticism* (2010) and *Debating Self-Knowledge* (with Gary Ebbs, Cambridge, 2012).

Tim Button is University Lecturer and a Fellow of St John's College, at the University of Cambridge. He is the author of *The Limits of Realism* (2013), and publishes mostly within metaphysics, logic and the philosophy of mathematics.

Igor Douven is Research Director of the French National Centre for Scientific Research. He has published extensively in leading journals, on topics in epistemology, metaphysics, philosophy of science and philosophy of language.

Gary Ebbs is Professor of Philosophy at Indiana University. He is author of *Rule-Following and Realism* (1997), *Truth and Words* (2009), and *Debating Self-Knowledge* (with Anthony Brueckner, Cambridge, 2012).

Janet Folina is Professor of Philosophy at Macalester College. She is the author of *Poincaré and the Philosophy of Mathematics* (1992) and many articles in leading journals on symbolic logic, philosophy of math, and philosophy of science.

Sanford C. Goldberg is Professor of Philosophy and Chair of the Philosophy Department at Northwestern University. He is author of *Anti-Individualism: Mind and Language, Knowledge and Justification* (Cambridge, 2007), *Relying on Others: An Essay in Epistemology* (2010), and *Assertion: A Philosophical Essay on Assertoric Speech* (2015).

Thomas Grundmann is Professor of Philosophy at the University of Cologne. He is the author of *Analytische Einführung in die Erkenntnistheorie* (2008), *Der Wahrheit auf der Spur: Ein Plädoyer für den erkenntnistheoretischen Externalismus* (2003), *Analytische Transzendentalphilosophie: Eine Kritik* (1994), and is co-editor of *Experimental Philosophy and its Critics* (with Joachim Korvath, 2012).

Jesper Kallestrup is Professor of Philosophy at the University of Edinburgh. He is the author of *Semantic Externalism* (2011), and is co-editor of *New Waves in Philosophy of Mind* (with Mark Sprevak, 2014) and *Being Reduced: New Essays on Reduction and Explanation* (with Jakob Hohwy, 2008).

Patricia Marino is Associate Professor of Philosophy at the University of Waterloo. She is the author of *Moral Reasoning in a Pluralistic World* (2015) as well as many articles in leading journals on topics in ethics, epistemology, the philosophy of sex and love, the theory of truth, and the philosophy of economics.

Duncan Pritchard holds the Chair in Epistemology and is Professor of Philosophy at the University of Edinburgh. He is author of *Epistemic Luck* (2005), *Epistemological Disjunctivism* (2012), *Epistemic Angst: Radical Skepticism and the Groundlessness of Our Believing* (2015) and co-author of *The Nature and Value of Knowledge: Three Investigations* (with Adrian Haddock and Alan Millar, 2010).

Chris Ranalli is a postdoctoral fellow at the National Autonomous University of Mexico (UNAM). He has authored and co-authored several articles on epistemic luck and skepticism.

Gila Sher is Professor of Philosophy at the University of California at San Diego. Her publications include *The Bounds of Logic: A Generalized Viewpoint* (1991), *Between Logic and Intuition: Essays in Honor of Charles Parsons* (co-edited with Richard Tieszen, Cambridge, 2000), and *Epistemic Friction: An Essay on Knowledge, Truth, and Logic* (2016).

Tim Sundell is Assistant Professor of Philosophy at the University of Kentucky. He has published articles on the philosophy of language, aesthetics, metaethics, and philosophical and linguistic methodology.

Acknowledgments

I first encountered Hilary Putnam's reflections on the brain-in-a-vat (BIV) scenario as a graduate student in one of Sidney Morgenbesser's courses in the early 1990s. I was quickly convinced of the significance of these reflections. Partly this was due to the power of Putnam's writing and the provocativeness of his conclusions in *Reason, Truth, and History* (including in the "Brains in a Vat" chapter). But it was also due in part to the twinkle in my teacher's eyes and the devious look on his face when, on those blustery autumnal days on the seventh floor of Columbia's Philosophy Hall, Morgenbesser ruminated on what could be said or thought if the BIV scenario were actual. (Then again, maybe it was the way Morgenbesser managed to connect the BIV scenario, now to the centerfield play of Yankees' great Joe Dimaggio, now to the interpretative debates surrounding the story of the Israelites' exodus from Egypt, now to the (by then) long-overdue fourth chapter of my dissertation.) But I pondered the BIV scenario even out of the classroom. To this day, one of my most cherished memories from graduate school remains going out to dinner with both Putnam and Morgenbesser (and several others) one evening after Putnam delivered one of his Dewey Lectures (subsequently published by Columbia University Press as *The Threefold Cord: Mind, Body, and World*). Since Putnam was still grappling at the time with the issues surrounding his "internal realism," those of us at dinner that night had the opportunity to discern the lingering effects of the BIV scenario on Putnam's thinking. It should come as no surprise, then, that the two greatest debts in my own thinking on these matters are to Hilary Putnam and to Sidney Morgenbesser. (I still can't read "Brains in Vats" without thinking of those twinkling eyes and that devious grin – let alone Dimaggio and the Israelite exodus.)

I have continued to think about the BIV scenario over the years, during which time I have benefited profoundly from relevant discussions with many people. With apologies to those I have forgotten to name, these people include Kelly Becker, Paul Boghossian, Jessica Brown, Tony Brueckner, Gary Ebbs, Sean Ebels-Duggan, Kati Farkas, Brie Gertler, Alvin Goldman, Peter Graham, Thomas Grundmann, David Henderson, Terry Horgan, Henry Jackman, Jesper Kallestrup, Jennifer Lackey, Jack Lyons, Brian McLaughlin, Susana Nuccetelli, Duncan Pritchard, Baron Reed, Sarah Sawyer, Ernie Sosa, Åsa Wikforss, Crispin Wright, and no doubt others; I would like to express my gratitude to all of them.

As always, I would also like to thank Hilary Gaskin, editor at Cambridge University Press. She suggested the idea for this volume and encouraged me to take it on, and I am grateful to her for her support, encouragement, and patience in seeing this come to fruition. I am also grateful to Rosemary Crawley and to the many other good people at Cambridge University Press, with whom it is always a pleasure to work.

Finally, I would like to thank my wife and best friend, Judy, and my children, Gideon, Ethan, and Nadia, for putting up with me – even during periods in which it seems that all I want to talk about are brains in vats (which, I have learned, is not good dinner conversation).

I dedicate this book, with love, to my father, Allen Goldberg, who, though not a philosopher in the narrow (academic) sense of the word, has pondered central issues in metaphysics and epistemology for longer than I have walked this earth. I continue to remain uncertain, however, whether he knows that he is not a brain in a vat.

1 Introduction: Putnam's reflections on the brain in a vat

Sanford C. Goldberg

1.1

In 1981, Hilary Putnam published a paper entitled "Brains in a Vat." In it, he reflected on a "science fiction possibility discussed by philosophers," which he describes as follows:

> a human being (you can imagine this to be yourself) has been subjected to an operation by an evil scientist. The person's brain (your brain) has been removed from the body and placed in a vat of nutrients which keeps the brain alive. The nerve endings have been connected to a super-scientific computer which causes the person whose brain it is to have the illusion that everything is perfectly normal. There seem to be people, objects, the sky, etc; but really all the person (you) is experiencing is the result of electronic impulses travelling from the computer to the nerve endings. The computer is so clever that if the person tries to raise his hand, the feedback from the computer will cause him to 'see' and 'feel' the hand being raised. Moreover, by varying the program, the evil scientist can cause the victim to 'experience' (or hallucinate) any situation or environment the evil scientist wishes. He can also obliterate the memory of the brain operation, so that the victim will seem to himself to have always been in this environment. It can even seem to the victim that he is sitting and reading these very words about the amusing but quite absurd supposition that there is an evil scientist who removes people's brains from their bodies and places them in a vat of nutrients which keep the brains alive. The nerve endings are supposed to be connected to a super-scientific computer which causes the person whose brain it is to have the illusion that ... (Putnam 1981b: 5–6)

This scenario, which will henceforth be called the brain-in-a-vat (or BIV) scenario, has generated a tremendous amount of philosophical commentary in the more than three decades since its publication.

Putnam's reflections on the BIV scenario have a familiar historical precedent, of course, in Descartes's reflections on the Evil Demon scenario. As Descartes had described that scenario in *Meditations on a First Philosophy*, an Evil Demon who is as evil as he is powerful aims to dupe you as much as possible, and so stimulates your mind so as to give you normal-seeming sensations and "experiences," under conditions in which there is no world beyond your mind at all (just the Evil Demon). Descartes employed the thought experiment in the course of employing the method of *systematic doubt*, through which he hoped to discern the "foundations" of all that he knew. Through this method he aimed to rid himself of any belief that was dubitable – any belief that *could* be doubted – until such time as he could certify the truth of the belief (in which case, and only in which case, he would endorse the belief). Accordingly, the Evil Demon scenario served two purposes for Descartes. The first was that it enabled him to determine the extent of what could be doubted: any belief that the Demon could render false is a belief that could be doubted. On reflection, it turned out that this included the belief in a world external to one's own mind, and the corresponding belief in the existence of objects and properties in that world. The second purpose served by the Evil Demon scenario was that of a heuristic. Having the Evil Demon in mind was a constant reminder that Descartes needed to take care not to simply endorse what he found himself naturally believing: here the thought of the possibility of an Evil Demon reminded him of the need for constant vigilance, lest he allow to slip into his system something that could be doubted (and hence might be false).

In contrast to Descartes's primarily epistemological motivations, Putnam's aim in reflecting on the BIV scenario was to defend some points about the nature of intentionality and related matters – in particular, (mental and linguistic) reference and representation. He asked the question, "Could we, if we were brains in a vat in this way, *say* or *think* that we were?" (7; original italics) The burden of his argument was to answer this in the negative. At the same time, he anticipated that his argument would have some implications not only for semantics and the philosophy of mind and language but also for epistemology (the nature and limits of our knowledge of the world; the nature of our knowledge of the meanings of our language and the contents of our thought) and metaphysics (metaphysical realism; the nature of truth).

Putnam's argument for the conclusion that a BIV could not say or think that it was a BIV appealed to the conditions on reference. Starting the paper off by repudiating what he called the "magical theory of reference," Putnam went on to argue that for a subject to be able to refer to an object or a property in thought or speech requires some sort of *causal contact* with the object or property. With this condition on reference in place, Putnam contends, neither a BIV nor an unenvatted (English-speaking) subject can say or think a truth with "I am a BIV." Consider first the BIV. Because the BIV is not in causal contact with the items of our ordinary environment – no tables, trees, or turtles exist in its environment – the causal contact principle forces us to hold that, when a BIV speaks of "tables" or "trees" or "turtles," we must regard its thought and talk as regarding something *other than* tables or trees or turtles. Perhaps it is referring to internal features of the computer. Alternatively, perhaps it is referring to features of its sensory or "perceptual" experiences: not trees, but whatever it is in the envatted circumstance that causally prompts the BIV's uses of "tree" – say, trees-in-the-mental-image; not tables, but tables-in-the-mental-image; not turtles, but turtles-in-the-mental-image. But the same point holds for a BIV's use of "brain in a vat": since it has not been in causal contact with any such thing, when it thinks "I am a brain in a vat," it should not be construed as referring to (or representing itself as) a brain in a vat, but as something else – in which case its thought is *false*. Of course, if the subject is an ordinary (unenvatted) English-speaking subject, then, while such a subject can use "brain in a vat" to refer to or pick out a brain in a vat, even so, the thought such a subject expresses with "I am a BIV" – namely, the thought that she herself is a BIV – is false. So we see that the thought expressed by "I am a BIV" is false whether the subject is a BIV or an ordinary (English-speaking) subject. Since this argument is perfectly general – the conclusion depends only on generic considerations about the nature of mental and linguistic reference in any natural language – the result is that *no one can truly think of oneself that one is a BIV*. Or so Putnam argued.

It is worth noting that, as offering an argument for a causal contact condition on linguistic representation, Putnam's paper "Brains in a Vat" reinforced a conclusion he had already famously advanced in his 1975 paper "The Meaning of 'Meaning.'" In that paper Putnam had sought to show that "meanings ain't in the head," by which he meant that the meanings of our words depend for their individuation on facts that are "external" to the speaker's bodily states. Putnam's preferred formulation of this claim appealed to the possibility of two doppelgängers – subjects who are type-identical as far as the history of their bodily states goes, and whose phenomenological experiences are subjectively indistinguishable. In these terms, the thesis that meanings "ain't in the head" was formulated as the thesis that there could be two doppelgängers who, owing to having grown up in different environments, think different thoughts when each thinks a thought which he would express with "Water is thirst-quenching": one of them refers to (linguistically represents) *water* (H$_2$O) as being thirst-quenching, the other refers to (linguistically represents) *another liquid* – call it twin-water (which shares superficial qualities with water, but which is of a different chemical kind) – as thirst-quenching. This difference in the meaning of 'water' in their respective idiolects reflects differences in the liquid kinds with which they have interacted in their respective environments: one has applied 'water' to water, the other has applied 'water' to the other (water-like) liquid kind. These facts about the environmental differences are relevant to determining what each doppelgänger means by 'water'; hence the meaning of 'water' "ain't in the head" (of either one). Such a view came to be known as a *semantic externalist* view about linguistic meaning.

In comparison with Putnam's (1975) argument for semantic externalism, two developments are noteworthy with respect to the (1981) argument in "Brains in a Vat." The first is that the 1981 argument extended the semantically externalist conclusion beyond the case of linguistic meaning, to the contents of thought. Those familiar with the history of these discussions will know that Burge (1979) had already argued for such an extension, albeit by appeal to another consideration first presented in Putnam's 1975 paper: the division of linguistic labor. Putnam's 1981 paper argues for its externalist conclusion about the contents of thought on the basis of cases that have nothing to do with the division of linguistic labor. He asks us to imagine a scenario in which ants trailing across wet send leave tracks that compose an image that is perceptually indistinguishable from a caricature of Winston Churchill (published in some newspaper); Putnam argues that, even so, if some alien from another planet were to view this image, the alien would not be mentally representing or thinking of Churchill, even if the alien's sensory state would be subjectively indistinguishable from a state in which it observed the caricature in the paper. The content of the alien's mental state depends on which item it has perceived – the ant trail or the caricature. Nor is this the only difference between Putnam's 1981 argument involving the BIV and his earlier 1975 arguments from "The Meaning of 'Meaning.'" A second difference is this: in the 1981 paper, Putnam explicitly uses his reflections on reference to develop what appears to be a profoundly new sort of anti-skeptical argument. What is more, as Putnam and others saw, this argument also appears to have implications for metaphysics – in particular, for the (im)-possibility of *metaphysical realism*, and for the lessons to be drawn from the possibility of non-standard models in model theory. That a thesis about the conditions on reference might have such dramatic epistemological and metaphysical implications perhaps explains why Putnam's reflections on the brain in a vat have attracted a good deal of attention.

I have organized the contributions to this volume to reflect the three main areas where the literature has discussed Putnam's reflections: intentionality and the philosophy of mind and language; epistemology; and metaphysics (including discussions of the implications of the so-called model-theoretic argument). Of course, the issues raised in one ramify to touch topics in the others, and this is something that will be seen throughout the papers in this volume. Still, it is helpful to group the papers according to the main contributions they seek to make. I begin with the papers in the philosophy of mind and language, as these go to the heart of the sort of argument Putnam was trying to make in 1981; and we move from there to epistemology, and then on to metaphysics.

1.2

It is no surprise that Putnam's semantic reflections on the BIV scenario generated discussions in the theory of intentionality (especially in the philosophy of mind and language), and it is with papers addressing these topics that this volume begins. (Other themes from philosophy of mind and language will loom large in several of the papers in the metaphysics section as well.)

One of the earliest influential assessments of the success of Putnam's argument was by Tony Brueckner. It is fitting to lead off this volume with a chapter from him, both to honor his memory – he passed away more than a year before this volume made it to press – and to acknowledge his central role in leading the assessment of the BIV-based arguments for anti-skepticism. In a series of very influential papers starting in the 1980s (see especially Brueckner (1986) and (1992a)), Brueckner sought to clarify the nature of the argument, and hoped to identify the (philosophy of mind and language) assumptions that underlie Putnam's anti-skeptical use of the BIV thought experiment. Brueckner originally and frequently did so in an attempt to *criticize* Putnam's argument; the charge of his seminal (1986) paper was that the argument was question-begging, and he often concluded that the argument failed to establish a serious anti-skeptical conclusion. However, in his contribution to this volume, "Putnam on brains in a vat," Brueckner limits himself to a re-assessment of the argument and various objections that he (and others) have levelled against it. (Or rather he re-assesses the *two* arguments through which the BIV scenario can be used to support an anti-skeptical conclusion, and he raises and replies to various objections to these ways.) As this re-assessment focuses on objections to assumptions in the philosophy of language, Brueckner's chapter serves to introduce the reader to a variety of topics in the philosophy of language, as these arise in connection with an assessment of the success of Putnam's anti-skeptical argument. Brueckner concludes his contribution by noting, as he had argued in his (1986) paper, that Putnam's anti-skeptical argument has certain limitations: it cannot be used to show that you are not a *recently envatted* BIV.

In his contribution, "How to think about whether we are brains in vats," Gary Ebbs aims to identify precisely Putnam's objective in his reflections on the BIV scenario. Ebbs begins by noting that in "Brains in a Vat" (Chapter 1 of *Reason, Truth, and History*), Putnam argues that, even if it is physically possible that there be brains that are always in a vat, it cannot actually be true that we are always brains in a vat. But Ebbs thinks that Putnam's readers have misunderstood the purport of this argument. The best-known reconstructions of the argument assume that its goal is to rule out *a priori* the supposedly coherent possibility that we are always brains in a vat.[1] While Ebbs agrees that this sort of argument cannot succeed, he thinks this was not the purport of the argument. On the contrary, the purport of that argument was "to dissolve a problem that apparently arises from *within* [one's] own *non*-skeptical account of the methodology of inquiry." Ebbs concludes that, so interpreted, Putnam's argument is both illuminating and successful.

Many philosophers (including several in this volume) suppose that Putnam's BIV-based anti-skeptical argument is motived by appeal to semantic externalism in the philosophy of mind and language. Those who endorse this supposition might well think that anyone who rejects the doctrine of externalism about the contents of thought cannot exploit the anti-skeptical conclusion Putnam sought to establish through his reflection on the BIV. In his contribution, "Brains in vats, causal constraints on reference and semantic externalism," Jesper Kallestrup takes aim at this impression. Kallestrup argues that we ought to distinguish the claim that there are causal *constraints* on reference from the doctrine known as the *causal theory of reference*; and he goes on to argue that, whereas Putnam's BIV-based anti-skeptical argument relies only on the former, externalism

---

[1] Although Brueckner's chapter in this volume does not weigh in on whether Putnam's argument succeeds in establishing a conclusion against the most *radical* forms of skepticism (according to which you are *and have always been* a BIV), many of his other papers had done just that. For a recent review by Brueckner himself, see Brueckner (2012).

about the mental relies on the latter. The result, according to Kallestrup, is that one need not be a semantic externalist to endorse Putnam's anti-skeptical argument. Kallestrup goes on to point out that there are theorists who embrace a causal constraint on reference, yet who reject the causal theory of reference; so if his argument from this chapter is correct, such theorists can embrace Putnam's anti-skeptical conclusions even as they reject semantic externalism about the mind.

Sven Bernecker's contribution to this volume, "Extended minds in vats," seeks to resist the anti-skeptical thrust of Putnam's argument. However, where many others do so by criticizing one or another of the argument's assumptions in philosophy of language or mind (see e.g. the contributions to this volume by Folina, Douven, Sher, and Sundell), Bernecker does so by appeal to an auxiliary thesis in the philosophy of mind. The auxiliary thesis in question is the *extended mind hypothesis*, according to which the mind as a cognitive system sometimes "extends" to include features of the environment. Such a view is often defended on the grounds that the manipulation of these environmental features is itself part of the information-processing that is done by the mind *qua* cognitive system. Bernecker motivates his appeal to this auxiliary claim by arguing, first, that Putnam's BIV-based anti-skeptical argument trades on semantic externalism about the mind, and second, that at least some of those who embrace semantic externalism also embrace the doctrine of the extended mind.[2] At the very least, then, Bernecker's argument targets such folks; it is with them in mind that he writes that "Given the extended mind hypothesis, the supercomputer and the envatted brain can be regarded as aspects of the extended mind of the evil scientist." The burden of Bernecker's chapter is to show that under these assumptions the distinctly anti-skeptical thrust of Putnam's reflections on the BIV "is lost."

1.3

Another part of the vast literature generated by Putnam's reflections on the BIV scenario concerns the anti-skeptical purport of these reflections. Here, several issues were discussed in the literature in epistemology.

In Chapter 6, "Putnam on BIVs and radical skepticism," Duncan Pritchard and Chris Ranalli argue that Putnam's reflections on the BIV fail in their anti-skeptical ambitions. However, unlike those attempts to show this by

---

[2] The doctrine of the extended mind goes beyond standard semantic externalism about the mind in that, where the latter is a thesis about the individuation of mental states, the former is a thesis about the mind *qua* cognitive system itself.

appeal to the falsity of one or another assumption about the nature of language or thought, Pritchard and Ranalli argue that it is the very transcendental pretensions of the argument that get it in trouble. In particular, they argue, Putnam's "proof" that we are not BIVs appears to fall victim to one of two influential criticisms of so-called transcendental anti-skeptical arguments. After revisiting Brueckner's (1986) reconstruction of Putnam's BIV-based anti-skeptical argument, Pritchard and Ranalli follow Crispin Wright in maintaining that Brueckner's reconstruction of the argument had misidentified the problematic nature of the argument. Whereas Brueckner (1986) thought that Putnam's "proof" was problematic for depending on an assumption pertaining to the identity of the language in which the argument was framed,[3] Pritchard and Ranalli argue that the problematic nature of the "proof" has to do with its transcendental nature. In particular, Pritchard and Ranalli argue that, as a transcendental argument, Putnam's BIV-based anti-skeptical argument appears to fall victim to remarks that Barry Stroud and Tom Nagel have directed against transcendental anti-skeptical arguments.

Another epistemological issue which has been much discussed in connection with the BIV scenario, and which touches on issues of skepticism, concerns the nature of epistemic justification itself. Admittedly, the discussion in question (to be described in what follows) is intelligible only if we can make sense of the radical skeptical possibility in which one oneself is a BIV, and so only if Putnam's "proof" to the contrary fails. Even so, it is worth considering this line of reflection on the BIV, if only because it has played such a central role in thinking about the nature of epistemic justification.

Consider Descartes's version of the scenario involving the Evil Demon. As noted above, Descartes had used this scenario to make vivid the idea that your perceptual beliefs regarding particular features of the external world, as well as your general belief in a world of objects and properties "external" to your mind, are more susceptible to skeptical doubts than you might have realized. In making this plain, Descartes's agenda was to render intuitive the claim that if any of these beliefs of yours are to be justified, you must first be justified in believing that the Evil Demon scenario itself is non-actual. But Stew Cohen (1984) came up with an alternative use for the Evil Demon scenario. Comparing you to your envatted twin doppelgänger, Cohen highlighted how intuitive it is to suppose that, given the subjective indistinguishability of your and your doppelgänger's internal history and perceptual experiences, your and your doppelgänger's perceptual beliefs are *equally*

---

[3] Brueckner's contribution to this volume acknowledges that this diagnosis was faulty.

well justified. If this is so, then whether or not you are a BIV envatted by the Demon *does not matter to how well justified your empirical (perceptual) beliefs are*. This intuition, which has been dubbed the "new" Evil Demon intuition, was used by Cohen to criticize reliabilist accounts of epistemic justification, according to which a belief is justified only if it was formed through a process that reliably produces true beliefs. Cohen's own favored view of epistemic justification was an "internalist" one, according to which the facts that determine one's degree of justifiedness supervene on one's "internal" (non-factive) mental states.

In Chapter 7, "New lessons from old demons: the case for reliabilism," Thomas Grundmann takes aim at this use of the BIV scenario. To do so he explicitly targets both Descartes's use of the Evil Demon scenario as well as Cohen's "new" use of that scenario. Grundmann argues that, contrary to what many epistemologists appear to suppose, considerations like those that motivated Descartes can be used to motivate reliabilism; and he argues further that reliabilism can accommodate something very much in the spirit of the intuition elicited by Cohen's "new" Evil Demon scenario.

One of the more robust discussions generated by Putnam's reflections on the BIV concerned the interplay of issues regarding external world skepticism and authoritative self-knowledge of the contents of one's thoughts and the meanings of one's terms. Admittedly, this discussion was generated even prior to Putnam's reflections on the BIV scenario; it began as early as his arguments for semantic externalism in Putnam (1975).[4] But it is clear that the worries discussed there were seriously reinforced by the would-be anti-skeptical proof offered in Putnam (1981b). What is more, the (1981) argument also suggested a renewed formulation of the problem. The worry itself can be stated, at least to a first approximation, as follows. Suppose that Putnam's "proof" succeeds at showing that anyone who utters (or thinks the thought expressed by the English sentence) "I am a BIV" says or thinks something false. Suppose further that, by reflecting on this perfectly general result, one can acquire the first-personal knowledge to the effect that one oneself is not a brain in a vat. Then it would seem that, given the nature of the considerations involved, one who reasons through the argument can come to

---

[4] I should note that *Putnam himself* did not think that his BIV-based argument raised problems for authoritative self-knowledge of one's thoughts or meanings. On the contrary, in his reflections on the BIV scenario, he assumed that subjects have such authoritataive self-knowledge, and used this assumption to draw conclusions about the nature of thought and language in relation to the world. But many other authors worried about this; and it is a topic that shows up in many of the contributions to this volume (for which see footnote 6).

know *a priori* (or at least from the armchair) that one oneself is not a BIV. But the impression remains that one *cannot* know this *a priori* (nor can one know it from the armchair). If this impression is correct, it underwrites a *modus tollens* inference. In particular, we can appeal to the impossibility of *a priori* or armchair knowledge that one oneself is not a BIV, in order to conclude that one of the two suppositions above must be false: either Putnam's "proof" is no such thing; or else what one knows, when one knows that "I am a BIV" is false, *is not tantamount to knowing that one oneself is not a BIV*. The latter option holds if (and perhaps only if) we call into question the subject's knowledge of what she herself has expressed with "I am not a BIV," and correspondingly if we call into question the subject's knowledge of the meaning of "BIV" in her mouth, as well as the thought content she herself expresses when she utters "I am not a BIV." Hence it appears that the "proof" succeeds only at the cost of calling into question the subject's authoritative knowledge of the meanings of her words and the contents of her thoughts.

As I say, this sort of worry has a history that goes back to Putnam's original argument for semantic externalism (Putnam 1975). For example, if the meaning of a natural kind term such as 'water' depends for its individuation on the scientific nature of the kind to which it applies, as Putnam (1975) had argued, then it would seem that a thinker who knew the philosophical argument for this conclusion would be in a position to reason, from her thought that water is thirst quenching, to the conclusion that her environment contains water. But then it seems that Putnam's (1975) argument has discovered an unexpected route to *a priori* (or at least armchair) knowledge of (some of) the features of one's environment! Insofar as one regards this as absurd, one will reject either the supposition that Putnam's argument succeeds at establishing semantic externalism, or else that the subject has authoritative knowledge of what she is thinking when she thinks a thought that she would express with such a natural kind term like "water." This worry was famously turned into an objection to externalist views of the mind by Michael McKinsey (1991), and it has been much discussed in the literature.[5]

In Chapter 8, "BIVs, sensitivity, discrimination, and relevant alternatives," Kelly Becker addresses this dialectic as it arises in connection with Putnam's (1981) "proof."[6] He considers how this dialectic looks if we assume a

---

[5] For one of the most influential monographs on this and related topics, see Brown (2004). See also Brown (1995, 2001) and Sawyer (2001) for earlier discussions.

[6] This issue is also touched on in this volume in the chapters by Folina (at the very end of her chapter) and Douven (at the end of Section 11.3).

sensitivity account of knowledge. Many have remarked on this account's twin virtues of (i) implying a discriminatory ability condition on knowledge, and (ii) generating the set of relevant alternatives within which to assess whether the subject has the discriminatory ability (and hence whether the subject has knowledge). Some theorists might think that since the sensitivity account has these two virtues it might illuminate the nature of self-knowledge of one's thoughts: to address whether the subject knows what she is saying or thinking, we might see how well she fares in discriminating the present circumstance (in which she is thinking a particular thought) from the other relevant alternatives generated by the sensitivity account itself (in which she would be thinking some other thought, one with a distinct content). Becker argues that such an application of the sensitivity account is mistaken: the sensitivity account of knowledge sheds no more light on self-knowledge of one's thoughts than we get from semantic externalism itself.

1.4

A central aspect of Putnam's semantic reflections on the BIV scenario concerns the relationship between the anti-skeptical purport of these reflections and their (alleged) implications for metaphysical realism. The remaining chapters in this volume address some of these issues. To see the linkage, consider how things stand from the perspective of the sort of skepticism that is motivated by the thought that you don't know you're not a BIV. This sort of skepticism, which we might call *BIV-based skepticism*, underwrites the possibility that the features of the world itself remain beyond your epistemological grasp; it raises the prospect that you are in no position to come to know how things are with that world. Since views of this sort embrace the idea that the features of the "external" world might forever evade human knowledge, they are standardly designated as "metaphysically realist" views. On Putnam's understanding, a view was metaphysically realist when (i) it endorsed a correspondence theory of truth, and (ii) it endorsed or implied that *what there is* is itself not constrained by *what we can know regarding what there is*. As we will see, several authors in this volume question the bearing of the doctrine of correspondence truth on metaphysical realism. But whatever the outcome of that debate is, so long as such a realism is committed to (ii), it would appear that BIV-based skepticism goes hand-in-hand with metaphysical realism. Consequently, if Putnam's "proof" that we are not BIVs succeeds, he appears to have come up with an argument against metaphysical realism.

Interestingly, Putnam developed what many regard as a "formal counterpart" (Douven, this volume) of this sort of argument in his so-called "model-theoretic" (MT) argument.[7] (While Putnam briefly alluded to model-theoretic considerations in the "Brains in a Vat" paper, with a passing reference to the Skolem–Löwenheim Theorem (1981b: 7), he developed the MT argument itself at length in the rest of *Reason, Truth, and History*.) To a first approximation, the thrust of the MT argument is as follows. For any empirically adequate theory of our world, there will be non-standard interpretations of the theory that nevertheless constitute models (rendering all of the theory's claims true). Consequently, the proponent of metaphysical realism has no resources with which to single out one of these as "the" favored interpretation: any attempt to do so would be "just more theory," which in turn could be provided a non-standard model. This is a problem for metaphysical realism precisely because such a view insists that truthmakers are mind-independent facts involving objects and their properties – whereas the guaranteed existence of non-standard models establishes that the set of sentences whose truth we aim to model can be modeled by interpretations pertaining to vastly different underlying realities.

Whether in his semantic reflections on the BIV scenario, or in his development of the MT argument, Putnam is targeting an assumption that is common to both BIV-based skepticism and metaphysical realism. To a very rough first approximation, the targeted assumption is that we can make sense of the question of what there is, and so can make sense of the idea that our words might fail to refer to what there is (and so might fail to enable us to frame true claims about what there is), *without having to appeal to our background theories about what there is*. Putnam himself rejects this assumption, and (in *Reason, Truth, and History*) he proposes to replace it with a view he calls "Internal Realism" (IR). IR amounts to the claim that "what objects does the world consist of is a question that it only makes sense to ask within a theory or description" (Putnam 1981a: 49). For those who embrace IR, truth is characterized, not as a relation of correspondence between sentences and some sort of theory- and mind-independent reality, but instead as the characteristic a sentence has when it is rationally acceptable under epistemically ideal circumstances.

Each of the six chapters in the final section of this volume addresses one or another of Putnam's arguments against metaphysical realism – whether these

---

[7] I want to express my thanks to my colleague Sean Ebels-Duggan, for a helpful discussion of the nature and scope of the MT argument.

arguments come in the form of Putnam's semantic reflections on the BIV scenario, or his reflections on the interpretative permutations at the heart of the MT argument.

Tim Button's chapter, "Brains in vats and model theory," is a great place to start, as it aims to make explicit the connection between Putnam's semantic reflections on the BIV and his MT argument. What is more, Button aims to offer a schematic defense of the arguments as he construes them. He considers three main anti-skeptical arguments: Putnam's BIV-based anti-skeptical argument, a "skolemist" anti-skeptical argument (based on a particular reply to Skolem's "paradox" regarding the possibility of countable models for the sentence "there are uncountable sets"), and Putnam's "permutation" argument. In each case, Button clarifies the nature of the argument and offers a schematic defense of its anti-skeptical upshot. He thinks that each of these anti-skeptical arguments makes a similar point: if the various forms of skepticism are to be interesting and worth taking seriously, they must avoid employing a "magical" theory of reference; but once they avoid employing such a theory, it will turn out that, on reflection, each kind of skepticism can be shown (by one or another of these anti-skeptical arguments) to be *incoherent because self-refuting*. The upshot is that we ought to reject any picture of language's or thought's bearing on the world on which such skeptical possibilities are left open. And this, of course, is to reject the picture of metaphysical realism.

In her chapter "Realism, skepticism, and the brain in a vat," Janet Folina takes aim at the allegedly anti-skeptical and anti-metaphysical-realist implications of Putnam's semantic reflections. Interestingly, she and Button appear to agree on one key point, namely, that the upshot of Putnam's reflections on the BIV scenario is that such a scenario is "unthinkable" to anyone who is in it. (Button makes essentially the linguistic version of this very point when he notes that "The lynchpin of all of the anti-sceptical arguments is just that, if the skeptical scenario were actual, then we would be unable to articulate this (barring magic).") But whereas Button regards this as showing that, for example, BIV-based skepticism is incoherent, Folina urges that it does not follow from the fact that the scenario in question is *unthinkable if actual*, that it is impossible or incoherent. Stronger, she argues that Putnam's attempt to derive the falsity of BIV skepticism itself begs the question of metaphysical realism: in her words, "the conclusion that global skepticism is either incoherent or false *presupposes* the falsity of metaphysical realism" (my italics). Over the course of her chapter, Folina revisits various aspects of Putnam's argument: its reliance on multiple languages (and perspectives) to make its point; the allegedly self-refuting status of "I am a BIV"; the possibility of an infinite regress in the semantic representation of the subject's self-directed thought when she wonders whether she is a BIV; and finally the role of the causal theory of reference in the argument itself. Folina concludes that Putnam's reflections fail to yield an anti-skeptical proof: either they are epistemically circular in a way that undermines their status as a "proof," or else (on an alternative construal) they beg the question against metaphysical realism itself.

Like Folina, Igor Douven (in Chapter 11, "Rethinking semantic naturalism") aims to show that Putnam's BIV-inspired reflections do not undermine metaphysical realism. However, where Folina focused on the BIV argument itself, Douven focuses instead on the MT argument. He begins by noting a point others have made: if it is to bear against metaphysical realism, this argument requires an additional assumption of semantic naturalism, the view that (in Douven's words) "semantics is an empirical science like any other." But Douven goes on to argue that the MT argument depends not only on semantic naturalism, but on a *particular version* of semantic naturalism, on which semantics is not an empirical science like any other unless it embraces a physicalist reduction of semantic properties. The burden of Douven's chapter is to challenge this physicalistic requirement on semantic naturalism. The lesson Douven draws is that, while metaphysical realists ought to embrace semantic naturalism, they should reject the demand for a *physicalistically reductionist* version. He goes on to outline some "promising" semantic frameworks that are scientific without being physicalistic; and he notes that each of these promising frameworks fails to support Putnam's MT argument against metaphysical realism. The result is that metaphysical realism remains a live option – Putnam's MT argument to the contrary notwithstanding.

Whereas Douven's focus is on the doctrine of semantic naturalism, Patricia Marino, in Chapter 12, "Internal to what? Contemporary naturalism and Putnam's model-theoretic argument," focuses her attention on the doctrine of naturalism more broadly. She is interested in comparing what she calls "contemporary naturalism," which is the doctrine, roughly, that science is our best guide to what there is, with the view Putnam favored, internal realism (IR). Marino is interested in exploring the similarities and differences between IR and naturalism. To focus her study, she relies on the naturalism articulated in Penelope Maddy's (2007) *Second Philosophy*. Among the similarities Marino finds between the two doctrines is a broad embrace of the idea that we can understand such notions as truth or reference only from within our best theories of the world. (Here she notes, as Douven notes in his chapter, that the development of deflationary theories of truth in the past two decades alters the resources that are available to us as we do semantics: the correspondence theory of truth is no longer regarded as the only serious game in town.) Among the important differences Marino finds between naturalism and IR, she points out what she regards as the most important one: their respective attitudes toward the question whether the methods of science have any special epistemological status. (Naturalism answers in the affirmative, IR in the negative.) Marino concludes her chapter by arguing that there are some grounds for favoring naturalism over IR on this score, and that in any case naturalism is a better fit with "contemporary understandings of the role of values in science and with contemporary practices having to do with disagreement."

In Chapter 13, "The model-theoretic argument: from skepticism to a new understanding," Gila Sher adds her voice to those who question the success of Putnam's case against metaphysical realism. She begins her chapter by distinguishing a "narrow" and a "broad" MT argument. According to Sher, the narrow argument, which appeals to the Löwenheim–Skolem Theorem, aims to show that for any theory formulable in first-order logic, a non-standard interpretation can be given that is a model of that theory. On Sher's reading, such a result is taken by Putnam to show that it is "impossible in principle to determine the reference of terms theoretically." She adds that this narrow result "applies both to theories of reference that list the referents of words one by one and to theories that determine their referents by means of general principles, e.g., by means of a *causal* principle of reference." Next, Sher moves on to the broad MT argument. This argument appeals to the Isomorphism Theorem; it aims to show that, for any theory formulable in first-order logic, there will be a model of the theory that assigns non-standard (unintended) referents to the referring expressions and non-standard (unintended) extensions to the predicates. Sher notes that Putnam regards this result as showing that (in her formulation) "no theoretical (as opposed to pragmatic) account of reference is adequate." For her part, Sher disputes the conclusion that no theoretical account of reference is possible. To this end she appeals to Tarski's motivation for constructing a model-theoretic semantics, in order to argue that this is not the appropriate framework within which to think about the determination of reference. Sher goes on to criticize Putnam's "permutation" argument, which had sought to use an analogue of the Isomorphism Theorem to establish a skeptical conclusion regarding reference-determination. And she concludes by arguing that nothing in what Putnam has shown undermines a position that combines the correspondence theory of truth with an "enlightened" form of realism (one which eschews any appeal to things-in-themselves or the God's eye point of view). But she also leaves us with a new question regarding the BIV: assuming that BIVs are possible, how (if at all) could a BIV find out about its world, and what (if anything) could we learn from thinking about this scenario?

In his contribution, "Eligibility and ideology in the vat," Tim Sundell also aims to defend a kind of realism against Putnam's reflections on the nature of reference. Starting with the assumption that David Lewis's (1984) doctrine of reference magnetism succeeds in addressing the worries raised by Putnam's MT argument, as many philosophers suppose, Sundell notes that, even so, work remains to show that the doctrine of reference magnetism addresses the other arrow in Putnam's anti-metaphysical realism quiver: the *BIV-based* anti-skeptical argument. Addressing himself to this argument, Sundell proposes a response on behalf of the metaphysical realist, based on the distinction between the *truth* of a theory and what Sundell calls its overall *epistemic success*. The upshot is that, Putnam's MT and BIV-based arguments to the contrary notwithstanding, the metaphysical realist "can maintain that there *are* genuinely radical yet non-self-refuting skeptical hypotheses, but that such hypotheses concern not the truth of a theory but a different aspect of epistemic success, namely the fundamentality of its ideology."

Part I

Intentionality and the philosophy of mind and language

2 Putnam on brains in a vat

Tony Brueckner

2.1 Skeptical hypotheses and the skeptical argument

The Cartesian skeptic puts forward various logically possible *skeptical hypotheses* for our consideration, such as that you are now merely dreaming that you are reading an entry on Hilary Putnam. The more radical *Evil Genius hypothesis* is this: you inhabit a world consisting of just you and a God-like Evil Genius bent on deceiving you. In the Evil Genius world, nothing physical exists, and all of your experiences are directly caused by the Evil Genius. So your experiences, which represent there to be an external world of physical objects (including your body), give rise to systematically mistaken beliefs about your world (such as that you are now sitting at a computer). Some philosophers would deny that the Evil Genius hypothesis is genuinely logically possible. Materialists who hold that the mind is a complex physical system deny that it is possible for there to be an Evil Genius world, since, on their view, your mind could not possibly exist in a matterless world. Accordingly, a modern skeptic will have us consider an updated skeptical hypothesis that is consistent with materialism. Consider the hypothesis that you are a disembodied brain floating in a vat of nutrient fluids. This brain is connected to a supercomputer whose program produces electrical impulses that stimulate the brain in just the way that normal brains are stimulated as a result of perceiving external objects in the normal way. (The movie *The Matrix* depicts *embodied* brains which are so stimulated, while their bodies float in vats.) If you are a brain in a vat, then you have experiences that are qualitatively indistinguishable from those of a normal perceiver. If you come to believe, on the basis of your computer-induced experiences, that you are looking at a tree, then you are sadly mistaken.

After having sketched this brain-in-a-vat hypothesis, the skeptic issues a challenge: can you rule out the possibility described in the hypothesis? Do you know that the hypothesis is false? The skeptic now argues as follows. Choose any target proposition P concerning the external world, which you think you know to be true:

(1) If you know that P, then you know that you are not a brain in a vat.
(2) You do not know that you are not a brain in a vat.

So

(3) You do not know that P.

Premise (1) is backed by the principle that *knowledge is closed under known entailment*:

(CL)   For all S, α, β: If S knows that α, and S knows that α entails β, then S knows that β.

Since you know that P entails that you are not a brain in a vat (for example, let P = *You are sitting at a computer*), by (CL) you know that P only if you know its entailed consequence: you are not a brain in a vat. Premise (2) is backed by the consideration that your experiences do not allow you to discriminate between the hypothesis that you are *not* a brain in a vat (but rather a normal human) from the hypothesis that you *are* a brain in a vat. Your experience would be the same regardless of which hypothesis were true. So you do not know that you are not a brain in a vat.

2.2 Semantic externalism and the Simple Argument

A Martian accidentally spills a jar of green paint. A blob forms, one which exactly resembles a *National Geographic* photo of a pine tree in Yosemite. The Martian forms a mental image that exactly resembles the image that I form as a result of seeing the magazine photo. Hilary Putnam's intuition is that the Martian's mental image does not *refer to* any trees, does not *represent* any trees, in contrast to *my* mental image.

An ant crawls through some damp, firm sand, tracing out a shape that exactly resembles a very good caricature of Winston Churchill that I recently saw in the *Times*. Our Martian sees the ant's tracing and comes away with a mental image exactly resembling mine. Again, the Putnamian intuition is that the Martian's mental image, unlike mine, does not refer to, does not represent, Winston Churchill.

The Putnamian intuition is not affected by complicating the examples: alongside the tree-resembling paint blob is a blob that looks like this: TREE; a second ant traces a shape alongside the Churchill-resembling tracing that looks like this: WINSTON CHURCHILL. For the Martian's mental images, again: no reference, no representation.

What explains the power of these semantic intuitions? It is that our Martian (and, we can assume, no other Martian) has had no causal contact of any kind – direct or indirect – with trees or with Sir Winston. Thus, the Martian examples violate a *causal constraint on reference/representation*.

Now we turn to *Putnamian brains in a vat*; call them *BIVs*. There are no trees in the vat-world, only brains in a vat, along with a supercomputer that electronically stimulates them, and nothing else – no cats, no Porsches, . . . A BIV "speaks" – well, *thinks in* and *appears to itself to speak* – a language that superficially resembles English. Call the language *vat-English*. The BIV mentally tokens the sentence 'Here is a beautiful tree'. Just as in the case of the Martian, the BIV's token of 'tree' does not refer to, does not represent, trees. This is because of the violation of the causal constraint on reference: no trees in the vat-world.

This (negative) semantic claim leads to the establishment of the first premise of a Putnamian anti-skeptical argument. Call it *SA* (for *Simple Argument*).[1]

(1) If I am a BIV, then my tokens of 'tree' do not refer to trees.

Call (1) the *semantic externalist* premise of the argument, relying as it does upon the view that the semantic properties of a language depend upon circumstances in the external, causal environment of the language users (trees present versus trees absent).

Now for premise (2). As a prelude, let us consider the *Knowledge of the Semantics of My Own Language Quiz* (*Quiz*, for short). Let us pause for a bit, and cleanse our minds of all concerns regarding Cartesian skepticism and semantic externalism. I am given a *Quiz* with just one question, as follows:

My word 'tree' refers to

(a) quantum-entangled systems
(b) cows
(c) milk
(d) Brazil
(e) trees

---

[1] See Brueckner (1992a). Putnam has said (in conversation) that even though SA was not explicitly formulated in Putnam (1981b), it nevertheless captures his considered intentions for generating anti-skeptical fuel from the semantic considerations discussed in his book.

What should my answer be to *Quiz*? Isn't it obvious that (e) is the answer that I ought to give? Accordingly, we can state the other premise in SA:

(2) My word 'tree' refers to trees.

From (1) and (2) we get SA's conclusion:

(3) I am not a BIV.

(In an appendix, I will discuss some other ways of putting Putnam's remarks about BIVs to anti-skeptical use.)

2.3 Objections to SA

The simplest and most powerful *First* objection to SA centers around an intuitive charge of question-begging. Charges of question-begging and circularity are thrown around too haphazardly in philosophy. It is obvious that SA does not exhibit *formal* circularity, in having its conclusion as a premise. So what drives the intuition that SA is somehow question-begging? What question might be being begged? Obviously, the question whether I am a BIV.

One sin that might be called begging the question is being *epistemically circular*.[2] You cannot tell whether a given argument is epistemically circular just by surveying its form (that will only tell you about formal circularity). Instead, you must inquire into the *justification* that the proponent of the argument offers for its premises. If the justification for accepting one of the premises in part consists in the assumption of the truth of the conclusion, then there is epistemic circularity in the putting-forward of the argument.

The *question-beggingness-cum-epistemic circularity* charge with respect to SA arises as follows. Assume that semantic externalism is true, thereby yielding premise (1). Then premise (2) is true only if the conclusion (3) is true: in the presence of (1), (2) entails (3). In other words, assuming semantic externalism, my language (including my 'tree') disquotes only if I am not a BIV. So given (1), we have to assume the truth of (3) in order to have justification for accepting (2). Epistemic circularity! Question-begging!

Not to put too fine of a point upon it, this is a ridiculous objection. The objection can be made to *any* argument with the *modus tollens* form of SA:

(I) If P, then Q
(II) ~Q
(III) ~P

---

[2] See Alston (1989c).

Assume that (I) is true (as we did with the semantic externalist premise (1) of SA). Then, in the presence of this assumption, premise (II) is true only if the conclusion (III) is true. So: *in order to have justification for believing (II), we must assume the truth of the conclusion (III)*. But no – Obviously not! We might well have a justification for believing (II) that does not advert to (III). This is what in fact holds for SA: my justification for believing (2) derives from my knowledge of the semantics of my own language, as is illustrated in the *Quiz*.

The *Second* objection to be considered links up with the foregoing reply to the First objection. It can be put in the following way, as a variant on the First. Either I am a non-BIV speaking English or instead a BIV speaking vat-English. In order to have justification for believing the disquotational premise (2) of SA, I need to assume that *I am speaking English*. Epistemic circularity! Question-begging!

The proper response to this Second objection is that whichever language, of the two that are in play in the context of SA, is the one that I am speaking, my language disquotes. This is true of both English, the language spoken by me and Babe Ruth and Winston Churchill if I am in a normal, non-vat world, and vat-English, the language spoken by me in a vat-world. I can have justification for believing that my language disquotes – and hence justification for believing (2) – without recourse to helping myself to an assumption that the conclusion (3) of SA is true. Before getting to the end of the argument, my attitude is this: I do not know which language I am speaking – one shared with the Babe or one used in a vat – but I nevertheless know that (2) is true.

The *Third* objection to contemplate is as follows. A BIV can consider in thought the sentences used to express SA. The argument expressed by those sentences as he uses them does *not* prove the conclusion that he is not a BIV; similarly, an argument that he considers whose conclusion is 'There are trees' does not prove that there are trees. An argument framed in vat-English cannot prove the foregoing conclusions. So if *I* am a BIV, then when *I* rehearse the sentences forming SA, I do not thereby prove the conclusion that I am not a BIV. I thereby prove something else, if I prove anything at all.

This worry is unfounded. If SA is sound, then it proves just what it appears to prove – that I am not a BIV. Just read the argument carefully when you work through it! It makes no difference to my argumentative situation if someone on Jupiter uses those very sentences with different meanings from mine and thereby proves that Mercury is hot.

The *Fourth* objection concerns the relation between SA and the ordinary, non-philosophical putative knower. What should be the anti-skeptic's goal with respect to the BIV hypothesis? On one way of thinking about the anti-skeptical project, the goal is to show that we know that we are not BIVs. Thus the BIV scenario is not a threat to our claims to know that there are trees, cats, Porsches, and so on. But how does SA achieve this goal? If someone runs through SA, then he can know that he is not a BIV by knowing that SA is sound, thereby knowledgeably ruling out the BIV possibility. But the average putative knower is not in a position to knowledgeably rule out the BIV possibility by thinking through SA – for example, he will know nothing about semantic externalism, nothing about BIVs. Given the soundness of SA, he is not a BIV, but he does not know this. The same problem arises for other anti-skeptical strategies: for example, the average putative knower has no familiarity with Descartes's anti-skeptical strategy concerning the non-deceptive nature of God. He is there in no position to knowledgeably rule out Descartes's skeptical possibility that he is a victim of Evil Genius deception.[3]

A *Fifth* objection is leveled at premise (2), but it is fueled by different reasons from those behind the First objection. To say that my utterances of 'tree' refer to trees seems to presuppose that *trees exist*. Otherwise, how could it be said that my utterances of 'tree' refer to them?[4] In putting forward premise (2), then, we seem to be presupposing that this world is *not* a treeless world. This is tantamount to the conclusion we wish to prove (that I am not a BIV in a tree-less, cat-less world).

Accordingly we must modify SA along the following lines:

(1′) If I am a BIV, then it is not the case that if my word 'tree' refers, then it refers to trees.
(2′) If my word 'tree' refers, then it refers to trees.
(4) I am not a BIV.

(1′) is licensed by semantic externalism. (2′) is licensed by my knowledge of the semantics of my own language; but clearly it does not presuppose that trees exist.

A *Sixth* objection concerns the scope of SA and its revised variant. These arguments cannot prove that I am not a *recently disembodied* brain in a vat (as opposed to a Putnamian BIV, who has always been envatted). If I have been speaking English up until my recent envatment, then my words will retain their English referents (to trees, for example). Thus the Putnamian

---

[3] This objection is made by Keith deRose and Ted A. Warfield in the introduction to deRose and Warfield (1999).
[4] This objection is due to Byeong-Uk Yi, in an unpublished paper.

semantic externalist considerations will find no purchase against the skeptical hypothesis that I am a fledgling brain in a vat.[5] However, in such a recent envatment scenario, the pertinent skeptical argument leaves unscathed many of my knowledge-claims (such as that I was born as a human baby in Indiana, that I have a black cat ...). So the recent envatment scenario lacks the skeptical power – the skeptical reach – of the Putnamian BIV scenario.

Appendix

There are some other ways of developing an anti-skeptical argument that proceeds from Putnamian semantic externalism. Let us call the first the *Disjunctive Argument* (DA for short). In a nutshell, DA goes as follows.[6] Either I am a BIV speaking vat-English or instead a non-BIV speaking English. In the first case, my utterances of 'Here is a green tree' have non-standard truth conditions that concern not trees but rather computer states that causally affect my brain so as to produce "tree-experience." Thus the vat-English truth conditions of my utterance of 'Here is a green tree' are satisfied, given that the supercomputer is running a program that affects my brain in such a way as to produce experiences just like those of a normal human who sees a green tree. So if I am a BIV, then the vat-English truth conditions of 'I am a BIV' are not satisfied, since no computer program features are running in such a way as to produce experiences representing me to be a disembodied BIV. So my utterances of 'I am a BIV' are false in the first case considered. In the second (non-BIV) case, in which my utterances of 'I am a BIV' have standard English truth conditions, those conditions are obviously *not* satisfied. Again, my utterances of 'I am a BIV' come out false. So I am not a BIV, by DA.[7]

There is an objection to DA that parallels the First objection to premise (2) of SA. The problem concerns the move from

(ML)   My utterances of 'I am a BIV' are false.

to

(DQ)   I am not a BIV.

We need to move first from the metalinguistic (ML) to

(ML′)   My utterances of 'I not a BIV' are true.

---

[5] See Brueckner (1992a) for an early statement of this objection.
[6] This argument is strongly suggested by Putnam (1981b). [7] See Brueckner (1992a).

This step is unproblematic. But then we need to move from the metalinguistic (ML′) to (DQ) via the use of disquotation:

(ML″)   My utterances of 'I am not a BIV' are true iff I am not a BIV.

The problem is that *knowledge* of (ML″) seems to presuppose that I know that I am in a non-vat world in which my utterances of sentences have standard, non-disquotational English truth conditions, which is tantamount to what we are trying to prove.

To cut to the heart of the matter, we could answer this objection by putting forward a variant of SA, using sentential variants of premises (1) and (2). The disquotational variant of (2) – namely (ML″) – could be defended along the same lines employed in defense of (2) itself: knowledge of the (truth-conditional) semantics of my own language.

Another way of developing a Putnamian anti-skeptical argument involves a transition from semantic externalism about reference and truth conditions to a parallel semantic externalism about mental content. When a BIV thinks a thought via the vat-English sentence 'Trees are green,' he does not think the thought *that trees are green*, since he cannot think thoughts that represent trees. A variant of SA emerges from this point:

(1″) If I am a BIV, then I am not thinking that trees are green.
(2″) I am thinking that trees are green.
(3) I am not a BIV.

(1″) is licensed by semantic externalism about thought-content. (2″) is justified in a manner which mimics the Quiz discussed earlier. This time, the pertinent Quiz knowledge of my current thought-contents.

3 How to think about whether we are brains in vats

Gary Ebbs

Imagine that duplicates of our brains are in a vat from the beginning to the end of their lives, stimulated by a computer in exactly the same way that our brains are stimulated, and that both the duplicate brains and the computer came into existence by quantum accident. Call these "brains that are always in a vat." I assume it is at least physically possible that there be such brains. This physical possibility becomes philosophically interesting when we find ourselves tempted to think that, despite our ordinary beliefs to the contrary, *we may actually be brains that are always in a vat*.

In Chapter 1 of *Reason, Truth, and History*, Putnam argues that even if it is physically possible that there be brains that are always in a vat, it cannot actually be true that we are always brains in a vat. The best-known reconstructions of Putnam's argument assume that its goal is – and ought to be – to rule out by strictly *a priori* reasoning the supposedly coherent possibility that we are always brains in a vat. Against this, I will argue that the goal of Putnam's argument is to dissolve a problem that apparently arises from *within* his own *non*-skeptical account of the methodology of inquiry. To motivate my non-standard reconstruction of Putnam's argument, I begin by reviewing some of the problems that standard reconstructions of it face.

3.1 Problems for standard reconstructions

What is the goal of Putnam's argument? Standard reconstructions of it assume

Answer 1: The goal of Putnam's argument is to show, by strictly *a priori* methods, that we are not always brains in vats.

Answer 1 implies:

(A)   Putnam's argument is successful only if a person who is agnostic about whether he or she is always a brain in a vat can reasonably accept all of its premises.

As Crispin Wright explains, "... the argument, if sound, should have the power to move an agnostic to the conclusion that he or she is not a brain in a vat" (Wright 1994: 222). Similarly, according to Anthony Brueckner, "that I am a normal human being speaking English rather than a BIV speaking vat-English ... must be *shown* by an anti-skeptical argument, not assumed in advance" (Brueckner 1986: 160).

Answer 1 also implies:

(B) Putnam's argument is successful only if his causal constraints on meaning and reference can be known strictly *a priori*.

According to Putnam, "[the] causal constraints on meaning and reference ... have roughly the following form: to refer to an object in the physical world, or to a physical property or relation, one must either have an appropriate kind of causal relation to the object, property, or relation ..., or be able to describe what it is one intends to refer to in terms of objects, properties, and relations to which one does have an appropriate causal connection." (Putnam 1994a: 284–5). Assumption (B) is that we can know of and accept these causal constraints without relying on any substantive or "empirical" beliefs.

Here is a representative example of a reconstruction of Putnam's argument that presupposes Answer 1 and assumptions (A) and (B).

Reconstruction 1 (due to Wright):

(i) My language disquotes.
(ii) In BIVese, 'brain in a vat' does not refer to brains in a vat. by casual constraints
(iii) In my language, 'brain in a vat' is a meaningful expression.
(iv) In my language, 'brain in a vat' refers to brains in a vat. (i), (iii)
(v) My language is not BIVese. (ii), (iv)
(vi) Therefore, I am not always a brain in a vat. (v), def. of "BIVese"

Wright assumes we can each know the premises of this argument *a priori*. The premise that at first seems most in need of defense and explanation is premise (ii). In support of premise (ii), presumably, Wright would reason roughly as follows. "A brain that is always in a vat does not satisfy the necessary conditions for being able to refer to brains or vats. Hence, whatever its expression 'brain in a vat' refers to, it is not to brains in a vat." Let us suppose that this reasoning is correct, and *a priori*, so that we are *a priori* justified in accepting premise (ii).

Now the problem for Reconstruction 1 is that if we are *a priori* justified in accepting premises (i) and (iii), then we may infer (iv) even if we suppose that we are always brains in a vat, and hence even if we suppose that our language is BIVese. We are therefore *a priori* justified in accepting the negation of premise (ii). But, as we just saw, we are also supposed to be *a priori* justified in *accepting* premise (ii).

Clearly, something has gone wrong. Perhaps we should conclude that we can accept premise (ii) only if we suppose we are *not* always brains in vats, and hence that we cannot know premise (ii) *a priori*, if we can know premises (i) and (iii) *a priori*. This would be to give up assumption (B), and to conclude that Putnam's argument fails, given Answer 1.

Alternatively, we might conclude, following Brueckner, that we can know premises (ii) and (iii) *a priori*, but we cannot know premise (i) *a priori*. In Brueckner's view, we can know premise (i) *a priori* only if we can know *a priori* that our language is not BIVese, hence only if we know *a priori* that we are not always brains in a vat. But Answer 1 and assumption (A) apparently imply that we cannot know *a priori* that our language is not BIVese. Brueckner concludes that premise (i) cannot be used as part of an *a priori* argument that establishes that our language is English, not BIVese.

Wright replies to this worry as follows:

> Let it be that I do not know whether I am speaking English or BIVese; still I do know that, whatever "snow" refers to in my language, I may identify its reference by *using* that very word. (Wright 1994: 225)

But this reply just pushes the question back to a more basic one: "If we suspend all our substantive or 'empirical' beliefs, as we would need to do in order to suppose that we are always brains in vats, are we in a position to *use* our words at all?" If we answer "yes," we separate standards for using, as opposed to mentioning, words from our actual practices of identifying competent and incompetent uses of words. Putnam observes that while standards for minimal competence in the use of words are context-sensitive and may vary across linguistic communities and times, we do not take a speaker to be using a word unless we take her use of the word to be minimally competent. I will not take a speaker to be using the English word 'Tiger,' for instance, if the only sentences with occurrences of 'T-i-g-e-r' in them that she accepts are, "Tigers are snowballs" and "Tigers melt at room temperature." Moreover, Putnam's observations about meaning and reference commit him to rejecting the analytic/synthetic distinction, understood as part of an account of *a priori* knowledge. If we accept Putnam's observations about meaning and reference, as Wright claims to do, we cannot explain our grasp of how to use our words as a grasp of rules that determine the truth-values of some of our sentences *a priori*. We therefore cannot *both* try to "suspend" all our substantive or empirical beliefs *and* take ourselves to be competent to *use* our words, in the logician's sense that contrasts with mentioning them.

One might think that, even if I try to "suspend" all my empirical or substantive beliefs, I nevertheless know that *whether or not* my language is English or BIVese, my sentence, "'Snow' refers to snow," is true in my language. But the reasoning of the previous paragraph implies that if I try to "suspend" all my substantive or empirical beliefs, I thereby in effect render myself linguistically incompetent, even in my own eyes, and so I cannot take myself to express, and hence do not know, the thought that 'Snow' refers to snow.

Wright objects to the claim that I am not in position to use my own words if I suspend all my substantive or "empirical" beliefs, calling it "mere legislation" (Wright 1994: 225).

> In order comprehendingly to disquote the sentence, "'Snow' refers to snow," I do not need, in any sense jeopardized by semantic externalism, to identify the thought that "Snow" refers to snow. It is enough if, courtesy of the appropriate external circumstances, I have that thought, on the appropriate cue. (Wright 1994: 225)

As I noted above, however, Putnam's semantic externalism is rooted in observations about our actual practices of taking speakers to be minimally competent in the use of English words. A speaker who suspends all of her substantive or "empirical" beliefs about what snow is, and does not affirm any demonstrative sentences that contain the word snow, such as, "That's snow over there," cannot be regarded as minimally competent in the use of the word 'snow.' This is not to say that in order to count as minimally competent in the use of the word 'snow,' one must be able to distinguish, for instance, between snow and twin snow, which is made up of frozen XYZ molecules. The requirements on minimal linguistic competence are in general not demanding. In some cases, a speaker may count as minimally competent in the use of a given word even though all the sentences containing the word that she accepts are false. All we can say generally is that to be minimally competent in the use of a given word one must have some idea of what thoughts one expresses by uttering sentences that contain the word. This observation supports and clarifies the truism that *to express a thought, one must have some idea of what that thought is*. Wright's defense of the *a priori* nature of premises (i) and (iii) is not compatible with that truism, and is therefore unsuccessful.

I conclude that if we accept Answer 1 and its consequences, assumptions (A) and (B), there is no satisfying reconstruction of Putnam's argument that we are not always brains in vats.

3.2 Transition to a different interpretation of the argument

The fault lies not with Putnam's argument, but with Answer 1. Putnam says he is

> *reasoning a priori* ... [n]ot in the old "absolute" sense (since we do not claim that magical theories of reference are *a priori* wrong), but in the sense of inquiring into what is *reasonably* possible *assuming* certain general premises, or making certain very broad theoretical assumptions. Such a procedure is neither "empirical" nor quite "a priori", but has elements of both ways of investigating. (Putnam 1981b: 16)

I propose that we understand these remarks as rooted in the following methodological assumption:

Methodological Assumption (MA):	In our inquiries we can do no better than to start in the middle, relying on already established beliefs and inferences, and applying our best methods for re-evaluating particular beliefs and inferences and arriving at new ones.

As I shall understand MA, it implies both that no belief, inference, or method is immune to revision, and that there are no epistemological standards higher or firmer than the ones we express in our actual endorsements of particular beliefs, inferences, and methods for arriving at beliefs.

MA may seem to dismiss skepticism altogether. Certainly it dismisses any purely *a priori* question of how knowledge is possible. Nevertheless, beliefs that I accept as part of my best current theory – beliefs that I am licensed to accept, by MA – may seem vulnerable to a *reductio ad absurdum* style of skepticism – what Putnam calls an "internal" skeptical challenge (Putnam 1994a: 284). On the one hand, it is part of my best current theory that I am not always a brain in a vat, and my acceptance of this belief therefore counts as reasonable, according to MA. On the other hand, I seem to be able to make sense of the skeptical hypothesis that I am actually always a brain in a vat. And if I am such a brain, it seems, then almost everything I believe is false. I might hope to dismiss this possibility by appealing to my best current theory, according to which I am not such a brain. But I realize that the proximal stimulations of my brain would be the same either way. I therefore seem to face a classic under-determination problem. It appears that I have no non-circular warrant for sticking with my prior theory, according to which I am not always a brain in a vat. I may therefore begin to feel that all my beliefs and theories are mere stabs in the dark, no more reasonable than any other beliefs and theories.

There is a huge literature in epistemology devoted to analyzing this kind of reasoning and trying to show that even if we suppose that the statement that we are always brains in vats describes how things may actually be, we have good reason to believe that we are not always brains in vats. Putnam's argument is a response of a very different kind. Its goal is to convince us that the statement that we are actually always brains in vats does not describe how things may actually be.

But how could an argument change our minds about whether a given statement describes how things may actually be? Wouldn't any such argument have to beg the question from the start? To address these questions, I need to introduce some terminology.

Bipolarity: Person P takes statement S to be bipolar (at t) if and only if P can make sense of S's being true (at t) and P can make sense of S's being not true (at t).

Example: I take the statement that *my computer is in my room at the Inn* to be bipolar. I believe that my computer is in my room at the Inn but I can make sense of its being not true that my computer is in my room at the Inn.

Unipolarity: P takes S to be unipolar (at t) if and only if P can make sense of S's being true (at t) or P can make sense of S's being not true (at t), but not both.

Example: I take the statement that *snow is white and snow is not white* to be unipolar, since I cannot make sense of its being true, but I can make sense of its being not true – indeed, I accept the negation of the statement.

Note that the sentences that we use to express false unipolar statements are meaningful.

I shall try to show that the key to understanding Putnam's argument is to see that *we may change our minds about whether a statement is bipolar.*

I start with a simple case in which we learn that a statement we (briefly) took to be bipolar is (we now think) unipolar:

(Δ) There is a barber who lives in Tisbury, Massachusetts, and who shaves all and only those who live in Tisbury, Massachusetts, but do not shave themselves.

This statement follows a familiar form that is known to be contradictory, and hence we know that the statement is not true. When one first encounters a statement of this form, however, one might very well suppose that it may actually be true, and hence that it is bipolar. It takes a bit of reasoning to see that it is inconsistent, hence unipolar, and not true. Without yet knowing whether the statement is consistent, we may try to get clearer about the conditions under which it would be true, if it were consistent. The obvious first step is to suppose that there is such a barber. And then we may ask if he shaves himself. Either the supposed barber shaves himself or he does not. If he shaves himself, then, since he shaves all and only those who live in Tisbury who do not shave themselves, and he lives in Tisbury, it follows from (Δ) that he does not shave himself. And if he does not shave himself, then since he lives in Tisbury, it follows from (Δ) that he does shave himself. Either way, there is a contradiction. We may at first have supposed that (Δ) may actually be true, but on further reflection we find that it is inconsistent, and hence unipolar.

Is this reasoning *a priori*? Not in the old 'absolute' sense, according to Putnam. Yes, the reasoning is logical. But if we accept MA, we are committed to rejecting any methodologically significant analytic–synthetic distinction, and cannot regard the logical laws on which the above reasoning relies, such as the law of non-contradiction, as analytic. Nor is there a non-circular argument for the law of non-contradiction, for instance. Still, the logical laws on which the above reasoning relies are part of our best current theory, and we cannot specify any way in which they may be false. This is enough, I submit, for us to be *entitled* to regard (Δ) as false (i.e. its negation as true).

These methodological reflections suggest that (a) our judgment that a given statement is unipolar or bipolar cannot be strictly *a priori*, in the traditional sense, and (b) for any statement S that we understand, if we cannot make sense of S's actually being true, we are entitled to accept the negation of S and to regard S as unipolar.

3.3 An alternative reconstruction

With these points in mind, let us now return to the question with which I began: What is the goal of Putnam's argument that we are not always brains in vats?

Answer 2: The goal of Putnam's argument is to show that for each of us, there exists a statement (one that we express by uttering "I am always a brain in a vat") that (a) we are at first strongly tempted to regard as bipolar, and hence as useable as part of an internal skeptical challenge to the coherence of MA, but that (b) we should regard, after more careful reflection, to be unipolar.

If we accept this answer, we may reconstruct Putnam's reasoning in a way that is compatible with our acceptance of MA. I propose the following:

Reconstruction 2 (adapted from Tymoczko 1989a):

(1) I can raise the question: Am I always a brain in a vat?
(2) If I were always a brain in a vat, I could not raise this question.
(3) Therefore, I am not always a brain in a vat.

Note that we start with MA, we presuppose substantive empirical background beliefs, and it is reasonable for us to accept premises (1) and (2), even if we could not accept them without presupposing any substantive empirical background beliefs. Our position at the start is not agnostic, contrary to assumption (A).

Among the beliefs that we are entitled to presuppose, according to MA, is that we are not always brains in vats. Of course, if we can accept from the start that we are not always brains in vats, we do not need Putnam's argument to convince us of this. *The point of the argument is not to convince us that we are not always brains in vats – we already believed that, anyway – but to convince us that, contrary to our initial impression that the statement that we are not always brains in vats statement is bipolar, in fact, it is unipolar.* If the argument is successful, it transforms our understanding of the statement that we are not always brains in vats. We thought at first that, even though we believe it, we could make sense of its being false, and so that statement is bipolar. The point of the argument is to convince us that the statement is unipolar – we cannot make sense of its being false.

The argument changes our understanding of the statement not by starting from an agnostic point of view, but by showing that if we start with all the beliefs to which we are entitled by MA, we are in a position to see that the premises of Putnam's argument, which might at first appear to be bipolar, are unipolar.

Consider (2) first. We are in fact committed to Putnam's causal constraints on meaning, which support (2). These constraints may seem like empirical claims that are bipolar, and hence may actually be false. But we are unable to specify any minimally plausible alternative to those constraints – we know of no minimally plausible theory of reference that does not imply them, and do not see how to construct one. In this respect, our acceptance of the causal constraints on meaning and reference is like our acceptance of the law of non-contradiction – we are unable to specify any way in which it may actually be false. Given MA, this is enough for us to be *entitled* to accept the constraints and to regard our statement of them as unipolar.

Now consider (1). We take for granted our background empirical beliefs. But can we specify any way in which (1) may actually be false? If we understand Putnam's observations about meaning and reference in the way I described above, we cannot even try to specify any way in which (1) may actually be false without presupposing substantive beliefs that suffice for minimal competence in the use of the words of premise (1). One might think we could know that premise (1) is true without knowing what thought it expresses. But, as I have argued in detail elsewhere, our knowledge of what thoughts our utterances of (1) express is itself an aspect of, and inextricable from, our minimal linguistic competence. Hence we cannot even try to specify any way in which (1) may actually be false without presupposing substantive beliefs that suffice for knowledge of what thoughts our utterances of (1) express. In short, if we presuppose substantive beliefs that suffice for minimal competence in the use of the words of premise (1), we may infer that we are not in any possible world in which (1) is not true.

By this reasoning I can conclude that I cannot express or understand the statement that I am always a brain in a vat without presupposing substantive beliefs and principles from which I may infer that I am not always a brain in a vat. I therefore conclude that the statement is self-undermining, in the following sense:

Self-undermining: P judges that S is self-undermining (at t) if P judges that P cannot express or understand S without presupposing substantive beliefs and principles from which P may infer that S is not true.

But if I judge that the statement that I am always a brain in a vat is self-undermining, I judge that I am unable to make sense of the statement's actually being true. I am therefore entitled to accept its negation, and to regard it as unipolar. More generally,

(*)   If P judges that S is self-undermining (at t), then P is *entitled* to accept the negation of S and to regard the negation of S as *unipolar* (at t).

We may summarize these points as follows. By (1)–(3), we can come to see that what at first seemed to be a challenge to our acceptance of our best current theory, as licensed by MA – the apparent bipolarity of the statement we express by "I am always a brain in a vat" – is in fact not such a challenge. Properly viewed, argument (1)–(3) shows us that the statement is self-undermining, in the sense that, to express and understand it, we need to presuppose substantive background beliefs from which we may infer that it is not true. By

(*), then, we may infer that we are *entitled* to accept the statement that we are not always brains in vats and to regard it as unipolar.

Coda

To see how far we have come from standard ways of thinking about Putnam's argument, consider the following objection to an argument like (1)–(3):

> I can conclude from this [argument] that I am a normal human being rather than a BIV – and thereby lay the skeptical problem to rest – only if I can assume that I mean by "I may be a BIV" what normal human beings mean by it. But I am entitled to that assumption only if I am entitled to assume that I am a normal human being speaking English rather than a BIV speaking vat-English. This must be *shown* by an anti-skeptical argument, not assumed in advance. (Brueckner 1986: 160)

This objection is natural and appropriate, given Answer 1, but completely off-target, given Answer 2. If we accept Answer 2, as I propose, then we will not see Putnam's argument as "anti-skeptical" in Brueckner's sense of that term. We will instead think of it as a contribution to Putnam's lifelong project of clarifying the methodology of inquiry. It shows that if we assume MA, then the statement that we are always brains in a vat is not bipolar, as we initially thought, but unipolar – we are entitled not only to regard it as false, but also to conclude that we cannot make sense of its actually being true.

4 Brains in vats, causal constraints on reference and semantic externalism

Jesper Kallestrup

Putnam's proof (1981b) that we are not brains in vats (BIVs) is often construed as a semantic response to epistemological skepticism. In particular, the proof has typically been assumed to rely on semantic externalism, that is, the view that the semantic contents of referring terms depend on features of the external environment in a constitutive sense. This chapter provides a critical assessment of that assumption. Crucially, all that the best formulation of the proof relies on is a causal constraint on reference, which should be distinguished from a causal theory of reference. Some semantic internalists accept such a constraint in virtue of combining their view with the claim that reference is determined by satisfaction of causal descriptions. It turns out the semantic content of such descriptions constitutively depends neither on internal features of speakers nor on the sorts of environmental features which semantic externalists typically point to. So, if semantic externalists can appeal to Putnam's proof as a semantic response to epistemological skepticism, then so can those semantic internalists who endorse causal descriptivism.

4.1 Reference and causation

Putnam (1981b: 5ff.) argued that words do not intrinsically represent what they are about. For instance, 'Churchill' and 'squirrel' do not by themselves represent the individual Churchill and the species *sciurus vulgaris*, respectively. At least two conditions must be met if a word is to play a representational role. First, a word can represent an object or a natural kind only when used by an individual (S) with the intention of representing an object or a natural kind. If an ant crawling in the sand accidentally draws a picture of Churchill, it does not succeed in representing Churchill because it does not intend the indentation to represent Churchill. Secondly, a word is capable of representing an object or a natural kind in the external world only if appropriate causal connections are in place between S using that word and the relevant object or instances of the relevant kind. Our ant on the beach sustains no causal connections whatsoever with Churchill. Putnam takes representational intention and causal connection to be individually necessary for S to use a word to successfully represent an object or a natural kind. Whether these conditions should also be regarded as jointly sufficient is neither a question Putnam addresses nor one that we shall settle here. On the face of it, the first condition seems highly plausible. Creatures or systems incapable of forming representational intentions are ones to which we would ordinarily hesitate to attribute representational powers. But how exactly such intentions are to be understood is a vexed issue which we shall not probe into here. In fact, we henceforth restrict attention to the second necessary condition, and we shall only be discussing the aspect of representation that concerns the use by S of a word to refer to objects or natural kinds. With that in mind, let's try to characterize in more detail the causal connection that must be in place between S and an object or a natural kind if S is to use a singular or natural kind term to pick out an object or a natural kind.[1] To require that S have had actual causal encounters with the relevant object or kind is unduly demanding. After all, one can surely use the name 'Barack Obama' to refer to Barack Obama without ever having met the current US President, or use 'red squirrel' to refer to the species *sciurus vulgaris* even though one has only seen grey squirrels. Putnam (1981b: 16) appears to allow for such possibilities:

> one cannot refer to certain kinds of things, e.g. trees, if one has no causal interaction at all with them, or with things in terms of which they can be described.

But what exactly are the things causal interaction with which would allow S to refer to objects or natural kinds in the external world when using singular or natural kind terms if not those objects and kinds themselves? In some cases, physical pictures might suffice, but any kind of mental imagery would clearly not. What Putnam has in mind is more likely that in the case of 'tree,' causal interaction with trunks, roots, branches, leafs, etc. would enable S to describe a tree in sufficient detail without having encountered one. However, requiring

---

[1] Natural kind terms arguably refer to abstract natural kinds, or properties themselves, rather than the concrete instances of those kinds, or the objects instantiating those properties. For instance, 'tiger' picks out the natural kind *panthera tigris*, or the property of being a tiger, as opposed to the concrete tigers which are the actual instances of that kind, or the objects instantiating that property. Those instances or objects constitute the actual extension of the natural kind term 'tiger,' and they are non-rigidly picked out by the natural kind predicate 'being a tiger.' We want natural kind terms to be rigid, but their extensions obviously vary from world to world. In contrast, neither the existence of the property of being a tiger nor the existence of the natural kind *panthera tigris* varies from world to world. On this view, natural kind terms are thus singular referring terms rather than plural referring terms.

causal connections with enough mereological parts of the relevant objects or natural kinds to be able to describe those objects or kinds may still be too demanding. In some cases, S can refer successfully in the absence of any causal connection to any parts. Thus, S can use 'scandium' to refer to the chemical element Sc with atomic number 21, merely in virtue of knowing that scandium is a rare earth element. Like most of us, S has never encountered scandium, nor does S know anything about its physical or atomic properties such as density or radius. In other cases, S refers successfully but causal connections to mereological parts do not enable S to uniquely describe the whole object or natural kind. For instance, Putnam uses 'beech tree' and 'elm tree' to refer to beech and elm trees, respectively, even though in both cases he associates the stereotypical concept **a big deciduous tree growing in the eastern parts of the US**, which does not discriminate between them.[2] These examples illustrate the division of linguistic labor: in every linguistic community some speakers have more expertise in applying certain terms than others do. So, experts on botany possess a method by which they can effectively recognize whether any given tree that falls under Putnam's associated stereotype is an elm or a beech. When agnostic, or in error, about the application conditions of a term, Putnam and other ordinary speakers defer to experts in the know. We would want the causal constraint on reference to reflect this phenomenon:

(CC) If individual S is to use a referring term 'n' to refer to an object n or natural kind k at the actual world, then S must have had causal interaction with (i) n or instances of k, or with (ii) mereological parts of n or parts of instances of k sufficient to describe n or k uniquely or at least in some detail, or with individual S* who has had interaction with (individual S** who has had interaction with ...) (i) or (ii).

As formulated, (CC) yields the contours of a positive statement of Putnam's causal constraint on reference pertaining to singular or natural kind terms. In keeping with Putnam's claims about the division of linguistic labor and semantic deference, (CC) allows for S to successfully refer in cases where S either sustains no causal interaction with the referents or their mereological parts, or lacks uniquely identifying descriptive information of those referents.

Importantly, to say that (CC) is about what constrains reference is not to say that (CC) is about what determines reference. (CC) is not a view in

---

[2] I use bold to indicate concepts or semantic contents.

foundational semantics about what makes 'n' have the reference that 'n' has, let alone a view in descriptive semantics about what the semantic content of 'n' consists in. (CC) merely imposes a necessary condition on a theory of reference, which may well be satisfied by several such theories. Take the causal (-historical) theory of reference (CTR), as initially developed by Kripke (1980) and Putnam (1975, 1978), and subsequently refined by Devitt (1981), Devitt and Sterelny (1999), and others. The gist of (CTR) is that the referent of 'n' at the actual world is determined (or specified or identified) as whatever plays a certain causal role vis-à-vis 'n.'[3] Proponents of (CTR) disagree over the details of that role, but the rough idea is that once a term 'n' is introduced into language by some act of baptism, 'n' retains the same reference as long as its users are linked to that original act via a causal-historical chain of successive users. S succeeds in referring with 'n' by intentionally borrowing the reference from S*, S**, etc., earlier in the chain, stretching back to the dubbing of the object or natural kind in question. (CTR) could also allow for the reference of 'n' to be fixed by causal encounters with mereological parts of the referent of 'n.' Recall Burge's (1982) example of a chemically uninformed speaker who, despite the absence of water, uses 'water' to think thoughts involving **water** in virtue of relying on those scientific experts who on the basis of separate causal encounters with hydrogen and oxygen construct a false chemical theory to the effect that these elements bond to form H_2O.[4] If (CTR) is finessed to accommodate such examples, (CC) and (CTR) both have it that a referential use of 'n' by S is dependent on the obtaining of causal connections between S, or those from whom S acquired 'n,' and the referent of 'n,' or its mereological parts.

Another point of similarity is that neither (CC) nor (CTR) makes any ontological commitments.[5] (CC) makes no assumptions about the ontological category to which the referents of 'n' belong. Likewise, (CTR) is silent on the question of which entities play which causal roles vis-à-vis which referring terms. We have so far restricted attention to terms which purport to refer to entities in the external world, but (CC) and (CTR) apply *mutatis mutandis* to terms which aim to pick out mental objects or properties. Suppose that S

---

[3] Putnam (1978: 58) calls this "the social co-operation plus contribution of the environment theory of the specification of reference."

[4] Burge (2010: 68–9) argues that scientists were able to think thoughts containing the empty concept **phlogiston** in virtue of bearing certain relations to other thoughts containing relevant non-empty, wide concepts, for example the concepts **physical body, burning** or **mass**. Thoughts containing **phlogiston** are constitutively related through inference and scientific theory to the latter thoughts. Moreover, a novice just learning phlogiston theory could be said to think thoughts containing **phlogiston** through communication with experts on such theory.

[5] Brueckner (1995) makes this point in the case of (CTR).

introduces 'n' as a term for a red after-image which S enjoys after intense light has ceased to stimulate the eyes. Because seeing such an after-image involves a causal relation, S can use 'n' to refer to that mental object, and so can S* provided S* intends to borrow the reference from S and that the right causal-historical links are in place.

There is nevertheless an important difference between (CC) and (CTR) in that only the latter is a theory about what determines reference. Only (CTR) makes a claim in foundational semantics about the facts in virtue of which 'n' has the reference that it has.[6] More precisely, what determines the reference of S's use of 'n' is the obtaining of certain causal-historical connections between S's use of 'n' and its referent.[7] Since, by the lights of (CC), these connections are precisely the ones that must be in place if S is to use 'n' to refer to its referent, it follows that if (CTR) is true, then so is (CC). But the converse is false. The best way to illustrate how (CC) may be true, while (CTR) is false, is to consider causal descriptivism, as developed and defended by Lewis (1984), Kroon (1987), and Jackson (1998). Thus Lewis (1984: 226–7) explicitly opts for a version of descriptivism according to which the associated descriptions are largely couched in causal terms, thereby incorporating a Putnam-style causal constraint on reference, while avoiding alleged problems for its rival (CTR). Let's work this view into shape by focusing on a causal version of what Soames (2005: 19, 69) calls weak descriptivism. We can define weak causal descriptivism (WCD) as the view that an associated causal description invariably fixes the reference of 'n,' that is, as the view that S associates with 'n' the description "the object or instance of a natural kind linked by a causal-historical chain to my present use of 'n'" such that S uses 'n' to refer to whatever object or natural kind satisfies that description at the actual world, no matter how the actual world turns out. Just as (CTR) is a view in foundational semantics, so is (WCD).[8] That is to say, both (CTR) and (WCD) offer an account in foundational semantics of the facts in virtue of which 'n' has the reference that it has. More precisely, according to (WCD), what determines (or specifies or identifies) the reference of S's use of 'n' is the satisfaction by an object or a natural kind of an associated causal description.

---

[6] For more on the distinction between descriptive and foundational semantics see Stalnaker (1997: 535).
[7] (CTR) is not a view about that which comprises the semantic content of 'n.' There is no claim that the causal-historical link of communicative exchanges through which 'n' is passed on from speaker to speaker yields its semantic content.
[8] (WCD) resembles (CTR) by not providing an account of what the semantic content of 'n' consists in. Neither (WCD) nor (CTR) is a view in descriptive semantics.

It should now be obvious why (WCD) is a counterexample to the inference from (CC) to (CTR). According to (WCD), S uses 'n' to refer to an object or an instance of a natural kind at the actual world only if there is a causal-historical connection between S's present use of 'n' and that object or natural kind instance. But if such a connection is in place, then S's use of 'n' satisfies the causal constraint in (CC). According to (CC), S can use 'n' to refer to an object or a natural kind at the actual world if S has had causal interaction with that object or instances of that kind. It follows that if (WCD) is true, so is (CC). So, (WCD) and (CTR) both entail (CC). Nevertheless, (WCD) and (CTR) are incompatible views about how reference at the actual world is determined. According to (WCD), reference is determined by satisfaction of associated causal descriptions. That applies not just at the time at which 'n' is introduced into language by some act of baptism, but even to S's current use of 'n.' According to (CTR), however, satisfaction of associated descriptions plays no role in accounting for S's current use of 'n.' True, (CTR) is consistent with the possibility of descriptions playing a role in fixing reference at a dubbing ceremony, but friends of (CTR) tend to follow Kripke (1980) in taking the reference of 'n' to be typically fixed by perception-cum-demonstration.

Here is the upshot. To think that adopting (CTR) is the only way to make (CC) true is mistaken. (WCD) also makes (CC) true, but since (CTR) and (WCD) are mutually exclusive theories, there is no valid inference from (CC) to (CTR).[9]

4.2 Putnam's proof that we are not brains in a vat

Putnam (1981b: 5–6) asked us to imagine the following brain-in-a-vat (BIV) scenario. Without S's knowledge, S's brain has been skillfully removed from the rest of her body, immersed in a vat full of nutrient fluid so as to stay alive, and hooked up to a super-scientific computer. S is a human being, but you can imagine S to be yourself. This computer, as controlled by an evil neuroscientist, feeds S's envatted brain sensory experiences just as if S were a perfectly normal human being going about her business in the external world. As normal embodied experiences and the BIV experiences are qualitatively indistinguishable, S has no inkling of the predicament she is in. The only difference between these experiences is causal: while S's embodied experiences are caused by objects in her immediate external environment, S's

---

[9] We take no stand on whether (WCD) is preferable to (CTR). Both views are associated with well-known problems which we shall not rehearse here.

illusory experiences are induced by features of the computer program. But such a difference in aetiology is undetectable from within those experiences. Putnam proceeds to envisage increasingly more radical scenarios: perhaps the evil scientist unwittingly removed S's brain from her body at birth and placed it in a vat, perhaps all human beings including the evil scientist suffer the same fate as S, or perhaps the entire universe happens to consist of automatic machinery tending a vat full of brains and nervous systems. We shall focus on the scenario mostly discussed in the literature according to which a single individual has always been envatted.

The BIV scenario presents a skeptical challenge to the effect that S cannot know she is not a BIV.[10] There are different ways to motivate this claim. Assume knowledge requires favoring evidence and all the evidence S has to go on is the totality of her experiences. Because the experiences S has when S perceives the external world are qualitatively indistinguishable from those S would have if S were a BIV, no evidence S has favors the former hypothesis over the latter. Suppose instead that knowledge requires a sensitive, experiential basis for belief. In that case, S's lack of knowledge that she is not a BIV is down to the fact that if S were a BIV, S would still believe that she is not a BIV on the experiential basis on which S actually holds that belief. From either conception of knowledge, the skeptic may then proceed via a closure principle of knowledge from S's lack of knowledge that she is not a BIV to the conclusion that S lacks swathes of knowledge of ordinary propositions such as that she has hands.

Some anti-skeptical responses are distinctively epistemic. If S's evidential base is expanded to include knowledge of the external world, which admittedly seems like a blatantly question-begging move, then S has evidence against the BIV hypothesis. Likewise, if all knowledge requires is a safe (experiential) basis for belief, then S can know the falsity of the BIV hypothesis. Putnam (1981b: 7–8), however, propounded a semantic response to the epistemic challenge presented by the BIV hypothesis. His line of thought was that given a certain constraint on the use of words to describe the hypothesis, its falsity is a condition on being able to so much as entertain thoughts about it. More precisely, once we appreciate how usage of referential terms requires causal links with their referents, it turns out S cannot think she is being radically deceived by the evil scientist unless she is not. Obviously, the skeptic has no argument if S is denied the thought that the BIV hypothesis

---

[10] Brueckner and Altschul (2010) detect some difficulties in using Putnam's description to formulate a skeptical scenario in which one is massively mistaken. For instance, recent envatment does not easily yield that result. They suggest instead a piecemeal procedure for producing a spate of skeptical arguments.

might be true. It follows that this hypothesis is false, not just as a matter of fact but necessarily so.

Against the backdrop of the BIV hypothesis, let's try to render Putnam's proof that we are not BIVs more precise. Since the proof depends for its cogency on each of us inferring the conclusion on the basis of knowing the premises while acknowledging its validity, we shall use the first-person pronoun.[11] For a start, consider the following simplified formulation:[12]

(1) I think the thought that I am not a BIV.
(2) I cannot possibly be a BIV if I think the thought that I am not a BIV.
(3) So, I cannot possibly be a BIV.

The argument from (1)–(2) to (3) raises the complication that (2) seems to presuppose a causal constraint on the possibility of thinking thoughts containing the semantic concept **BIV** which no BIV can satisfy. However, (CC) was limited to the referential use of words. We need an additional premise to the effect that my thinking a thought is causally constrained in the same way the sentence that I use to express that thought is causally constrained. While such a premise seems plausible as long as my thought is fully captured by the proposition that is expressed by the sentence which says what my thought is about, Lewis (1983a: 143–54), Loar (1996: 186–8), Bach (1997: 235), and Jackson (2003: 68) have argued that in general we have to tread carefully when drawing conclusions about the contents of intentional states from premises about the semantics of sentences that report such states.[13] In particular, one might worry that causal constraints on the use of terms need not carry over seamlessly to contents of the thoughts that can be expressed by sentences containing those terms. In any case, we shall restrict attention to a formulation of Putnam's proof that is centered on the idea of disquotation, thus avoiding commitment to a causal constraint on thoughts. To say that my language disquotes means that I can use any meaningful, referring term to characterize its own reference. Knowing such semantic features as the meaning of 'refer' and of quotation marks furnish me with *a priori* knowledge that

---

[11] Wright (1992: 91ff) discussed the intriguing possibility that we might be radically deceived in ways that for us are unthinkable. For instance, Putnam's proof leaves unanswered the possibility that someone else could truly use the sentence 'he is a BIV' to think the thought that I am a BIV.

[12] Compare also with Warfield (1999: 78).

[13] In particular, Loar (1996) argued that psychological content, that is, roughly, whatever individuates beliefs in commonsense psychological explanations, is poorly captured by that-clauses of belief reports, and Bach (1997) denied that that-clauses capture any sort of belief content in that such content is much more fine-grained than the content of such clauses.

my own language is subject to disquotation. Here is Wright's succinct rendition (1992: 74), where vat-English is the language of the BIV:

(4) My language disquotes.
(5) In vat-English 'BIV' does not refer to BIVs.
(6) In my language, 'BIV' is a meaningful expression.
(7) In my language, 'BIV' refers to BIVs.
(8) So, my language is not vat-English.
(9) But if I am a BIV, my language is vat-English.
(10) So, I am not a BIV.

Whether, as advertised, (4)–(10) amount to a proof that I am not a BIV is a vexed question which we shall not settle here, apart from making one pertinent observation. Brueckner (1986, 1999) argued that premise (7) is question-begging: my tokens of 'BIV' refer to BIVs only if my language is not vat-English, but if I am a BIV, then my language is vat-English, so my tokens of 'BIV' refer to BIVs only if I am not a BIV.[14] The worry is that appeal to the device of disquotation is illegitimate in an argument against a skeptic who claims I cannot know which language I speak because I cannot know whether I am a BIV.[15] Following Brueckner, the argument yields at most the conclusion that my tokens of 'I am not a BIV' are true. Before I can disquote that sentence and arrive at (10), I need knowledge that I speak English rather than vat-English, which I have only when I know that I am not a BIV.[16]

Brueckner's response raises the question of what justifies (7) and (5) in the first place. Clearly, the reason Putnam (1981b: 12–17) thinks that a BIV who speaks vat-English cannot refer to BIVs is that there is no causal connection between a BIV's use of 'BIV' and actual BIVs (apart from the triviality that the BIV's use of 'BIV' depends on the presence of itself, but such a connection

---

[14] English is qualitatively (e.g. syntactically and phonologically) similar to vat-English, but they count as numerically distinct languages in virtue of their different descriptive semantics.

[15] At this juncture, Wright's (1992: 74–5) distinction between being permitted to disquote my own language and possessing identifying knowledge of reference should be borne in mind. To allow for knowledge that 'n' refers to n is not to attribute any knowledge of who or what n is. Similarly, Falvey and Owens (1994: 126–36) argued that any proficient English speaker has knowledge of propositions expressed by a homophonic theory of truth for that language. I can therefore know that my sentence tokens have disquotational truth conditions. Such disquotational knowledge is different from knowing the empirical propositions expressed by a non-homophonic truth-theory for English.

[16] Brueckner (1986) went on to argue that Putnam's proof gives rise to epistemological skepticism about the meanings of our own language. From now on we assume that 'my language' in (7) refers to English, and hence set the question of whether (7) is question-begging aside. For the record, Putnam (1981b) displayed little interest in these epistemological issues.

obtains between the BIV's use of any term in vat-English and this particular BIV).[17] Indeed, owing to the lack of any (special) causal connections between any token terms in vat-English and external physical objects, BIVs are incapable of referring to any such objects. One option is instead to say that the BIV, just like the ant in the sand, fails to refer to anything at all. Pretty much all token words in vat-English that aim to refer are simply empty. A less dramatic option floated by Putnam (1981b) is to say that the BIV refers to what typically causes its word tokens. So, when the BIV uses 'BIV,' it might be referring to the electronic impulses that cause BIV experiences, or the features of the computer program that are causally responsible for those electronic impulses, or perhaps to a BIV-in-the-image. After all, there is a close causal connection between the use of 'BIV' in vat-English and the presence of such impulses or BIVs in the images. Putnam's text is strikingly non-committal on this point, arguably because all his proof needs (in premise (5)) is the negative claim that a BIV cannot refer to BIVs, and so cannot use 'BIV' to express the concept **BIV**. Reflect also that, even though a token in vat-English of 'I am a BIV' expresses the false proposition **I am a BIV-in-the-image** (or some similar deviant proposition), the BIV need not be massively mistaken. For instance, a token in vat-English of 'there is a sheep in the field' might then express the true proposition **there is a sheep in the field-in-the-image**. Be that as it may. For our purposes, the key point is that, following Putnam, only an embodied human being who speaks English can use 'BIV' to refer to BIVs, and hence express the (false) proposition **I am a BIV** by uttering 'I am a BIV', because only such a being sustains the right causal connections to BIVs.

The foregoing makes it evident that Putnam took causal considerations to play a crucial role in accounting for why a word in a given language has a particular reference. Since Putnam (1975, 1978) also arguably advocated the causal (-historical) theory of reference (CTR) from Section 4.1, many commentators have uncritically assumed that Putnam's proof rests on such a theory. Tichý (1986), Dell'Utri (1990), David (1991), Ludwig (1992), Brueckner (1992b, 1995), Steinitz (1994) and Warfield (1995) are cases in point. To my knowledge, Wright (1992: 171) was the first to observe that such an assumption is premature. Even though Putnam at times writes as though the justification of (5) and (7) is driven by (CTR), his proof does not strictly need (CTR). That is to say, while (5) and (7) certainly follow from (CTR), those two premises could be true even if the referent of 'BIV' at the

---

[17] Obviously, BIVs do not literally speak a language, or use words in the way we do in utterances of sentences. Such talk merely implies that words run through their minds in some sense.

actual world is not determined as whatever plays a certain causal role vis-à-vis 'BIV.' All the proof needs is the weaker claim that a use of 'BIV' must be causally constrained by its reference. Not in the strong sense that every single token of 'BIV' in English must have been caused by a BIV if that token is to refer to a BIV. For any such token to refer to a BIV, it suffices that there are suitable causal connections between other such tokens and BIVs. Indeed, (5) and (7) would be true if what was required for a use in English of 'BIV' to refer to a BIV was that some tokens of 'BIV' were causally connected either to mereological parts of BIVs sufficient to describe a BIV, or to a use by some other English speaker of 'BIV' which was causally connected to BIVs, or mereological parts thereof. Assuming such a relatively weak constraint, it still follows that only tokens of 'BIV' in English refer to BIVs. The point is now that such a causal constraint is exactly what is captured by (CC) from Section 4.1. But we also argued in Section 4.1 that weak causal descriptivism (WCD) entails (CC). The rest of this section shows that (5) and (7) accord with (WCD).

To recapitulate, the two theories of reference (WCD) and (CTR) offer incompatible accounts of what makes a term have the reference that it has. The disagreement is about whether reference at the actual world is determined by satisfaction of associated causal descriptions. Thus both involve imposing a causal constraint on reference, as encapsulated by (CC). When it comes to the term 'BIV,' (WCD) says that its reference is fixed at the actual world, no matter how it turns out, by satisfaction of the causal description "the object linked by a causal-historical chain to my present use of 'BIV.'" This means that when I use 'BIV' in the actual world I refer to whatever object is causally-historically linked to my present use of that term. Now suppose I am an embodied human being who speaks English and causally interacts with BIVs. In that case, (WCD) predicts in accordance with (7) that I use 'BIV' to refer to BIVs. Suppose instead that I am a BIV who speaks vat-English and causally interacts with features of the computer program, or perhaps with features in the image. Putnam (1981b) was explicit that such a supposition involves considering a possible world as a candidate for the actual world rather than a counterfactual world. That is to say, we are asked to consider the possibility that the actual world turns out in such a way that I am a BIV. In that case, since (WCD) is a view about reference-fixing at the actual world regardless of how it turns out, (WCD) implies that my tokens of 'BIV' refer to features of the computer program, or perhaps to a BIV-in-the-image, but not to BIVs. That is exactly what (5) says. So, both (7) and (5) are consonant with (WCD).

4.3 Semantic externalism and semantic internalism

Let's take stock. In Section 4.1 we argued that Putnam's causal constraint on reference (CC) is entailed by both weak causal descriptivism (WCD) and the causal (-historical) theory of reference (CTR), which are incompatible views in foundational semantics. In Section 4.2 we first presented Putnam's proof that we are not BIVs, and then argued that the two crucial disquotational steps are supported by (CC), irrespective of whether (CTR) or (WCD) holds. In this final section we turn to the implications for the debate over wide or narrow content. Our contention is that if the semantic internalist adopts a stronger version of causal descriptivism, then she can embrace Putnam's proof as pertaining to meaning without conceding the existence of the kind of wide concepts that her externalist opponent upholds.

So far we have shown that (CC) implies a difference in reference between English and vat-English tokens of 'BIV.' Where an embodied human being refers to BIVs, her envatted counterpart refers to BIVs-in-the-image (or the like). Since they are internally identical in terms of sharing physical properties (of the brain) and undergoing qualitatively identical, perceptual experiences, what they refer to when using 'BIV' is not completely fixed by their internal, physical or experiential, features. Moreover, stereotypical or purely descriptive concepts are also insufficient to determine the reference of those terms with which they are associated. Bear in mind Putnam's example of 'beech' and 'elm' from Section 4.1. What matters is the obtaining of appropriate causal connections between tokens of 'BIV' in English and BIVs, and tokens of 'BIV' in vat-English and features of the image (or whatever).

We also followed Putnam (1981b: 15) in taking tokens of 'BIV' in English and vat-English to express the (semantic) concepts **BIV** and **BIV-in-the-image** (or a similar non-standard concept), respectively. But what justifies the claim that an embodied human being and a BIV's use of 'BIV' not merely differ in reference, but also express distinct concepts? After all, (CC) pertains only to reference. What is needed to make the connection is the principle that meaning (in the sense of semantic content) determines reference such that two terms have the same reference if their meanings are identical. Once that assumption is on board, it follows from the fact that English and vat-English tokens of 'BIV' differ in reference that they must also have different meanings, that is, express distinct concepts. Again we can point to the fact that an embodied human being and a BIV are internal duplicates in terms of sharing physical properties (of the brain) and perceptual experiences.

Consequently, if meaning determines reference, and their respective tokens of 'BIV' differ in reference, the question of which concepts those tokens express is not entirely settled by their internal, physical or experiential, make-up. For if meaning were exclusively a matter of such internal features, then these tokens would express the same concept. What makes for a difference in meaning is rather the obtaining of appropriate causal connections between on the one hand tokens of 'BIV,' and on the other hand BIVs and features of the image (or whatever).

The foregoing has led a number of commentators to maintain either that Putnam is using semantic externalism directly to support the premises of his proof, or that those premises rest on a causal constraint on reference which gives expression to semantic externalism. DeRose (1999, 2000), Bernecker (2004), Brueckner (1992b, 2005), Stern (2007) and Madden (2013) are cases in point. Whether these commentators are correct depends very much on how semantic externalism is understood. Contrast the following two formulations:

Negative external dependence (NED):	The meaning of singular or natural kind term 'n' as used by S is not completely dependent in a constitutive sense on internal facts about what's going on physically or experientially inside S's brain.
Positive external dependence (PED):	The meaning of singular or natural kind term 'n' as used by S is at least in part constitutively dependent on the underlying scientific nature of the object or natural kind (instances) with which S, or a fellow speaker of S, has been in causal contact.

We can thus characterize semantic externalism in terms of either (NED) or (PED). The interesting observation is that in so far as Putnam's proof is concerned only (NED) is supported by (CC) in conjunction with the principle that meaning determines reference. Here's why. We argued in Section 4.2 that all premises (5) and (7) need for their support is (CC). That is to say, if (CC) holds, then an embodied human being uses 'BIV' to refer to BIVs, whereas a BIV, who sustains no causal connection with BIVs, cannot use 'BIV' to refer to BIVs. Putnam tentatively suggests that a BIV refers to BIVs-in-the-image, or perhaps to electronic impulses, but what exactly the BIV is picking out is strictly irrelevant as far as Putnam's proof goes. Now, if we add the principle that meaning determines reference, it follows that an embodied human being and a BIV mean different things by tokens of 'BIV.' The former expresses the concept **BIV**, but just as in the case of reference, Putnam does not commit to any particular concept being expressed by the latter. If, say, the BIV refers to BIVs-in-the-image by 'BIV,' then that token expresses the concept **BIV-in-the-image**. There is no claim that either **BIV** or **BIV-in-the-image** depends constitutively on the underlying scientific nature of their referents. That is to say, neither the proof itself nor Putnam's accompanying text supports the positive claim that tokens in English and in vat-English express distinct concepts which depend for their constitution on the underlying scientific nature of their referents. What matters is that a BIV cannot use 'BIV' to express the concept **BIV** that an embodied human being expresses, regardless of such positive dependencies of constitution. Since the two beings are internal duplicates whose tokens of 'BIV' express distinct concepts, what they mean by 'BIV' is not wholly dependent on internal facts about what's going on inside their brains. So, (NED) is sufficient to support Putnam's claim that English and vat-English tokens of 'BIV' express distinct concepts. (PED) is arguably supported by Putnam's Twin Earth argument (1975), and (PED) would, if true, lend support to Putnam's claim, but its truth does not hang on (PED).

In the remaining part of this section we argue that the semantic internalist has the resources to accommodate Putnam's claim that 'BIV' has different meanings in English and vat-English. Just as (NED) and (PED) capture two distinct kinds of semantic externalism, we can define by negation two corresponding versions of semantic internalism. Which formulation is more accurate? The view that meaning is constitutively dependent on nothing but internal facts about what's going on inside the brain is not one that many contemporary internalists would want to embrace. For example, Jackson and Pettit (1993: 271–3) characterize narrow concepts as intra-world narrow, where a property P of x is intra-world narrow if and only if in every possible world where x has P any internal duplicate of x has P. Intra-world narrow properties are only shared by internal duplicates within the same worlds. Jackson and Pettit deny that any narrow concept is inter-world narrow in the sense that internal duplicates across possible worlds are also concept duplicates.[18] As these philosophers hold that narrow concepts depend on general features of the world, they would endorse (NED). They would, however, reject (PED). The reason is that (PED) allows for the possibility that internal duplicates within the same world fail to be concept duplicates in virtue of causally interacting with objects or (instances of) natural kinds

---

[18] See also Stalnaker (1989: 289–91) and Kallestrup (2011b: 119–22).

whose possibly unknown scientific natures are very different. Putnam's Twin Earth argument, remember, provides a familiar illustration. Since semantic internalism is consistent with (NED) but inconsistent with (PED), the debate between friends and foes of this view is best characterized in terms of disagreement over (PED).[19]

Now suppose our semantic internalist adopts weak causal descriptivism (WCD) from Section 4.2. In that case, she can offer an explanation of the truth of premises (5) and (7) in Putnam's proof. We argued that (WCD) entails (CC), and the truth of (CC) is all (5) and (7) require. So, it looks like our semantic internalist is home and dry. The problem is that (WCD) is merely a view about how reference is fixed in the actual world. In particular, (WCD) is silent on the question of which concepts are expressed by English and vat-English tokens of 'BIV.' Since we take it as common ground that those tokens differ in reference, and that meaning determines reference, the challenge for our semantic internalist is to provide a consistent account of how they can express distinct concepts when produced by internal duplicates. After all, semantic internalism pertains to the constitutive dependency of meaning on internal features. For this purpose, we need a view in descriptive semantics.[20] Let strong causal descriptivism (SCD) be the view that an associated causal description gives the meaning of a singular or natural kind term 'n.' According to (SCD), the description "the object linked by a causal-historical chain to my present use of 'n'" as associated with 'n' by S yields the semantic content of 'n' such that 'n' refers to whatever object satisfies that description at a possible world. Suppose now that we combine semantic internalism with (SCD).[21] In that case, an utterance by an embodied human being of 'BIV is F' is true if and only if the object linked by a causal-historical chain to that being's present use of 'BIV' is F. In contrast, a use of the same sentence by a BIV is true if and only if the object linked by a causal-historical chain to that BIV's present use of 'BIV' is F. Given that a difference in truth conditions implies a difference in semantic content, an embodied human being uses 'BIV' to express the concept **the object linked by a causal-historical chain to that being's present use of 'BIV,'** while a BIV expresses the concept **the object linked by a causal-historical chain to that BIV's**

---

[19] Here we restrict attention to the natural kind externalism that Putnam (1975) defended, but nothing much would change had we instead formulated a social externalist version of (PED).
[20] The same is true of semantic externalism. Mere appeal to (CTR) cannot furnish an account of which concepts are expressed by English and vat-English tokens of 'BIV.' What is called for is a view in descriptive semantics such as (PED), or perhaps the direct reference view according to which the reference of 'BIV' exhausts its meaning.
[21] See also Jackson (1998, 2003).

present use of 'BIV.' Owing to the occurrence of the indexical 'my' the two tokens of the same sentence type differ in truth conditions, and therefore also in the concepts that are expressed.

The foregoing shows that if, as we suggested, the disagreement between semantic externalists and internalists is a dispute over (PED), that is, the claim that meaning is partially dependent on the underlying scientific nature of the referents, then our semantic internalist can adopt (SCD) in order to explain how English and vat-English tokens of 'BIV' express different concepts, without having to accept (PED). For (SCD) has it that any conceptual difference between English and vat-English tokens of 'BIV' stems from a difference in contextual parameters, that is, the identity of the speaker, rather than differences in the underlying scientific nature of the referents. Indeed, any two English (or vat-English) tokens of 'BIV' would also express different concepts. Our semantic internalist can thus explain why such tokens express distinct concepts without invoking (PED). Still, a residual worry remains. Even if semantic internalism is understood as the negation of (PED), is the spirit of the view not compromised by the fact that (SCD) allows for a BIV and a normal human being to express distinct concepts by tokens of the same word type? We noted earlier that semantic internalists deny that narrow concepts are inter-world narrow. So, the fact that two internal duplicates fail to be concept duplicates poses no problem if only they are located in different possible worlds. One might then go on to argue that an embodied human being and a BIV must be located in worlds governed by different laws of nature. However, the BIV hypothesis is not obviously nomologically impossible, and in any case (SCD) allows for the possibility that internal duplicates who inhabit the same world fail to express the same concept. At this juncture our semantic internalist should concede that just as inter-world internal duplicates can fail to be concept duplicates, so can intra-world duplicates as long as any conceptual difference is merely down to contextual parameters. To hold such a view admittedly represents a slight departure from a more traditional internalist position, but the important point is that our internalist remains uncommitted to (PED), which defines the semantic externalist position in any robust sense.[22]

---

[22] Our semantic internalist might also argue that, even though sentences containing 'BIV' have different truth conditions in English and in vat-English, and so an embodied human being and a BIV's use of 'BIV' express distinct concepts, that need not imply a difference in their belief content. Perhaps, following Lewis (1979), they believe alike in that they both self-ascribe the property of presently using 'BIV' in a way that is linked by a causal-historical chain to an object. For more details see also Jackson (2003) and Kallestrup (2011a).

4.4 Conclusion

We argued in Section 4.1 that Putnam's causal constraint on reference (CC) is entailed by his causal theory of reference (CTR), but (CC) does not entail (CTR). Weak causal descriptivism (WCD) also entails (CC), yet is inconsistent with (CTR). In Section 4.2 we turned to Putnam's proof. The two key premises that English tokens of 'BIV' refer to BIVs, whereas vat-English tokens of 'BIV' refer to BIVs-in-the-image (or something similar) rest merely on (CC). Hence, it is possible to opt for (WCD) rather than (CTR) in support of those premises. In Section 4.3 we then considered Putnam's claim that English and vat-English tokens of 'BIV' also express distinct concepts. The semantic externalist thesis that certain concepts are constitutively dependent on the underlying scientific nature of their referents (PED), allegedly established by Putnam's Twin Earth argument, supports that claim. But so does strong causal descriptivism (SCD), according to which English and vat-English tokens of 'BIV' express distinct concepts in virtue of a hidden indexical element. A semantic internalist who avails herself of (SCD) can thus account for the difference in meaning between English and vat-English tokens of 'BIV' without any commitment to (PED). The downside is that such an internalist must admit that not all internal duplicates are concept duplicates, but that never was or should be a claim that defines her view. The upshot is that semantic externalists are no better placed than semantic internalists in terms of being able to appeal to Putnam's proof as a semantic response to epistemological skepticism.

5 Extended minds in vats

Sven Bernecker

Hilary Putnam has famously argued that "we are brains in a vat" is necessarily false. The argument assumes content externalism (also known as semantic externalism and anti-individualism), that is, the view that the individuation conditions of mental content depend, in part, on external or relational properties of the subject's environment. Recently content externalism has given rise to the hypothesis of the extended mind, whereby mental states are not only externally individuated but also externally located states. This chapter argues that when content externalism is combined with the extended mind hypothesis it is robbed of its anti-skeptical power. Given the extended mind hypothesis, the supercomputer and the envatted brain can be regarded as aspects of the extended mind of the evil scientist. On this view, the thought contents of the coupled brain–computer–scientist system do not differ from those of a normal human. But without a difference in thought contents Putnam's anti-skeptical argument crumbles.

Apart from giving rise to the extended mind hypothesis, content externalism has given rise to the thesis of embedded cognition, that is, the view that cognition depends not just on the brain but also on the body and its interaction with the environment. This chapter argues that when content externalism is combined with the thesis of embedded cognition, the vat has to fill in everything the world provides for the brain to realize the kind of mind we have. But if the vat fills in everything the world provides, then the skeptical problem evaporates.

Section 5.1 explains content externalism and gives a brief account of Putnam's refutation of the brain-in-a-vat scenario. Section 5.2 discusses the hypothesis of the extended mind. Section 5.3 argues that adding the extended mind hypothesis to content externalism undermines Putnam's refutation of the brain-in-a-vat scenario. In Section 5.5 it is shown that the thesis of

---

For helpful comments on an earlier version of this chapter I am grateful to Peter Baumann and Maura Priest.

embedded cognition takes away the skeptical sting the brain-in-a-vat scenario is said to have. Section 5.5 offers some concluding remarks.

5.1 Putnam on brains in vats

External world skepticism states that we don't know many of the worldly propositions that we take ourselves to know. Skeptical arguments typically take as their starting point skeptical scenarios. A skeptical scenario introduces a possibility concerning how the world really is that is incompatible with how we experience the world and that, given our empirical evidence, we are ostensibly unable to rule out. The skeptical conclusion follows from my inability to rule out this possibility. A classical skeptical scenario is Descartes's Evil Demon scenario:

> I will suppose ... that ... some malicious demon of the utmost power and cunning has employed all his energies in order to deceive me. I shall think that the sky, the air, the earth, colors, shapes, sounds and all external things are merely delusions of dreams that he has devised to ensnare my judgment. I shall consider myself as not having hands or eyes, or flesh, or blood or senses, but as falsely believing that I have all these things. I shall stubbornly and firmly persist in this mediation ... I am like a prisoner who is enjoying an imaginary freedom while asleep. (Descartes 1984: 15)

Hilary Putnam's brain-in-a-vat scenario is a contemporary version of Descartes's Evil Demon story. Here is Putnam's classic passage:

> [I]magine that a human being (you can imagine this to be yourself) has been subjected to an operation by an evil scientist. The person's brain (your brain) has been removed from the body and placed in a vat of nutrients which keeps the brain alive. The nerve endings have been connected to a super-scientific computer which causes the person whose brain it is to have the illusion that everything is perfectly normal. There seem to be people, objects, the sky, etc; but really all the person (you) is experiencing is the result of electronic impulses traveling from the computer to the nerve endings. The computer is so clever that if the person tries to raise his hand, the feedback from the computer will cause him to 'see' and 'feel' the hand being raised. Moreover, by varying the program, the evil scientist can cause the victim to 'experience' (or hallucinate) any situation or environment the evil scientist wishes. He can also obliterate the memory of the brain operation, so that the victim will see himself to have always

been in this environment. It can even seem to the victim that he is sitting and reading these very words about the amusing but quite absurd supposition that there is an evil scientist who removes people's brains from their bodies and places them in a vat of nutrients which keep the brains alive. The nerve endings are supposed to be connected to a super-scientific computer which causes the person whose brain it is to have the illusion that ... (Putnam 1981b: 5–6)

While the brain-in-a-vat scenario "violates no physical law," and is "perfectly consistent with everything we have experienced," Putnam (1981b: 7) still insists that it "cannot possibly be true, because it is, in a certain way, self-refuting." The statement "we are brains in a vat" is said to be *necessarily* false. If we are not brains in vats, then the statement "we are brains in vats" is obviously false. But Putnam argues that the statement "we are brains in vats" is also false if uttered or thought by a brain in a vat. This part of the argument rests on *content externalism*. Content externalism is the view that the meanings of my words and the contents of my thoughts depend in part on causal relations that I bear to aspects of my social and/or physical environment rather than only on internal properties of my mind and brain. What my words mean and my thoughts refer to is determined by the environmental features their usage or tokening is causally connected to.

A common strategy for motivating content externalism is to describe a situation in which there are two individuals who share all their intrinsic properties, but who differ in respect to some mental properties because they inhabit different environments. In "The Meaning of 'Meaning'" Putnam asks us to consider this thought experiment. Suppose Oscar is an English-speaker who uses the word 'water' in the same way as the other members of his linguistic community. He doesn't have any considerable knowledge of the chemical properties of water. Suppose that there exists somewhere in a nearby galaxy a Twin Earth, that is, a planet that is a molecule-for-molecule duplicate of Earth. The only difference between the two planets is that no water is present on Twin Earth. What is found there instead is a liquid which looks, tastes, and behaves like water but has the chemical composition XYZ and not H_2O. Like each one of us, Oscar has a molecular duplicate on Twin Earth.[1] Twin S has endured experiences that are just like Oscar's, except that where

---

[1] Here and elsewhere I follow the tradition in neglecting the fact that strictly speaking none of Oscar's molecules are identical with those of his twin, for Oscar's molecules contain H_2O while Twin Oscar's contain XYZ. The thought experiment can be changed to accommodate this fact.

Oscar has encountered H_2O, he has encountered XYZ; and neither of them is aware of the constitution of the liquids they refer to as 'water.'

The reference of Oscar's 'water' expression is different from the reference of his twin's 'water' expression. Oscar's expression refers to H_2O while Twin Oscar's refers to XYZ. Given that reference is part of the meaning, the meaning of Oscar's 'water' expressions is distinct from the meaning of Twin Oscar's 'water' expressions. And if the meaning of an expression is determined by the concepts of the speaker, then the concept expressed by Oscar's term 'water' is different from the concept expressed by Twin Oscar's term 'water.' To translate the concept expressed by the Twin Earthian word 'water' into English we have to coin a new word, perhaps *twater*. Owing to the difference in concepts, Oscar and Twin Oscar express different thoughts when both of them utter, for instance, "Gee, water is wet!" – and this in spite of their molecular identity. Putnam concludes that mental states involving natural kind terms don't supervene on physical states of our brains but on the physical states of our environment.[2] In Putnam's (1975: 227) famous phrase, "meanings ain't in the head."[3]

Let's get back to the brain-in-a-vat argument. Given content externalism, just as Twin Oscar's term 'water' does not have the sorts of causal connections to water needed for it to refer to water, a brain in a vat's usage of "vat" does not refer to vats. As Putnam (1981b: 14) puts it, "'vat' refers to vats in the image in vat-English, or something related (electronic impulses or program features), but certainly not to real vats, since the use of 'vat' in vat-English has no causal connection to real vats." If we were brains in a vat,

---

[2] Twin Earth cases assume a narrow notion of environment according to which a person's content-determining environment is limited to the planet he resides on. If, however, the notion of an environment is construed broadly, then the environment is made up of everything in the person's universe. Given the broad notion of environment, Twin Earth belongs to the environment of Earth, and vice versa. Oscar's word 'water' then refers to both liquids – H_2O and XYZ.

[3] Putnam's Twin Earth example exploits the fact that in the case of a natural kind term such as 'water,' the nature of the referent plays an essential role in individuating the concept associated with the word. A notorious objection to this thought experiment states, first, that it is limited to natural kind terms and, second, that it rests on the contentious idea that, just as the chemical composition (as opposed to the color, taste, density, or boiling point) is said to be the defining characteristic of water, every natural kind is supposed to have an essential property. While this is still a popular criticism of the Twin Earth example, it seems pretty clear that Putnam's overall position in "The Meaning of 'Meaning'" doesn't presuppose any substantial type of metaphysical essentialism and is intended to apply to most terms in our language (cf. Salmon 1979). Since writing "The Meaning of 'Meaning,'" Putnam (1990b: 70) has become skeptical of the search for necessary and sufficient conditions. "Is it clear that we would call a (hypothetical) substance with quite different behavior water in these circumstances? I now think that the question, 'What is the necessary and sufficient condition for being water in all possible worlds?' makes no sense at all. And this means that I now reject 'metaphysical necessity'."

then our word "vat" would not refer to vats. Consequently, the mere fact that we can raise the possibility that we are brains in a vat shows that we are not. In other words, "[i]f we can consider whether it is true or false, then it is not true ... Hence it is not true" (Putnam 1981b: 8).

Putnam's anti-skeptical argument crucially depends on the claim that the use of 'vat' in vat-English has no causal connection to real vats. Someone who was just recently subjected to envatment by an evil scientist could have had causal contact with vats before being envatted. Content externalists agree that the conceptual shift caused by an environmental shift takes time. Only if one remains in the vat long enough is one's concept of vat substituted for one's concept of vat-in-the-image. Thus for the brain-in-a-vat argument to work it has to be assumed that the brain has been envatted from "birth."

Another embellishment that has to be added to the brain-in-a-vat scenario for the anti-skeptical argument to work is that brains in a vat don't interact with normal people. For if such an interaction were possible the brain in a vat could think the following true thought: "I am what N.N. means when she says 'Sven is a brain in a vat,'" where N.N. is a normal person whose term 'brain' refers to brains and whose term 'vat' refers to vats. Following Putnam, I use the phrase "brain in a vat" to refer to a brain in a vat from birth living in a community of fellow brains in vats.

Many formulations and (alleged) improvements on Putnam's anti-skeptical argument have appeared in the literature. For present purposes, the following reconstruction of Putnam's argument will do:[4]

(1) My language disquotes. [From disquotation principle]
(2) In vat-English, 'brain in a vat' does not refer to a brain in a vat. [From content externalism]
(3) In my language, 'brain in a vat' is a meaningful expression.
(4) In my language, 'brain in a vat' refers to a brain in a vat. [From (1) and (3)]
(5) My language is not vat-English. [From (2) and (4)]
(6) If I am a brain in a vat, my language, if any, is vat-English. [Definition of vat-English]
(7) Therefore, I am not a brain in a vat. [From (5) and (6)]

To be sure, the argument does not prove that I am not a brain in a vat; it makes the weaker point that if I were a brain in a vat I could not coherently

---

[4] This reconstruction is due to Wright (1994: 224). Putnam (1994a: 284) seems to endorse this reconstruction.

think that I were. But from this it does not follow that the skeptical scenario that I might be a brain in a vat could not be true. This would only follow if the brain-in-a-vat scenario violated a physical law or contained a logical contradiction. But this is not what Putnam says. His claim is that the scenario is 'self-refuting' in the sense that the fact of its being entertained makes it false.

Putnam's anti-skeptical argument is clearly valid. What isn't clear is whether we have an *a priori* entitlement to the premises and whether they are true. Some have challenged Putnam's argument by questioning the *a priori* knowability of the fourth premise (see e.g. Brueckner 1986: 103). Since I don't have *a priori* access to the environmental factors that determine what my expression 'brain in a vat' refers to, I cannot know *a priori* that in my language 'brain in a vat' refers to brains in vats. To know that I would have to know whether I am speaking English or vat-English, and I could only know that if I already knew that I was not a brain in a vat.

A different line of attack challenges the *a priori* knowability of premise (4). Some have argued that content externalism has the consequence that I cannot tell, on the basis of reflection, what my words mean and what the contents of my thoughts are. The worry is that I can only know the contents of my thoughts after having investigated the content-determining environment. Elsewhere I have argued that content externalism and privileged self-knowledge are indeed compatible, but that the notion of privileged self-knowledge reconcilable with externalism is weaker and less interesting than the Cartesian notion of self-knowledge (cf. Bernecker 1996, 1998, 2000). Here I will not defend the compatibility of externalism and self-knowledge, but rather assume its truth.

The most fundamental critique of Putnam's anti-skeptical argument concerns the truth of premise (2). Some have argued that, because it seems perfectly coherent to suppose that I am a brain in a vat, premise (2) must be false. The plausibility of skeptical hypotheses swamps the considerations in favor of content externalism. Content externalism is false because skeptical hypotheses are coherent (see, e.g., Falvey and Owens 1994; Stroud 1984).

5.2 Extending content externalism

Some have argued that content externalism doesn't go far enough in repudiating the Cartesian picture of mentality as intrinsic to the subject. Whereas content externalism locates mental states inside the head or body of an individual, the *hypothesis of extended mind* (HEM) claims that the role of the physical or social environment is not restricted to the determination of mental content. Mental states are not only externally individuated but also externally located states. The reason they are externally located states is that they are realized by cognitive processes that are, in part, constituted by physical or bodily manipulations of environmental states. Cognitive processes are hybrid entities, made up in part of what is going on inside the brain of the creatures who have them, but also made up in part of what is going on in the environment of those creatures. Mental states are externally constituted in the sense that they are composed not only of the internal states of the individual in question but also of objects, properties, or events in his environment together with the appropriate relation connecting the two. "[T]he human organism is linked with an external entity in a two-way interaction, creating a coupled system that can be seen as a cognitive system in its own right" (Clark and Chalmers 1998: 8). In slogan form: the mind is not exclusively in the head.

The hypothesis of extended mind goes under a number of aliases. To distinguish the view expressed by HEM from content externalism it has been labeled *active externalism, vehicle externalism, enabling externalism, locational externalism,* and *environmentalism*. Proponents of HEM tend to embrace content externalism. Yet it is important to see that, though mutually consistent, content externalism is distinct from HEM.[5] It is one thing to say, as content externalism does, that the contents of mental states are individuated by the relations those states bear to certain environmental features. And it is quite another thing to say, as HEM does, that the cognitive processes that realize mental states are constituted in part by an individual's environment. The external individuation of mental contents does not entail the external location of mental states. And just as content externalism doesn't imply HEM, the latter doesn't imply the former. Instead of embracing content externalism, proponents of HEM could endorse some other semantic theory such as conceptual role semantics.

In their seminal paper "The Extended Mind," Andy Clark and David Chalmers provide two arguments in favor of HEM. First, they argue that the mind's cognitive processes can partially consist in processes performed by

---

[5] Sometimes HEM (or active externalism) is defined so as to include content externalism. Tollefsen (2006: 142n), for instance, writes: "Content externalism holds that the content of a mental state is determined by environmental or causal factors. My twin on Twin Earth does not have the same water beliefs as me because Twin Earth contains XYZ, not H_2O. The content differs. The vehicle, however, [i.e. the pattern of neurological activity] remains ... the same and inside the head. Active externalism argues that the vehicle of content need not be restricted to the inner biological realm. The idea is that both cognitive contents and cognitive operations can be instantiated and supported by both biological and non-biological structures and processes."

external devices. Consider, for instance, the cognitive process of rotating shapes when playing the game Tetris. According to Clark and Chalmers, the computer's rotation of a shape plays the same sort of role, in a person's cognitive economy, as the corresponding internal process of imagining how the shape would appear if it were rotated in various ways (see also Clark 2008: 70–3).

Clark and Chalmers's second argument in favor of HEM takes the form of a thought experiment that is meant to show that standing beliefs (such as memories and dispositional beliefs) can be partially constituted by factors external to the skin. The thought experiment involves two characters, Inga and Otto. Inga wants to visit the Museum of Modern Art in New York. At first she doesn't remember where the museum is located. She thinks for a moment and recalls that it is on 53rd Street. Clark and Chalmers note that it is uncontroversial to assume that Inga has had this belief about the museum's location all along, even if it has not always been occurrent. The belief was stored in memory, waiting to be accessed. Next consider Otto, who suffers from Alzheimer's disease. Owing to his failing memory, Otto always carries around a notebook in which he jots down information. He too decides to go to the same museum as Inga, and he too doesn't remember the location of the museum. Unlike Inga, Otto cannot retrieve the desired piece of information from his memory. Instead he consults his notebook, which says that the museum is on 53rd Street.

Clark and Chalmers argue that the information in the notebook plays the same functional role for Otto that an ordinary non-occurrent, but explicitly encoded, belief plays for Inga. We should therefore count the notebook as part of Otto's mind, and the location of the museum as one of Otto's beliefs. This inference rests on the *parity principle*:

> If, as we confront some task, a part of the world functions as a process which, were it to go on in the head, we would have no hesitation in recognizing as part of the cognitive process, then that part of the world is (so we claim) part of the cognitive process. (Clark and Chalmers 1998: 8)

If external devices act as memory traces, then they can be treated as memory traces, notwithstanding the difference in their location. Given the parity principle, Otto has the (dispositional) belief that the Museum of Modern Art is on 53rd Street even before he consults his notebook because the notebook plays the same role for Otto that memory traces play for Inga and because any alternative explanation involving intermediate beliefs about the contents of the notebook introduces "one step too many" (Clark and Chalmers 1998: 13) to the description of Otto's mental life.

Clark and Chalmers are careful not to trivialize the proposed extension of the boundaries of the mind. The external aids that count as part of an individual's mental processing must meet the following requirements (Clark and Chalmers 1998: 17; Clark 2010: 46): they must be (i) consistently available, (ii) readily accessible, (iii) automatically endorsed, and (iv) present (internally or externally) because they were consciously endorsed in the past. Clark and Chalmers are confident that constancy, direct accessibility, and present endorsement are constitutive of believing but they concede that it is debatable whether past endorsement belongs to the necessary conditions for belief. Without the past-endorsement condition there doesn't seem to be a difference between remembering and relearning. Yet adding this condition seems to rob HEM of its attraction. For if an extended belief requires conscious endorsement and if conscious endorsement is ultimately an internal process, then HEM is not really that different from the received picture whereupon the mind does not extend beyond the skin.

A problem for HEM is that it seems to take very little to satisfy the four criteria for inclusion of external props into an individual's cognitive system. In response to the worry that, given HEM, there is no stopping the 'leakage' of mind into the world Clark and Chalmers (1998: 8) also require that "the human organism is linked with an external entity in a two-way interaction, creating a coupled system." Clark dubs this two-way interaction continuous reciprocal causation (CRC), and Menary (2007) calls it cognitive integration. "CRC occurs when some system S is both continuously affecting and simultaneously being affected by activity in some other system O" (Clark 2008: 24). Unlike conditions (i)–(iv) above, CRC is intended only as a sufficient, not a necessary condition on HEM.

5.3 Outsourcing the mind

Clark and Chalmers's Otto is not so different from a brain in a vat. Otto relies on a notebook to acquire the belief that the Museum of Modern Art is on 53rd Street. If a brain in a vat comes to believe that the Museum of Modern Art is on 53rd Street it does so because it relies on the supercomputer. In both cases there is a systematic coupling between a brain, on the one hand, and on the other hand an external device that feeds the brain information. The coupling conditions are met in both cases: (i) the notebook and the computer are reliably available and typically invoked, (ii) information retrieved from the notebook and the computer is automatically endorsed, and (iii) information provided by the notebook and the computer is easily available as and when required. What distinguishes the case of Otto from that of the brain in a vat is the kind of external device they rely on. The brain in a vat relies on a computer while Otto relies on a notebook. We can further approximate the case of Otto to that of a brain in a vat by imagining a Twin Earth where Otto's brain has been envatted and where a supercomputer plays the role of the notebook.

How does embodied Otto differ from his envatted twin? One difference is that envatted Otto uses the laptop not only for selective tasks such as figuring out the whereabouts of the Museum of Modern Art but for acquiring all kinds of beliefs. But surely this isn't a relevant difference. It doesn't matter how often a brain forms a coupled system with an external device. Besides relying more heavily on external devices, envatted Otto differs from embodied Otto in that he is not aware of his reliance on external devices. Embodied Otto can tell whether and when he is using an external device (notebook) to form a belief. Envatted Otto, by contrast, would be very surprised if he found out about the physical and computational operations underlying his cognitive processes. But, once again, this is not a relevant difference (cf. Clark 2008: 164). HEM allows for cognitive integration to be opaque. A cognitively integrated system need not conceive of itself as such but may instead take itself to be wholly intra-cranial.

Given HEM, embodied Otto remembers the whereabouts of the Museum of Modern Art (even before he consults the notebook) because the notebook plays the same kind of functional role vis-à-vis information storage and retrieval as Inga's biological memory. Given the parity principle, if Inga's biological memory counts as part of the cognitive process *she* employs, then Otto's notebook counts as part of the cognitive process *he* employs. But just as there is a functional parity between Inga and embodied Otto, there is a functional parity between embodied Otto and his envatted twin. The vat and the connected supercomputer play for envatted Otto the same kind of functional role that the notebook and the rest of the external world play for embodied Oscar. The parity principle does away not only with unwarranted 'metaphysical bio-prejudice' (Clark 2008: xxvi) but also with the kind of techno-prejudice that makes us treat brains in vats like second-class citizens. "Otto in a vat," Clark claims, "shares all the standing beliefs of our worldly Otto. This should not come as much of a surprise because envatted Otto just *is* (functionally speaking) Otto the extended mind" (Clark 2008: 164).[6]

---

[6] "It would seem, then, that Otto and his duplicate will share their unquestionably mental lives, and may or may not share the aspect of their life that is anyway questionably mental" (Horgan and Kriegel 2008: 362).

To say that envatted Otto has beliefs if embodied Otto does is one thing; to say that the two Ottos hold the very same beliefs is quite another. HEM states conditions for when a system is minded; it does not specify conditions for the individuation of thought content. HEM leaves it open whether envatted Otto's beliefs have the same content as those of his embodied twin. As was explained before, HEM is compatible with different theories of mental content. When HEM is combined with a position whereby the meaning-bestowing relations are intra-linguistic or intra-cognitive,[7] then embodied Otto comes out as having the very same thought contents as envatted Otto. On this theory of mental content Putnam's semantic critique of external-world skepticism would not get off the ground.

But what happens when HEM is combined with content externalism? As was explained in Section 5.1, content externalism has it that the contents of an agent's thoughts depend on causal relations she bears to aspects of her physical and social environment. Whether envatted Otto has the same thought contents as embodied Otto crucially depends on what counts as envatted Otto's content-determining environment. Given Putnam's interpretation of content externalism, the content-determining environment of envatted Otto differs from that of embodied Oscar. This is why Putnam claims that a brain in a vat lacks the conceptual tools to entertain the thought that it is a brain in a vat. But when content externalism is combined with HEM the difference between the content-determining environment of the brain in a vat and that of a regular person disappears. For, just as the brain in a vat forms a coupled system with the supercomputer that feeds it all of its sensory-input signals, the supercomputer forms a coupled system with the evil scientist who programs it.[8] So even though the brain in a vat lacks *direct* causal contact with real brains and real vats, given HEM, it has *indirect* causal contact with real brains and real vats, for it has direct contact with the evil scientist who has direct contact with real brains and real vats. So, given HEM, the brain in a vat is sufficiently connected to the external world to 'speak' English and to have the same thoughts as the evil scientist.

To see that the combination of content externalism and HEM has the consequence of leveling the semantic difference between envatted and

---

[7] Examples of internalist semantics are meaning holism, functional role semantics, conceptual role semantics, causal role semantics, and the like.

[8] "Envatted-brain scenarios usually involve a systematic coupling between the brain, on the one hand, and on the other hand the external device (usually envisioned as a super-computer) that monitors the brain's motor-output signals and feeds it sensory-input signals. Arguably, the states of the external device could be regarded as aspects of an extended mind that is physically realized by the coupled brain–computer system as a whole" (Horgan and Kriegel 2008: 370–1, fn 30).

embodied brains it is helpful to compare the evil scientist in Putnam's skeptical scenario with Clark and Chalmers's Otto who is suffering from Alzheimer's disease. Just as the notebook is a record of Otto's thoughts, the brain in a vat is a record of the evil scientist's thoughts. And just as Otto can consult the notebook to find out what he used to think, we can consult the brain in a vat to find out what the evil scientist is thinking right now and can consult the brain in a vat's memories to find out what the evil scientist used to think. But if the notebook counts as an extension of Otto's mind, as Clark and Chalmers claim, then the brain in a vat should count as an extension of the evil scientist's mind. For the brain in a vat is like a mirror website which republishes information verbatim from another (originating) site without exercising independent editorial control. And if the envatted brain's mind is an extension of the evil scientist's mind, then the envatted brain's thought contents don't differ from those of the evil scientist. For what makes it the *same* mind (or the same mental process) that is located both in the evil scientist's head and in the brain in a vat? Intuitively it is the same mind if it thinks the same thoughts. And two thoughts are the same if they have the same content. Thus when applied to the brain-in-a-vat scenario HEM suggests that the evil scientist and the brain in a vat think the same thoughts. But if there is no difference in thought contents between the brain in a vat, on the one hand, and an ordinary person who has causal contact with brains and vats, on the other, then Putnam's semantic critique of external-world skepticism crumbles.

Let's go over the argument once again. We have started from the observation that the brain in a vat forms a coupled system not only with the supercomputer but also with the evil scientist operating the computer. The second step of the argument is to realize that coupling or cognitive integration is taken to be a sufficient condition on HEM. This was explained in Section 5.2. The upshot of the first two steps is that the evil scientist's mind extends to the brain in a vat. The third step of the argument is to say that the evil scientist's mind can only extend to the brain in a vat if they think the same thoughts. Sameness of mind requires sameness of thoughts. Two thought tokens belong to the same type if they have the same content. Thus, for the mind of the evil scientist to extend to the brain in a vat the scientist's brain and the envatted brain have to entertain the same thought contents. The fourth step says that since the evil scientist has the required causal contact with brains in vats to think the thought *I am a brain in a vat* and since the brain in a vat thinks the same thoughts as the evil scientist it too thinks the thought *I am a brain in a vat*. And if we assume that the indexical 'I' refers to the local realization of the thought in question, then the brain in a vat is having a true thought when it thinks that it is a brain in a vat. So, contrary to Putnam's contention, it is not the case that the thought *I am a brain in a vat* is necessarily false. When content externalism is combined with HEM it loses its anti-skeptical punch.

Note that it doesn't help to change the skeptical scenario by increasing the distance between the evil scientist and the brain in a vat. We can imagine a version of Putnam's famous Twin Earth where 'brain' refers to something other than brain, say, computer programs, and where vat refers to something other than vat, say, vat holograms. We can further suppose that the evil scientist and the supercomputer are located on Earth while the brain in a vat is located on Twin Earth. The brain in a vat on Twin Earth is connected to the computer on Earth by a very long cord. Would changing the skeptical scenario in this way make a difference regarding the brain in a vat's thought contents? The answer is "no." To the extent that the brain in a vat forms a coupled system with the evil scientist, both of them think the same thoughts, regardless of the distance between them.

Given HEM, for the brain in a vat to lack the conceptual resources necessary to think the thought *I am a brain in a vat* the evil scientist who is coupled with the brain in a vat via the supercomputer would also have to be unable to think the thought *I am a brain in a vat*.[9] But under what circumstances would the evil scientist be unable to think this thought? One possibility is that the evil scientist who programs and operates the computer is Davidson's Swampman. This is Davidson's Swampman thought experiment:

> Suppose lightning strikes a dead tree in a swamp; I am standing nearby. My body is reduced to its elements, while entirely by coincidence (and out of different molecules) the tree is turned into my physical replica. My replica, the Swampman, moves exactly as I did; according to its nature it departs the swamp, encounters and seems to recognize my friends, and appears to return their greetings in English. It moves into my house and seems to write articles on radical interpretation. No one can tell the difference. (Davidson 2001: 19)

---

[9] A critic might object that the referents of 'I' are different when the evil scientists thinks *I am a brain in a vat* and when the brain in a vat thinks *I am a brain in a vat*. This would mean that the evil scientist and the brain in a vat cannot share indexical thoughts. I disagree. Following Fost (2013), I think that we sometimes think of our identities as being extended, in more or less the sense of HEM. When the evil scientist talks about 'I' he is referring not only to himself but also to the coupled system consisting of the supercomputer and the brain in a vat.

But, Davidson argues, there is a difference because the Swampman cannot "be said to mean anything by the sounds it makes, nor to have any thoughts." The reason is that Swampman lacks the proper causal-historical connections to the world which underpin meaning and thought content.[10]

We can combine the brain-in-a-vat scenario with the Swampman scenario by imagining that the supercomputer has been built and is operated by Swampman. The brain in a vat has now turned into a *brain in a swamp*. If Swampman does not have thoughts, neither does the envatted brain that is 'cognitively' integrated with Swampman. So if we assume that the supercomputer is built and operated by a mindless creature like Swampman, the hypothesis of the extended mind doesn't get a foothold. For if there is no mind in the first place, then there isn't anything that can be extended to the envatted brain.

Putnam too considers a version of the brain-in-a-swamp scenario, for he worries that a brain in a vat still has indirect causal connections to real vats and real brains through the evil scientist who programs the supercomputer that feeds the brain in a vat sensory information. To sever this last connection a brain in a vat has with the real world Putnam modifies the scenario in such a way that the vat and automated machinery are no longer designed by an intelligent scientist, but rather are "supposed to have come into existence by some kind of cosmic coincidence" so that they "have no intelligent creator-designers" (Putnam 1981b: 12). Putnam's point is that that if brains in *vats* don't have our concepts neither do brains in *swamps*.

> For there is no connection between the *word* 'tree' as used by these brains and actual trees. They would still use the word 'tree' just as they do, think just the thoughts they do, have just the images they have, even if there were no actual trees. Their images, words, etc., are qualitatively identical with images, words, etc., which do represent trees in *our* world.[11] (Putnam 1981b: 12–13)

The skeptical worry raised by the brain-in-a-swamp scenario differs from that raised by the brain-in-a-vat scenario. The brain-in-a-vat scenario illustrates

---

[10] According to Hawking (1993: 112–13), Swampman is a physical possibility. Millikan (1984: 93) says of her Swampwoman: "that being would have no ideas, no beliefs, no intentions, no aspirations, no fears and no hopes ... this because the evolutionary history of the being would be wrong."

[11] Horgan and Kriegel (2008: 371) imagine a scenario similar to the brain-in-a-swamp scenario discussed here: "Let the pertinent scenario be an envatted brain that receives randomly-generated inputs from a long-term surrounding electrical storm that just happens, via cosmic coincidence, to give the brain an ongoing phenomenal mental life that exactly matches yours."

the possibility that my thoughts have determinate contents but that these contents differ from those of its embodied duplicate thereby making it impossible for the brain in a vat to even consider the possibility of external-world skepticism. The brain-in-a-swamp scenario, by contrast, illustrates the possibility that I am a propositional zombie that lacks a mind and lacks thoughts. As I have argued elsewhere (Bernecker 2000, 2004) content externalism makes it impossible to rule out zombie skepticism. For if mental content consists in the nomic dependence of brain states on environmental conditions, a type of configuration in my brain is a mental state only if it is normally tokened by some environmental condition. But I cannot know *a priori* whether there is any systematic relationship between my internal states and states of an external kind. I am unable to know *a priori* whether my so-called thoughts are indeed thoughts as opposed to some other kind of states lacking mental content. Content externalism implies that I am unable to know *a priori* that I am a minded being rather than a propositional zombie.

Elsewhere (Bernecker 2000, 2004) I have argued that even though I cannot know *a priori* I am having thoughts as opposed to contentless states I *can* know *a priori* what my thoughts are about, provided they have content. I can know what I am thinking – the specific content of the thought – without knowing that I am thinking – the fact that my so-called thoughts are not contentless states. *A priori* knowledge of what I am thinking about is consistent with me lacking the ability to rule out, on the basis of *a priori* reasoning, the possibility that I don't have any propositional attitudes. That's why the inability to rule out the brain in a swamp scenario doesn't undermine the kind of self-knowledge presupposed by the fourth premise of Putnam's brain-in-a-vat argument.

Let's take stock. We saw that adding HEM to content externalism has the consequence of undermining Putnam's refutation of the brain-in-a-vat scenario. For given HEM, the brain in a vat is sufficiently connected to the external world to 'speak' English and to entertain the thought *I am a brain in a vat*. But if the brain in a vat can think the thought that it is a brain in a vat then Putnam is wrong in claiming that external-world skepticism is self-refuting. For the brain in a vat to not have the ability to think the thought that it is a brain in a vat no one may be interacting with the supercomputer who is able to think this thought. One way of spelling out this possibility is to imagine a brain in a swamp. Content externalism is unable to rule out the brain-in-a-swamp scenario.

The upshot is that content externalism loses its anti-skeptical force when it is combined with HEM. And if it is a motivation for content externalism that it refutes the brain-in-a-vat scenario, then adding HEM makes content externalism less appealing. So contrary to Clark's (2008: 78) contention, HEM is not "orthogonal to the more familiar Putnam–Burge style externalism"; instead HEM and content externalism are in tension with one another.

5.4 Embedding the vat

The hypothesis of the extended mind (HEM) states that the boundaries of the mind extend beyond the boundaries of individual organisms. There are a number of theses in the vicinity of HEM that are easily mixed up with HEM. The thesis of *embodied cognition* states that cognition depends not just on the brain but also on the body. The thesis of *enactive cognition* proposes that cognition is not something that occurs inside of an agent, but is a product of the interaction between agents and their environment. The thesis of *distributed cognition* states that cognition and knowledge are not confined to an individual but are distributed across objects, individuals, artefacts, and tools in the environment. Each of these theses contributes to a picture of mental activity as dependent on the context in which it occurs, whether that context is relatively local (as in the case of enactivism and embodiment) or relatively global (as in the case of distribution and extension). According to my usage, *embedded cognition* is the genus, and embodied, enactive, embedded, and distributed cognition and their ilk are species. This usage isn't standard but it seems as good as any.

In the previous section we have seen that, assuming the extended mind thesis, the brain-in-a-vat scenario is coherent but Putnam's argument against this scenario fails. The goal of this section is to show that, assuming the thesis of embedded cognition, the brain-in-a-vat scenario is incoherent.

In Putnam's version of the brain-in-a-vat story, one is asked to imagine that one's brain has been removed from one's body and placed in a vat of nutrient fluids, and that all of its normal neural inputs and outputs are being simulated by a supercomputer. The brain has no way of knowing whether it is in a skull or in a vat. Can we be sure that this is not our current situation? How do we know that anything beyond our brains is real rather than virtual? The moral of the brain in a vat story is that the neural representations of body and world are only indirectly related to real external things. But for the brain-in-a-vat story to make sense we have to assume that a suitably working human brain is sufficient all on its own for the instantiation or realization of our mental life. And this very assumption is challenged by the thesis of embedded cognition. Clark writes:

> The mistake, then, is to infer that the sufficient mechanism is the biological stuff alone, just because the biological stuff, in the special vat-context, helps support thinking and experience. At the limit of this thought experiment we have the single neuron in a dizzyingly complex vat ... We would not conclude that experience and thought constitutively depend only on the activity of that single neuron. (Clark 2009: 980–1; see also Clark 2008: 163–4; Shapiro 2004: 218; 2011: 162)

Assuming the thesis of embedded cognition, the mind is not realized simply in the brain but its realization is integrated throughout the body. Mental processes are not the deliverances of only the brain, but a brain that is intimately enmeshed with a body. Damasio explains:

> It might be argued that if it were possible to mimic, at the level of the dangling nerves, realistic configurations of inputs as if they were coming from the body, then the disembodied brain would have a normal mind. Well, that might be a nice and interesting experiment 'to do' and I suspect the brain might indeed have *some* mind under those conditions. But what that more elaborate experiment would have done is create a body surrogate and thus confirm that 'body-type inputs' are required for a normally minded brain after all. And what it would be unlikely to do is make the 'body inputs' match in realistic fashion the variety of configurations which body states assume when those states are triggered by a brain engaged in making evaluations. (Damasio 1994: 228; see also Heylighen 2012)

If the mind depends on the body, then envatment is impossible. And if it were possible for an isolated brain to have our mental life, then the entire body and local environment would have to be envatted as well. Thompson and Cosmelli remark:

> Careful examination of this thought experiment indicates that ... any adequately functional 'vat' would be a surrogate body, that is, that the so-called vat would be no vat at all, but rather an embodied agent in the world. Thus, what the thought experiment actually shows is that the brain and body are so deeply entangled, structurally and dynamically, that they are explanatorily inseparable. Such entanglement implies that we cannot understand consciousness [and cognition] by considering only the activity of neurons apart from the body, and hence we have good explanatory

grounds for supposing that the minimal realizing system for consciousness [and cognition] includes the body and not just the brain.[12] (Thompson and Cosmelli 2011: 163)

So given the thesis of embedded cognition, the vat and the supercomputer have to do all the complex work of body, action, and world. But the vat can only do the work of the body, action, and world if the vat contains the body and the world. And if the vat contains the world, the brain in vat is not cut off from the world in the way suggested by the skeptic. Envatting the world thus goes hand in hand with disarming the skeptic. So in the end we are left with a kind of dilemma: If the vat *does not* fill in everything the world provides, then the brain-in-a-vat scenario is incoherent; and if the vat *does* fill in everything the world provides, then the skeptical threat evaporates.

5.5 Conclusion

I have argued for two conditional claims. If content externalism is combined with the extended mind thesis, Putnam's refutation of the brain-in-a-vat scenario collapses. And if content externalism is combined with the embedded mind thesis, the brain-in-a-vat scenario ceases to pose a skeptical problem. Provided these claims can be believed there are a number of conclusions we can draw. First, we can either reject the embedded mind thesis because it renders the brain-in-a-vat scenario incoherent or reject the brain-in-a-vat scenario because it violates the embedded mind thesis. Second, we can either reject the extended mind thesis and hold on to Putnam's anti-skeptical argument or embrace the extended mind thesis and reject Putnam's anti-skepticism. Third, we can simply abandon the brain-in-a-vat story and work with a skeptical scenario that does not violate extension, embedding, and content externalism. A case in point is Descartes's waking dream scenario. In this scenario my words and thoughts do refer to objects in my

---

[12] "When theorists invoke the notion of a brain in a vat, they invariably take a unidirectional control perspective and view the brain as a kind of reflexive machine whose activity is externally controllable. Yet numerous neurobiological considerations count against this viewpoint and indicate that the brain needs to be seen as a complex and self-organized dynamical system that is tightly coupled to the body at multiple levels" (Cosmelli and Thompson 2010: 362; see also Thompson and Stapleton 2009: 27). "So I hold that the supposed consciousness of a causally detached brain – say, a living brain floating listlessly in a vat, as in Hilary Putnam's famous thought-experiment – even though it seems both conceivable and logically possible, just would not be a consciousness like ours. On our view, a consciousness necessarily involves a brain that is causally-dynamically coupled with all the other vital systems, organs, and processes of our living body" (Hanna 2011: 21).

environment and my mind is entirely within the physical boundaries of the brain and skull. The third option strikes me as the most promising. But this is not the point of the paper. The point of the paper is that buying into the content externalist's critique of brain-in-a-vat skepticism comes at the price of rejecting popular theories of the mind that have grown out of content externalism.

I have assumed, and not argued for, the truth of the extended mind thesis.[13] But even if the extended mind thesis turns out to be indefensible, the problems for Putnam's anti-skepticism don't go away. For on some versions of content externalism one can possess the concept X even if one has never had causal contact with the referent of X. Burge (1982), for instance, claims that the inhabitants of Putnam's waterless Twin Earth *can* have water thoughts provided that there exists sufficient knowledge of chemistry among the Twin Earthian experts to distinguish water from various twin-concepts such as twater.[14] These experts qualify for possession of the concept *water*. And if dry-Oscar defers to the experts when it comes to his use of 'water,' then he too qualifies for possession of the concept *water* despite not knowing anything about chemistry and never having interacted with water. Now assuming Burge's version of content externalism, we can imagine a community of brains in vats theorizing about brains (as opposed to brains-in-the-image) and vats (as opposed to vats-in-the-image) and thereby coming to possess the concepts *brain* and the concept *vat* despite never having had (direct) contact with brains and vats. Thus we don't even need to buy into the extended mind thesis to conclude that a brain in a vat can think the true thought *I am a brain in a vat*.

---

[13] In Bernecker (2014) I argue for the following conditional claims: if the extended mind debate is a substantive dispute, then we have only superficial understanding of the extended mind hypothesis. And if we have deep understanding of the extended mind hypothesis, then the debate over this hypothesis is nothing but a verbal dispute.

[14] Burge is not alone. See also Ball (2007), Goldberg (2006a), Korman (2006), and McLaughlin and Tye (1998a).

Part II
Epistemology

6 Putnam on BIVs and radical skepticism

Duncan Pritchard and Chris Ranalli

6.1 Putnam's BIV argument

A familiar way of arguing for radical skepticism is by appeal to radical skeptical hypotheses, such as the hypothesis that one might be a brain in a vat (BIV) which is being radically, and undetectably, deceived about its environment. Roughly, the skeptical argument goes that since such skeptical hypotheses are by their nature indistinguishable from normal experience, so one cannot know that they are false. Furthermore, if one cannot know that they are false, then it follows that one can't know much of what one believes, most of which is inconsistent with radical skeptical hypotheses.

This last step will almost certainly require some sort of closure-style principle, whereby knowledge is closed under known entailments. Thus, if one does have knowledge of the 'everyday' propositions which one takes oneself to know (e.g. that one has hands), and of the fact that these propositions entail the denials of radical skeptical hypotheses (e.g. the BIV hypothesis, because BIVs don't have hands), then one could come to know that one is not a BIV. Conversely, insofar as one grants that it is impossible to know that one is not a BIV, then it follows that one cannot know the everyday propositions which are known to be inconsistent with the BIV hypothesis either.

There are many ways of responding to radical skepticism of this form, which we will refer to as *BIV skepticism*. One might deny the relevant closure principle, for example, or one might put forward an epistemology according to which one could know the denials of radical skeptical hypotheses, and so on.[1] On the face of it, Hilary Putnam's (1981b) famous argument against BIV skepticism would appear to be a variation on this last anti-skeptical strategy,

---

We thank Jesper Kallestrup and Sandy Goldberg for helpful comments.
[1] The rejection of closure as a response to BIV skepticism was famously advanced by Dretske (1970) and Nozick (1981). For two very different defenses of an epistemological proposal according to which it is possible to know the denials of radical skeptical hypotheses, see Pritchard (2002c, 2005) and Pritchard (2008, 2012). For a general overview of the contemporary literature on radical skepticism, see Pritchard (2002b).

in that he also seems to be, effectively, claiming that one can know that one is not a BIV.

The parallels between these two anti-skeptical approaches are superficial, however, and the differences significant. In particular, Putnam's overarching goal is not to make the *epistemological* claim that such anti-skeptical knowledge is possible, but rather to motivate the *semantic* claim that one cannot truly think the thought that one is a BIV. But these claims are logically distinct, in both directions. That one can know the denial of the BIV hypothesis is obviously consistent with the possibility that one can truly think the thought that one is a BIV. And while admittedly not so obvious, that one cannot truly think the thought that one is a BIV is consistent with being unable to know that one is not a BIV (we will return to consider this particular non-entailment claim below).

In order to understand Putnam's semantic argument we first need to get to grips with the variety of content externalism that he advances. For the starting point of Putnam's BIV argument is the idea that in order to be able to even think thoughts with a particular content, then certain external conditions – in particular, causal conditions – need to be met. For example, if one is a Martian who has never encountered trees, or been part of a linguistic community which has an established practice for referring to trees, then one cannot even think thoughts about trees. One's thoughts would instead be about something altogether different, insofar as they had content at all.

If we grant the truth of this content externalist thesis to Putnam, then one can immediately see how it can create a problem for BIV skepticism, at least so long as this form of radical skepticism is formulated in a particular way (the reason for this *caveat* will become apparent in a moment). For what goes for our Martians when it comes to having thoughts about trees will also apply to a BIV. In particular, a BIV can no more think thoughts about trees than a Martian can, since neither have enjoyed the right kind of causal connections to trees to make this possible. Insofar as one is able to think thoughts about trees, then, it follows that one is not a BIV. More generally, what Putnam is disputing is the idea, common to presentations of radical skepticism, that BIVs and their non-envatted counterparts are thinking exactly the same thoughts, the only difference being that, while the former thoughts are massively false, the latter thoughts are mostly true.

In order to bring this anti-skeptical line of argument into sharper relief, consider Putnam's claim that one cannot truly think that one is a BIV, such that this claim is in a sense necessarily false. Of course, if one is not a BIV, then this thought trivially expresses a falsehood. But what if one is a BIV? This is where Putnam's content externalism comes into play, since he maintains that such a thought still expresses a falsehood. After all, if one is a BIV, then one cannot even think the thought that one is a BIV, but must inevitably think a thought with a different content instead. Given Putnam's brand of content externalism, it is thus *impossible* to truly think the thought that one is a BIV, and one can, it seems, derive this conclusion on purely *a priori* grounds.

In order for this argument to go through, of course, it is important that being a BIV is analogous to being a Martian in the relevant respects. This is where it becomes important to Putnam's argument – and he is quite explicit about this point – that the BIV hypothesis is construed a certain way, such that the brain in question has always been envatted, and such that the stimulation of the BIV is undertaken by supercomputers (and always has been). So construed, there is no route, whether direct or indirect, whereby the BIV could become causally related in the appropriate way to the kinds of things that normal non-envatted agents have thoughts about, such as trees. In contrast, had the envattment been recent, for example, then it would have been possible in principle for the BIV to have had the right kind of causal connections to trees prior to succumbing to this predicament.[2]

One consequence of this point is that Putnam's response to BIV skepticism is essentially limited, in that it will not apply to all forms of BIV skepticism, but only those formulated in terms of a specific rendering of the BIV hypothesis. Even so, if Putnam's argument goes through it is still a startling result. For is it really possible to argue on purely *a priori* grounds that even this specific form of BIV skepticism is false? Henceforth, we will grant to Putnam that the BIV hypothesis is construed in the way that he stipulates in order to further evaluate this claim.

6.2 Brueckner's critique of the BIV argument

We can divide the criticisms of Putnam's anti-skeptical argument into two broad categories. The first type says that the argument is in some way *question-begging*, while the second type says that the argument is in some way *self-refuting*.

---

[2] There are interesting questions to be asked about such non-permanent envattment cases, such as whether the BIV will eventually lose the capacity to think ordinary thoughts (e.g. about trees), though we will be setting these concerns to one side here. For a classic discussion of issues of this type – albeit focused not on BIV cases but rather parallel concerns which arise in 'Twin Earth' cases – see Boghossian (1989).

Anthony Brueckner's (1986) core criticism of Putnam's anti-skeptical argument falls into the first category. In particular, he argues that Putnam's anti-skeptical argument begs-the-question against the skeptic in the following sense: the argument seeks to show that we're not BIVs, but establishing that conclusion requires us to know a principle which is alone sufficient for that anti-skeptical conclusion. In order to see how Brueckner's criticism works, let's consider his reconstruction of Putnam's argument:

(P1) Either I am a BIV (speaking vat-English) or I am not a BIV (and, instead, I'm an English-speaking human).
(P2) If I am a BIV, then my utterances of "I'm a BIV" are true iff I'm a BIV*.
(P3) If I am a BIV, then I'm not a BIV*.

So, from (P2) and (P3):

(C1) If I am a BIV, then my utterances of "I'm a BIV" are false.
(P4) If I am not a BIV, then my utterances of "I'm a BIV" are true iff I'm a BIV.

So, from (P4):

(C3) If I am not a BIV, then my utterances of "I'm a BIV" are false.

Therefore, from (P1), (C1), and (C3):

(C) My utterances of "I'm a BIV" are false.

How can (C) enable one to know that one is not a BIV? First, knowledge is closed under competent deduction. So, if I know that the premises of the argument are true, and I competently deduce (C) from the premises, I'm thereby in a position to know that (C). And (C) says that when I say "I'm a BIV," I express something false. So, I know that when I say "I'm a BIV," I say something that's false. However, as Brueckner points out, the argument for (C) has not established the crucial anti-skeptical premise, namely:

(*) I know that I'm not a BIV.

According to Brueckner, in order to show that I'm not a BIV, and thereby establish (*), the following principles have to be invoked:

(A) My utterances of "I'm not a BIV" are true.
(B) My utterances of "I'm not a BIV" are true iff I'm not a BIV.

From (A) and (B), that I'm not a BIV follows. From the principle that knowledge is closed under competent deduction, it follows that I'm in a position to *know* that I'm not a BIV. However, (B) seems dubious here. After all, as (P2) and (C1) highlight, not all languages are *disquotational*. Indeed, vat-English is one such non-disquotational language. So this raises the question of whether the language in which I utter "I'm not a BIV" is a disquotational language (like English, for normal non-envatted speakers) or not (like vat-English, for envatted speakers). But according to Brueckner:

> I cannot claim to know that I am not a BIV until I can claim to know that [*the anti-skeptical argument*] is a sound argument and that it somehow allows me to know that I am not a BIV... Can I claim to know this without assuming that I am speaking English? (Brueckner 1986: 159)

Brueckner issues the proponent of Putnam's anti-skeptical argument a challenge here: can one claim to know that their utterances of "I'm not a BIV" are true without *presupposing* that their utterances have disquotational truth conditions? On Brueckner's view, it can't be done because "this must be shown by an anti-skeptical argument, not assumed in advance" (Brueckner 1986: 160). In other words, vat-English is not disquotational, while English is. BIVs can't speak English. But since the Putnamian anti-skeptical argument cannot establish that I'm not a BIV without presupposing that I'm speaking English – and therefore not vat-English – it thereby presupposes what it seeks to prove: that I'm not a BIV.

6.3 Wright's reconstruction of the BIV argument

In the last section we saw that Putnam's anti-skeptical argument seems to depend on two core assumptions: that the language in which the anti-skeptical argument is framed is disquotational, and that, in the BIV's language, "BIV" does not refer to BIVs. We also saw how the first assumption might be problematic. As Brueckner argued, since the anti-skeptical argument seems to require the assumption that the speaker's language is disquotational, and this assumption presupposes that the speaker's language is *not* the BIV's language, it follows that the speaker presupposes that the language in which their argument is framed is not the BIV's language. But isn't this a crucial step in Putnam's anti-skeptical argument – one that is meant to be shown, rather than presupposed?

At this stage, one might wonder whether Brueckner's reconstruction of Putnam's anti-skeptical argument is the most charitable reconstruction. In addition, one might wonder whether, even if Brueckner's reconstruction is correct, these two core assumptions are as problematic as Brueckner suggests. Crispin Wright (1992) follows Brueckner in treating those two assumptions as core, but he argues that the disquotation assumption is far less problematic than Brueckner suggests. On Wright's view, it is the second assumption that is the more problematic of the two.

In order to understand Wright's objection against the second assumption, let's start with his reconstruction of Putnam's anti-skeptical argument.[3] First, we begin with the *prima facie* plausible thought that "BIV" is meaningful. After all, it didn't seem to us that Putnam's explanation of the BIV hypothesis was incoherent, in the same way that a set of nonsense sentences immediately strike us as incoherent. So, phrased in the first person:

(1) In my language, "BIV" is meaningful.

Now, from (1) and the principle that my language is disquotational, it follows that:

(2) In my language, "BIV" refers to BIVs.

From (2) and the principle that, in the BIV's language, "BIV" does not refer to BIVs, it follows that:

(3) My language is not the BIV's language.

However:

(4) If I am a BIV, then my language *is* the BIV's language.

Therefore, from (3) and (4):

(5) I am *not* a BIV.

Let's focus on the step from (2) to (3). As we said earlier, Wright maintains that the second assumption of Putnam's anti-skeptical argument is the more problematic assumption. What makes it problematic, on his view, is how it enables the transition from (2) to (3). For while it might allow the speaker to conclude that their language is not the BIV's language, it is far from clear that it should allow the speaker to conclude that other speakers do not speak the BIV's language. But according to Wright, if the argument is valid, then it ought to make no difference whether the argument is framed in the first person or the third person.

---

[3] Putnam (1994) has said that Wright put "more clearly than I myself did ... the premises and the deductive steps involved in my argument."

We might imagine Putnam running his anti-skeptical argument past us, where the first-person pronoun featured in its premises refers to him. Imagine further that Putnam then asks us to consider whether the argument is valid and sound. Reflecting on his argument, we reformulate it so that the first-person pronoun is replaced with a co-referential third-person pronoun. We then state the argument as follows:

(1*) In Putnam's language, "BIV" is meaningful.

From (1*) and the assumption that Putnam's language is disquotational, it follows that:

(2*) In Putnam's language, "BIV" refers to BIVs.

Therefore, from (2*) and the assumption that, in the BIV's language, "BIV" does not refer to BIVs:

(3*) Putnam's language is not the BIV's language.

However:

(4*) If Putnam is a BIV, then his language is the BIV's language.

And with an application of *modus tollens* on (3*) and (4*), it follows that:

(5*) Putnam is not a BIV.

But isn't it altogether incredible that we should be able to prove, *a priori*, that *Putnam* is not a BIV?

According to Wright, it is. As he puts the objection:

> Without supplementary information, you cannot validly infer anything from [*the assumption that Putnam's language is diquotational*] and [*the assumption that in Putnam's language, "BIV" is meaningful*] about how to *specify* what is the reference of 'brain-in-a-vat', as used in [*Putnam's*] language. All you can infer is that a specification in [*Putnam's*] language would be homophonic. That is the same thing as [*premise (2*)*] only if it is presupposed that your language – the language in which the argument is presented – is [*Putnam's*]. (Wright 1992: 77)

Wright thinks that the move from (1*) and (2*) to (3*) is invalid, unless of course we presuppose that our formulation of the argument above is framed in the same language as Putnam's. But this might be contentious. After all, from the fact that our languages are homophonic – that we sound the same, and have the same phonetic and lithographic representations – it doesn't follow that the meanings of our terms are the same. Indeed, this point flows from semantic externalism. Wright's point is that, for all we know as the assessors of the above argument, "BIV" in Putnam's language means *Frenchman*. We're not in a position to know that "BIV" as used in the argument means what it does in our language without additional information (AI). What kind of additional information? Wright suggests the following:

(AI)   The previous anti-skeptical argument was formulated in Putnam's language, and Putnam's language coincides with the language of the assessor of the argument, inasmuch as the meaning assigned to all of the referring expressions therein are the same.

Now (AI) would be quite useful, in that we would now be in a position to make a valid inference from (1*) and (2*) to (3*). But Wright's issue with (AI) is with whether we are in a position to *know* that our use of "BIV" means for us, the assessors of the argument, what it means for Putnam, the proponent of the argument. For example, with (AI), we can now see that the sub-conclusion (3*) follows from the premises. But what's left open is how we should understand (2*). After all, we could claim that "BIV" means whatever it does in our language, but with (AI) that's just trivial. This raises the issue of what "BIV" *means* in our language, and how we know what it means. In short, Wright worries that semantic externalism problematizes one's *knowledge of content* in the following sense: the kind of knowledge of content that externalism seems to forbid (or at least problematize) is the same kind of knowledge that is needed to make Putnam's anti-skeptical argument work.[4] In particular, semantic externalism calls into question the kind of knowledge of content that is needed to secure our knowledge that "BIV" means what we think it means.[5]

6.4 Putnam's argument *qua* transcendental argument

According to Wright (1992: 85), the most charitable interpretation of Putnam's anti-skeptical argument is that it's a "transcendental argument," and Putnam (1981b: 16) himself also describes the argument in these

---

[4] Compare with Wright: "The worry is whether fully exorcising the sceptical doubt which brain-in-a-vat examples and other similar stories raise would not require precisely the kind of identifying knowledge of content which semantic externalism itself proscribes" (Wright 1992: 78–9).

[5] This connects to a general worry which has been raised regarding content externalism, which is the extent to which it is compatible with the idea that we can have *a priori* access to our own mental states. For some of the core literature on this topic, see Boghossian (1989), McKinsey (1991), Davies (1998), Wright (2000), and the articles collected in Nuccetelli (2003). See also Pritchard (2002a).

terms.[6] What makes the argument 'transcendental'? Put generally, an anti-skeptical argument is transcendental when its conclusion is about non-psychological reality, and its premises are about our psychology, and the non-psychological, necessary conditions for having that type of psychology.

So construed, Putnam's anti-skeptical argument does seem to fit the bill. Consider this reconstruction of the argument:

(T1) A necessary condition of the possibility of thinking that *I'm not a BIV* is that I'm not a BIV.
(T2) I can think that *I'm not a BIV*.
(TC) I'm not a BIV.

I can think that "I'm not a BIV" says something that's true.[7]

But the sentence is ambiguous. After all, recall the point that the sentence "I'm not a BIV" in the BIV's language is true iff I'm not a BIV-in-the-image, while the sentence "I'm not a BIV" in English is true iff I'm not a BIV. In either case, whatever proposition we express with "I'm not a BIV," it's a true proposition. The pressing question is *which* true proposition are *we* expressing? That is to say, when we say or think *I'm not a BIV*, which true proposition are we expressing? We could say that it expresses the proposition that *I'm not a BIV* rather than the proposition that *I'm not a BIV-in-the-image*. But how are we supposed to know this?

Brueckner puts this objection to the Putnam transcendental argument as follows:

> If I am in a vat world, then my sentences do not have disquotational truth-conditions and my beliefs do not have disquotational contents. If I am instead in a normal world, then my sentences do have disquotational truth-conditions and my beliefs do have disquotational contents. If I do not yet know which sort of world I am in (this is what the Putnamian argument is supposed to settle), then it appears that I do not know which sorts of truth-conditions and contents are mine. So it appears that the Putnamian

---

[6] For example, here's how Putnam discusses his reasoning: "[M]y procedure has a close relation to what Kant called a 'transcendental' investigation; for it is an investigation, I repeat, of the preconditions of reference and hence of thought – preconditions built in to the nature of our minds themselves, though not (as Kant hoped) wholly independent of empirical assumptions" (Putnam 1981b: 16).

[7] Compare with the following formulation of argument, which highlights the potential ambiguity:
(T1) A necessary condition of the possibility of thinking that the sentence "I'm not a BIV" is true is that that sentence is true.
(T2) I can think that the sentence "I'm not a BIV" is true.
(TC) The sentence "I'm not a BIV" is true.

argument is epistemically circular ... That is, in order to know, or have justification for believing, the argument's self-knowledge premise [*That I can think that I'm not a BIV*], I need to know, or have justification for believing, its conclusion [*that I'm not a BIV*]. (Brueckner 2010: 95)

Brueckner's criticism puts considerable pressure on a proponent of the anti-skeptical efficacy of the Putnamian transcendental argument. The benefit of using an anti-skeptical *transcendental* argument over any other kind of anti-skeptical argument is that the self-knowledge premise of the transcendental argument is supposed to be safe from skeptical criticism. That is, it is supposed to be a premise that even a skeptic should accept. However, as Brueckner highlights, a skeptical predicament easily arises for the self-knowledge premise of the Putnamian transcendental argument. It arises because the kind of epistemic support one would need in order to know that *I am thinking that I'm not a BIV* is the same type of epistemic support one would need in order to know that *I'm not a BIV*.

6.5 Stroud's dilemma for transcendental arguments

In the previous section, we construed Putnam's argument as a transcendental argument. The basic objection to the argument was that it doesn't seem to put us in a position to know that we are not BIV's. Instead, it seems only to establish that the sentence "I am not a BIV" expresses a true proposition, but the arguer is not in a position to know which true proposition that sentence expresses. As Brueckner (1986, 2010) expressed the point, it seems that the transcendental arguer would have to know that s/he wasn't a BIV in order to know that their utterance or representation of the sentence "I'm not a BIV" expresses the proposition *that I'm not a BIV*.

We can sharpen this objection as follows. One can grant that the Putnamian transcendental argument establishes the conclusion that our utterance or representation of *the sentence* "I am not a BIV" *is true*. The problem, however, is whether this helps us to undercut skepticism, since it is compatible with the truth of the sentence "I am not a BIV" that we *are* BIVs, so that the proposition our sentence expresses is that *I am not a BIV-in-the-image*. Putnam's transcendental argument from content externalism establishes that the sentence has to be true, because it would be true whether we are in the normal, non-envatted world, or instead in the non-normal, envatted world. But what we want to know is which world we are in; or which true proposition *our* use of "I'm not a BIV" expresses.

Even if one is unmoved by Brueckner's criticism of the Putnamian transcendental anti-skeptical strategy, Barry Stroud famously argued that transcendental arguments *in general*, despite appearances to the contrary, aren't effective as anti-skeptical arguments. In brief, Stroud's argument goes like this. In order for a transcendental argument to have anti-skeptical consequences, it has to presuppose idealism or verificationism (or some sort of anti-realist principle). But these doctrines are themselves *sufficient* to block skepticism, thus rendering the transcendental argument *superfluous*. The dilemma, then, is that either we dispense with idealism or verificationism, and thereby lose the anti-skeptical consequences of the transcendental argument, or else we keep idealism or verificationism, and then render the transcendental argument superfluous. In either case, the transcendental argument is itself ineffective.

Stroud's criticism of transcendental arguments comes in three parts. The first part is the "hedging" move; the second part is the "bridge of necessity" move; and the third part is the "sufficiency" move. The transcendental arguer begins with a mind-to-world thesis, such as that:

(T)   A necessary condition for the possibility of having psychological states P with content S is that *S is true*.

For example, in Putnam's argument, (T) would be construed as: a necessary condition for the possibility of thinking that *I'm not a BIV* is that *I'm not a BIV*. However, Stroud insists that the transcendental thesis can always be 'hedged' into a weaker mind-to-mind thesis:

> The sceptic can always very plausibly insist that it is enough to make language possible [*or thoughts, beliefs, or representations of certain types*] if we believe that S is true, or if it looks for all the world as if it is, but that S needn't actually be true. (Stroud 1968: 255)[8]

So, applying the hedging move to the transcendental premise of Putnam's argument, we get:

---

[8] One might wonder whether the hedging move is fair to the proponent of transcendental arguments. After all, part of the Kantian project is show that there are interesting mind-to-world relations which can be known by *a priori* reasoning. So, it seems Stroud's hedging move challenges a major part of the Kantian project. However, even Stroud's challenge lacks adequate support, and is in this way unfair; the thrust of Stroud's concern here is that the proponent of the transcendental argument *has* to reply in ways which remove the anti-skeptical efficacy of the transcendental argument. For example, she'll have to say that the hedging the mind-to-world thesis to a mind-to-mind thesis isn't enough to establish the transcendental conclusion, and this is where Stroud challenges the proponent of the transcendental argument to explain why this is so without invoking an idealist or verificationist principle. Cf. Brueckner (2010: 109).

(T1*) A necessary condition of the possibility of thinking that *I am not a brain in a vat* is that *I must not seem to be a brain in a vat.*

With (T1*) replacing (T1), the most that a proponent of Putnam's transcendental argument could infer is (TC*): that I must not *seem* to be a BIV. But it's not clear how that conclusion could have any anti-skeptical import. For the skeptic can plausibly agree with (TC*), and argue that: "It's true that you can think that you're not a BIV, and it's true that a necessary condition of your thinking that you're not a BIV is that you must not seem to be a BIV. And I grant that you don't seem to be a BIV. What I'm suggesting is that, although you don't seem to be a BIV, you nevertheless *don't know* that you're not a BIV."

Now the bridge of necessity move comes into play on (T1*). The argument here would be that, in order for the proponent of the transcendental argument to bridge the explanatory gap from *seeming not to be a BIV* to *not being a BIV* one would need to invoke an idealist principle or a verificationist principle (or more broadly, an anti-realist principle). Why? *Prima facie* at least, it's hard to see how there could be a *necessary* connection between *seeming not* to be a BIV and actually *not* being a BIV that wasn't anti-realist friendly. After all, the BIV hypothesis is set up so that how everything perceptually and introspectively seems to us to be is radically different from how things actually are. Because the world exists independently of us – *independently* of our conceptual schemes, language, and thought – it is possible for the world to be radically different from how it perceptually seems to us to be.

According to Stroud, an idealist principle or a verificationist principle is sufficiently anti-skeptical already, rendering the need for a transcendental argument superfluous. In particular, such an argument doesn't do any special anti-skeptical work that couldn't have been done by the idealist principle or the verification principle on its own. As Stroud puts the point more generally:

> Even if we can allow that we can come to see how our thinking in certain ways necessarily requires that we also think in certain other ways . . . and we can appreciate how rich and complicated the relations among those ways of thinking must be, how can truths about the world which appear to say or imply nothing about human thought or experience be shown to be genuinely necessary conditions of such psychological facts as that we think and experience things in certain ways, from which the proofs begin? It would seem that we must find, and cross, a bridge of necessity from the one to the other. That would be a truly remarkable feat, and some convincing explanation would surely be needed of how the whole thing is possible. (Stroud 2000: 158–9)

Stroud's complaint here is that it's hard to see how the truth of certain contingent, non-psychological propositions about the world could be necessary conditions of the truth of certain psychological propositions.

However, a proponent of the Putnamian transcendental argument can argue that content externalism provides the explanation of how that "bridge of necessity" is to be crossed without invoking an idealist or verificationist principle.[9] After all, for the content externalist, the contents of some of our thoughts are in part *world-dependent*, whereas idealism entails that the world is *mind-dependent*. For the idealist, for it to be possible for anything to be a BIV is for it to be possible to represent something as being a BIV. The former metaphysical possibility depends on the latter conceptual possibility. Content externalism allows for the combination of world-dependence *and* mind-independence.[10]

6.6 Ineffable skeptical hypotheses

Even if Putnam's transcendental argument doesn't fall victim to Stroud's general critique of the anti-skeptical import of transcendental arguments, it

---

[9] Interestingly, treating Putnam's BIV argument as a transcendental argument also draws it closer to Davidson's (1983; cf. Davidson 1990, 1999) famous anti-skeptical strategy, particularly since Davidson also (at least in later work) described his anti-skepticism as being transcendental in form. The other obvious parallel, of course, is that both philosophers primarily motivate their anti-skepticism by appeal to a form of content externalism. Although it would take us too far afield to explore these issues here, we think there is much to be gained by examining Putnam's BIV argument and Davidson's anti-skepticism in tandem. For a recent discussion of Davidson's response to radical skepticism, see Pritchard (2013).

[10] Consider these remarks by Brueckner:

> Granted, if idealism is assumed, then the existence of various psychological facts will entail that a world of mountains, lions, and cars exists. And the fact that such a world exists will (at least at first blush) seem to be a non-psychological fact. However, the sort of transcendental argument I would like to investigate does not at all depend on idealism of any kind. According to the anti-sceptical content externalist, the existence of content-bearing mental states requires that non-psychological reality be a certain way. But its being that way is not constituted by some sustaining psychological reality. (Brueckner 1999: 230)

> However, one might worry that Stroud's second concern arises here. The verificationist maintains that the sentence "I'm not a BIV" is true if and only if "I'm not a BIV can be verified. One might think that one implication of Putnam's anti-skeptical argument is that "I'm not a BIV" is always verifiable, since it's verifiable in English or in natural language more generally (e.g. verified as true) and verified as true in vat-English (or in envatted form of a natural language) as well. Whether this is a collapse into verificationism is unclear, however, because the proponent of Putnam's transcendental argument can plausibly suggest that no *general* verificationist principle is being invoked. Instead, they can say that some *special* sentences turn out to be always verifiable as being true (e.g. sentences like "I'm not a BIV").

might fall victim to another general concern. Thomas Nagel (1986) presents a number of criticisms against Putnam's BIV argument,[11] but his core complaint is, first, that the conclusion of this argument constitutes a *reductio* of Putnam's semantic externalism and, second, that even if it did work against the BIV hypothesis, there are so many more ineffable skeptical hypotheses that it cannot refute.

The crux of the first argument is that it is manifestly obvious that it is possible that we're BIVs, so that any theory which implies that it is not possible is false. According to Nagel:

> Such theories [*as semantic externalism*] are refuted by the evident possibility and intelligibility of skepticism, which reveals that by "tree" I don't mean just anything that is causally responsible for my impressions of trees, or anything that looks and feels like a tree, or even anything of the sort that I and others have traditionally called trees. Since those things could conceivably not be trees, any theory that says they have to be is wrong. (Nagel 1986: 73)

One reading of Nagel's criticism of the semantic externalist response to skepticism is that the possibility that skepticism is true provides at least *prima facie* grounds for thinking that what fixes the reference of our referring-expressions is not whatever is "causally responsible" for our typical use of those expressions (Nagel 1986: 73).

More generally, Nagel claims that, if anything, Putnam's BIV argument actually exacerbates the skeptical difficulty, for all it actually shows is that one can't truly think that one is a BIV *even if one is a BIV*:

> If I accept the argument, I must conclude that a brain in a vat can't think truly that it is a brain in a vat, even though others can think this about it. What follows? Only that I cannot express my skepticism by saying "Perhaps I am a brain in a vat." Instead I must say "Perhaps I can't even think the truth about what I am, because I lack the necessary concepts and my circumstances make it impossible for me to acquire them!" If this doesn't qualify as skepticism, I don't know what does. (Nagel 1986: 73)

---

[11] For example, Nagel criticizes Putnam's causal theory of reference, from which he argues that BIV's couldn't refer to trees (etc.). According to Nagel (1986: 72), while the skeptic might not be able to provide an explanation of how our terms refer without the referents existing, the skeptic is nevertheless "not refuted unless reason has been given to believe such an account impossible." For a defense of this criticism, see Zagzebski (2009).

The crux of Nagel's second argument is that the BIV hypothesis is simply a *template* for making vivid what might be our actual epistemic predicament. As Nagel puts the point:

> The traditional skeptical possibilities that we can imagine stand for limitless possibilities that we can't imagine. In recognizing them we recognize that our ideas of the world, however sophisticated, are the products of one piece of the world interacting with part of the rest of it in ways that we do not understand very well. (Nagel 1986: 73)

This brings to the fore the real challenge that radical skepticism poses in this regard. The BIV hypothesis is among the limited ways we can understand how our epistemic predicament might be radically different than what we take it to be. But there are skeptical hypotheses which are among them that we cannot conceive. This just registers that there might be some possible truths that we not only don't know but cannot conceive. *Prima facie* it's hard to see why some of those possible truths are not skeptical, representing our epistemic predicament in ways that we cannot conceive.

7 New lessons from old demons: the case for reliabilism

Thomas Grundmann

Our basic view of the world is well supported. We do not simply happen to have this view but are also equipped with what seem to us very good reasons for endorsing it. But it still seems possible that the real world is in fact very different from the way it epistemically appears to us, even if the way it appears to us is informed by our best epistemic sources (including the sciences). One radical way of considering the world as being very different from the way it appears to us is to think of our cognitive perspectives as being manipulated by a powerful being, traditionally called "the Evil Demon," who intends to deceive us about almost everything in the world. Nothing much depends on what exactly we think about the nature, motivation, and mode of operation of this demon, for example, whether we conceive of it as an evil god (as Descartes suggested), as a mad scientist (as in Putnam's seminal brain-in-a-vat case), or as a giant machine (as in the movie *The Matrix*). If some kind of Evil Demon hypothesis were true of the actual world, our well-established view of the world would be massively mistaken.

What is the epistemic significance of the fact that the Evil Demon hypothesis might be true of our world, although we currently don't have any evidence that suggests that this possibility is actualized?[1] There are two

---

Earlier drafts and parts of this chapter were presented on a number of different occasions: at a workshop on *New Perspectives on External World Scepticism* at the Munich Center for Mathematical Philosophy in July 2013; at a workshop on *Epistemic Justification and Reasons* at the University of Luxembourg in November 2013; at the University of Califorma, Santa Barbara, in April 2014; and at the workshop *Epistemische Standards, Ziele und Gründe* at the Technische Universität Dresden in May 2014. Substantial comments from David Enoch, Joachim Horvath, Jens Kipper and Merrie Bergmann helped me to work out a significantly revised final version of this chapter. I am extremely grateful to all of them.

[1] Pritchard (2012: 126–7) argues that we cannot in principle have empirical evidence that suggests that we are victims of skeptical deception: "Because it is in the very nature of radical skeptical hypotheses that they call one's empirical beliefs into question en masse, it is therefore inevitable that they will call into question whatever empirical basis one takes oneself to have for supposing such a hypothesis to be true" (127). But this view is implausible. Suppose, for example, that a voiceover tells us that she is persistently manipulating our experience. She then correctly predicts all kinds of surprising events in our future stream of experience. The best explanation of this pattern of

rather different intuitive responses that are usually addressed separately. On the one hand, many people share what I will call the *Old Evil Demon* (OED) intuition, according to which one must be justified in believing that the Evil Demon hypothesis is false in order to have any justified beliefs about the external world. Descartes maintained a similar view with respect to knowledge. In order to know that p, Descartes claimed, one has to rule out all propositions that are incompatible with the truth of p, including the hypothesis of radical demon deception. Currently, BonJour takes such a requirement as obviously applying to epistemic justification: "to admit that no response to the sceptic is possible ... destroys the claim of ... epistemic justification ... in the first place" (BonJour 1985: 14). Although not everyone will share BonJour's intuition, it seems to be accepted by a significant number of epistemologists and non-philosophers. On the other hand, there is the currently very prominent *New Evil Demon* (NED) intuition, according to which we can have justified beliefs about the external world even if the Evil Demon hypothesis of massive deception is *actually true*. Many people feel quite attracted to the fallibilist idea that even a false belief can be justified, and the NED intuition looks like a plausible generalization of justificatory fallibilism. Here are examples of two current proponents of the NED intuition. Cohen claims: "It strikes me as clearly false to deny that under these circumstances [i.e. if the mental perspective in the demon world looks fully normal; TG] our beliefs could be justified" (Cohen 1984: 281). Similarly, Foley (1985: 190) claims: "Even if ... our world is w [i.e. a demon world; TG], it still can be epistemically rational for us to believe many of the propositions we do."

The exact relationship between the OED intuition and the NED intuition is only rarely addressed in the literature. Are these intuitions compatible? And if they are, what meta-epistemological view of justification do they suggest? To the extent that the relation between the two intuitions is explicitly addressed, the prevailing view seems to comprise the following two claims (compare Pryor 2000; BonJour 2010):

(1) The NED intuition suggests *mentalism*, that is, the view that justificatory properties are fully determined by facts about non-factive mental states

---

experience would be that what the voice says is true. Hence, contrary to what Pritchard assumes, we do not need objective empirical evidence to support the claim that we are deceived by some powerful being. We can rely on our introspective knowledge about our experience, which is not called into question by the skeptical hypotheses under consideration.

of the cognizer.[2] If mentalism is true, justificatory properties do not depend on any facts external to one's mental perspective. Given that a belief-producing mechanism is reliable only if it produces mostly true beliefs in the actual and close possible worlds, mentalism implies that beliefs need not be reliably produced in order to be justified. Hence the NED intuition seems to suggest that reliability is not necessary for epistemic justification.

(2) The OED intuition is compatible with mentalism, that is, even if justification does not require reliability, there is an explanation why having justified beliefs about the world requires one to be justified in believing that the evil demon hypothesis is false.

In this chapter, I will argue for the contrary of both (1) and (2). In the next section, I will argue that at least some variants of the OED intuition strongly suggest that justification implies reliability after all. In Section 7.2, I will argue that, interestingly, this is compatible with the NED intuition, or, at least, with something very near to it. I will conclude by taking a somewhat broader perspective on the results of this chapter.

7.1 Why the OED intuition suggests that justification requires reliability

Isn't there an obvious explanation of why one must be justified in believing that the Evil Demon hypothesis is false in order to have justified beliefs about the external world – an explanation that is completely independent of any reliability requirement and that is fully compatible with epistemic internalism? The explanation runs like this: Considering the Evil Demon hypothesis constitutes a defeater to one's *prima facie* justified beliefs about the external world. Having the impression of massive deception "from the inside" defeats our *prima facie* justification even if justification does not require objective reliability. This defeater will remove the justification of one's beliefs about the world unless it is itself defeated by evidence against the demon hypothesis.[3] However, considering the mere possibility of a scenario of massive deception does not suffice to constitute a defeater. This is because regarding a proposition as possible neither amounts to believing that it is true (as doxastic

---

[2] Until more recently, all proponents understood mentalism in this way (see e.g. Feldman and Conee 2004). There are now some dissident views that include factive mental states such as perception (see e.g. Pritchard 2012) or knowledge (Williamson 2000) in the mentalist basis.
[3] This internalist explanation of the OED intuition was suggested to me by David Enoch.

defeaters require) nor does it provide us with any evidence for its truth (as normative defeaters require).[4]

On the other hand, one might think that there is a very short argument that establishes the reliability requirement for justification based on the OED intuition: Some skeptical hypotheses (SH), for example, the dreaming hypothesis, are incompatible with the reliability of our beliefs about the world; if we need good reasons for ruling out such hypotheses in order to be justified in our beliefs about the world, as the OED intuition requires, then (so the argument goes) there cannot be justified beliefs about the world unless we are in fact reliably connected to the world. However, this argument suffers from a severe defect. It presupposes that "having good reasons for ruling out SH" means the same as "having *infallible reasons* for believing that SH is false." A more charitable reading of the OED intuition, however, only requires that one has sufficiently good reasons for believing that SH is false. As long as one is fallibilist about justification, one can be justified in believing a proposition that is in fact false. The OED intuition is thus compatible with the idea that even an inhabitant of a demon world may justifiedly (but not infallibly) believe that the demon-world scenario does not apply to the actual world. Therefore, the OED intuition does not seem to require that justification involves reliability.

Further, one might doubt that the OED intuition can be explained unless justification requires reliability.[5] Specifically, why should one try to justify the belief that demonic hypotheses are false if one's intention is not to justify the belief that one is reliably connected to the world as is required by epistemic justification? There is, however, an answer to the question of why one should try to justify the belief that demonic hypotheses are false that is completely independent of a reliability requirement for justification. Consider a plausible version of the closure principle for justification: *in order to be justified in her ordinary belief that p, an epistemic agent must be justified in believing that all known alternatives to p are false* (see e.g. Wright 1986). Whenever we consider Evil Demon hypotheses we quickly realize, i.e., come to know, that some of them are incompatible alternatives to the propositions we ordinarily assume ourselves to be justified in believing. Consider my ordinary claim that

---

[4] For a comprehensive discussion of epistemic defeaters, see Grundmann (2011).
[5] In what follows, it is important to keep in mind that the order of justification differs from the order of explanation. The justification starts with immediate intuitions about demon worlds. From here we infer to explanatory principles from which what is intuited can be deductively derived. The explanations I offer below are not meant to be inferential justifications of what is intuited. The relation between justification and explanation is similar to that in hypothetico-deductive methods.

I am justified in believing that *I have two hands*. Having two hands is obviously incompatible with either living in a demonic void or being a handless brain in a vat. Hence, in order to be justified in believing that I have two hands, the closure principle requires me to be justified in believing that I am neither living in a demonic void nor a handless brain in a vat. Thus, there is a good and straightforward explanation of our OED intuition that does not imply that justification requires reliability.

On my view, there is a better argument for claiming that the OED intuition calls for an externalist reliability condition on epistemic justification. But the argument is more complex than the ones just considered. To explicate this argument, we need to distinguish two different kinds of skeptical hypotheses.[6] Skeptical hypotheses of the first type (SH1) are hypotheses that are incompatible with the *truth* of everything we ordinarily believe about the world. The best version of such a *hypothesis of global deception* seems to be Descartes's hypothesis of a demonic void without any material external world. This hypothesis of global deception must be distinguished from skeptical hypotheses of the second type (SH2), which describe scenarios in which *the sources of our beliefs about the world are epistemically inadequate*. While dreaming or hallucinating one seems to lack good perceptual reasons for what one dreams or hallucinates, even if what one dreams or hallucinates is true – which can surely be the case.[7] Consider dreaming that one is sleeping in one's bed or dreaming about one's actual name or profession. Therefore, SH2 – which I will generically call the "dreaming hypothesis" – conflicts with one's ordinary belief being justified rather than with it being true.

Given this distinction between skeptical hypotheses that are incompatible with the *truth* of our ordinary beliefs and skeptical hypotheses that are incompatible with the *justification* of what we ordinarily believe, let us reconsider the original OED intuition, which claims that in order to have justified beliefs about the world, we must be justified in believing that the relevant skeptical hypothesis is false. When one takes into account that there are two different types of skeptical hypotheses (SH1 and SH2), it seems quite natural to distinguish the following two different readings of the OED intuition:

OED*: In order to have justified beliefs about the world, we must be justified in believing that the *skeptical hypothesis of global deception* about the world is false.

---

[6] For this distinction, see Grundmann (2003: 71–2).
[7] See, for example, G. E. Moore (1959: 245–6), Stroud (1984: 16–17), and Wright (1986: 432–3).

OED**: In order to acquire justified beliefs about the world on the basis of sense experience, we must be justified in believing that the *dreaming hypothesis* is false.

It is easy to show that OED* can be explained without relying on the premise that justification involves reliability. We can give the required explanation by way of the following deductive argument:

(1) For all p, in order to be justified in believing that p we must be justified in believing that all things we know to be alternatives to p are false.
(2) We know that the skeptical hypothesis of global deception about the world (SH1) is an alternative to whatever we believe about the world.

Therefore,

OED*: In order to have justified beliefs about the world, we must be justified in believing that the *skeptical hypothesis of global deception* about the world is false.

This argument is clearly valid. Premise (2) seems obvious, since SH1 is defined as being incompatible with the truth of everything we believe about the world. Premise (1) is a version of the *closure principle* for justification. So the argument is sound. But then no premise about the reliability of justification is needed to explain OED*.

Consider, in contrast, OED**. This intuition cannot be explained in a way analogous to OED*. Why not? Because, as I said before, dreams may and sometimes do correspond to reality. Hence, the closure principle does not require that one is justified in believing that the dreaming hypothesis is false. So, we have to look for some other explanation of OED**. In what follows I will offer what I take to be the best explanation. I won't be able to rule out all possible alternatives. But I will argue that at least the most salient alternatives do not work. Here is one deductive argument that has OED** as its conclusion and hence offers an explanation, E1, of OED**:

(1) We acquire justified beliefs about the world on the basis of sense experience only if we are justified in believing that we acquire justified beliefs about the world on the basis of sense experience.
(2) We know that one cannot acquire justified beliefs about the world on the basis of sense experience when one is dreaming.
(3) If we are justified in believing that we acquire justified beliefs about the world on the basis of sense experience and if we know that one cannot acquire justified beliefs about the world on the basis of sense experience

when one is dreaming, then we are justified in believing that we are not dreaming that p.

Therefore,

OED**: In order to acquire justified beliefs about the world on the basis of sense experience, we must be justified in believing that we are not dreaming.[8]

What is the rationale behind the premises of this valid argument? Premise (1) expresses a kind of JJ–principle for propositional justification. In order to acquire justifiers (of a certain kind), we need to have good reasons that we acquire those kinds of justifiers. I will discuss the plausibility of this premise below. Premise (3) expresses a special instance of the previously introduced closure principle for justification. What about premise (2)? If one knows that one cannot acquire justified beliefs on the basis of sense experience when one is dreaming, then one cannot acquire justified beliefs on the basis of sense experience when one is dreaming. This is so because knowledge is factive. But why should it be impossible to acquire the justified belief that p on the basis of dreaming that p? One plausible answer is that (i) one's sense experience is unreliable as long as one is dreaming and (ii) one can acquire new justification only on the basis of reliable sources. The upshot of the above argument is that this explanation of OED** presumes that justification requires reliability.

The OED** intuition is sometimes used in skeptical arguments against the empirical justification of our beliefs about the world (see e.g. Wright 1991; Grundmann 2003: 216–26). Here is a schema for such arguments, driven by the OED** intuition:

(P1) In order to acquire justified beliefs about the world on the basis of sense experience, we must be justified in believing that the dreaming hypothesis is false.

(P2) We cannot be justified in believing that the dreaming hypothesis is false.

---

[8] More formally, the argument runs like this:

(1) $J_e p \rightarrow J J_e p$
(2) $K(J_e p \rightarrow \neg D p)$
(3) $(J J_e p \, \& \, K(J_e p \rightarrow \neg D p)) \rightarrow J(\neg D p)$

Therefore,

OED**: $J_e p \rightarrow J(\neg D p)$

The capital J stands for *justification*, with the index $_e$ it stands for *empirical justification*, K stands for *knowledge*, and D for *dreaming*.

Therefore,

(C)   We cannot acquire justified beliefs on the basis of sense experience.

Premise (P1) is equivalent to the OED** principle. If we accept this principle, the force of the skeptical argument depends entirely on premise (P2). Opinions differ on this premise. Some argue that one surely can have good empirical reasons against the dreaming hypothesis.[9] Doing so commits one to a kind of bootstrapping or epistemically circular justification. If one does not accept any of these justificatory strategies, one might still claim that one can have good *non-empirical* reasons against the dreaming hypothesis: either *a priori* reasons or some kind of default justification.[10] So, even if OED** is a crucial step in the skeptical argument against empirically justified beliefs about the world, it is not by itself sufficient to generate justificatory skepticism.

So far, I have argued that there is not a unified OED intuition, but rather two different intuitions that claim that being justified in believing that the Evil Demon hypothesis is false is necessary for being justified in believing ordinary propositions on the basis of sense experience. One of these intuitions, OED*, can be fully explained on the basis of closure. But to make sense of the other intuition, OED**, we apparently have to assume that epistemic justification requires reliability. Proponents of mentalism might respond that it is not clear that we all share the OED** intuition. But even if we do have this intuition, it might be explained away by claiming that the primary intuition about the old Evil Demon is OED*, and that we somehow do not distinguish clearly enough between this case and the dreaming hypothesis because dreams often falsely represent the environment. Hence we confuse OED* with OED**. If this were true, we would not need any additional explanation of OED**, for it would then be shown to be untrustworthy.[11] But this strategy would seem to be a desperate move. Given that many epistemologists still find OED** intuitively appealing, we can safely ignore this move here.

---

[9] For example, Austin (1962: 49) claims that dream experience is qualitatively different from waking experience. For a more timely defense that relies on experimental dream research, compare also Grundmann (2002). Similar views were held by Descartes, Hobbes, and Locke.

[10] For an *a priori* argument against skeptical hypotheses, see BonJour (1985: chapter 8). Wright (2004) employs the idea of default justification against the skeptical challenge.

[11] Something along these lines was suggested to me by Anthony Anderson.

Here is a more substantial objection to the explanation of OED** suggested above. One might argue that there is a much simpler and more straightforward way of explaining OED** than the one I suggested (i.e. E1):[12]

(1) If we are justified in believing that p on the basis of sense experience and if we know that if p is true and we are experiencing that p, we are justified in believing that we are not dreaming that p, then we are justified in believing that we are not dreaming that p.
(2) We know that if p is true and we are experiencing that p, we are justified in believing that we are not dreaming that p.

Therefore,

OED**: In order to be justified in believing anything on the basis of sense experience, we must be justified in believing that the *dreaming hypothesis* is false.

Let us discuss the premises in reverse order. Premise (2) seems plausible since it is very likely that true experiential representations do not constitute dreams. It is true that dreams can be factive, but only accidentally. Premise (1) expresses an instance of a transitivity principle for justification. More formally: $Jp \& K(p \rightarrow Jq) \rightarrow Jq$.[13] However, transitivity for justification is in danger of being too permissive. To see the worry more clearly, suppose that the justification for my belief is constituted by the degree of probability of the believed proposition given the evidence available to me. We may stipulate, for the sake of argument, that the probability of a belief must be higher than 0.6 for the belief to count as justified in the absolute sense. Now suppose that an epistemic agent A believes that p with a probability of 0.7 and also believes that the conditional probability of q given p equals 0.7. If she infers from this to q, her conclusion has a probability of 0.49. This is below the threshold for justification in the absolute sense. So this case constitutes a counterexample to the general principle of transitivity for justification. Of course, this is not a knockdown argument, since one might spell out justification in non-probabilistic terms.[14]

So far it has been argued that among the OED intuitions there is at least one intuition, namely OED**, whose best explanation involves a reliabilist constraint on epistemic justification. If one looks more carefully at this

---

[12] This objection was raised by Marian David. David Enoch helped me to make the objection as strong as possible.
[13] The capital J stands for *justification*, K stands for *knowledge*.
[14] This reply was suggested to me by Joachim Horvath.

explanation, it turns out that it depends in part on a highly controversial principle, the JJ-principle (premise 1 in E1). This principle is problematic for at least two reasons. First, if one always needs some kind of meta-justification for any kind of first-order justification, this looks like an over-intellectualized account of justification. Second, the JJ-principle directly leads to a vicious regress.[15] So the best explanation seems to be no good explanation after all. But then we are at the following impasse: there is an epistemic intuition, OED**, that can only be explained by epistemic principles that are, at least in part, dubious. For this reason, I won't rest my further argument on this version of the OED intuition and will bracket OED** for the rest of this chapter.

The interesting question now is whether there is any intuition in the vicinity of OED** (i) that does not rely on the highly controversial JJ-principle and (ii) that cannot be explained without assuming that justification requires reliability. On my view there is indeed such an intuition. Consider whether your current perceptual beliefs about the world are justified. When you ask yourself this, you treat it as an open question, that is, you are looking for reasons to decide the issue that do not presuppose any specific answer. Moreover, when you ask this question, you are looking for justifying reasons in order to decide whether your beliefs have first-order justification. How can you answer this second-order question positively? Intuitively, it would seem absurd to argue that you have justified perceptual beliefs just by referring to your *introspective knowledge* that your perceptual beliefs correspond to your sense experiences. You cannot tell whether your beliefs about the world are justified on the basis of nothing but introspection. When you rationally claim that you have justified perceptual beliefs you seem to be committed to the further claim that you are currently not dreaming. So, in order to give any justified affirmative answer to the question of whether you have justified perceptual beliefs, you need to be justified in believing that you are currently not dreaming.[16] This, then, is the intuition we have been looking for:

OED***: If you are justified in believing that you have acquired justified beliefs about the world on the basis of sense experience, you need to be justified in believing that you have not been dreaming.[17]

---

[15] Compare Alston (1989c). [16] Compare Grundmann (2003: 265).
[17] OED*** does not claim that you have to justify that you are not dreaming *before* or *independently* of any justified beliefs about the world. It is, for example, compatible with the view that you justify that you are not dreaming on the basis of bootstrapping from your justified first-order beliefs about the world.

We can explain this intuition without appealing to any controversial JJ-principle. Here is the explanation:

(1) You know that you cannot acquire justified beliefs about the world on the basis of sense experience when you are dreaming.
(2) If you are justified in believing that you have acquired justified beliefs about the world on the basis of sense experience and if you know that you cannot acquire justified beliefs about the world on the basis of sense experience when you are dreaming, then you are justified in believing that you have not been dreaming.

Therefore,

OED***: If you are justified in believing that you have acquired justified beliefs about the world on the basis of sense experience, you need to be justified in believing that you have not been dreaming.[18]

The OED*** intuition can obviously be explained without the dubious JJ-principle. We just need an instance of justificatory closure under *known* implication (premise 2) and the assumption that we know that we do not acquire perceptual justification merely by dreaming (premise 1).

Is it really true that the best explanation of premise (1) is that justification requires reliability? I want to defend this explanation by way of considering four different explanations of why the acquisition of empirically justified beliefs is incompatible with dreaming that do not depend on the assumption that justification requires reliability. Here is a *first* such explanation: dreaming states are neither perceptual nor experiential but are states of imagining. There are many differences between perception and imagination.[19] In contrast to sense perception, imagination is, e.g., not causally responsive to stimuli in the environment and is under our voluntary control (McGinn 2004: 12–17). Hence, dreams cannot provide us with *perceptual* justification for our beliefs about the world. Moreover, imagination lacks the affirmative character of representation, that is, the property of representing its content *as*

---

[18] Here again is a more formal version of the argument:

(1) $K(J_e p \rightarrow \neg Dp)$
(2) $(JJ_e p \,\&\, K(J_e p \rightarrow \neg Dp)) \rightarrow J(\neg Dp)$

Therefore,

OED*** $JJ_e p \rightarrow J(\neg Dp)$

The capital J stands for *justification*, with the index $_e$ it stands for *empirical justification*, K stands for *knowledge*, and D for *dreaming*.

[19] For a comprehensive discussion of these differences, see McGinn (2004: 7–41).

being actually true, which is necessary for being a justifying reason.[20] Being a mental state with the relevant (propositional) content is clearly not enough for justifying one's belief. This is the reason why the *desire* that a particular person is around or the *supposition* that she is around cannot justify the belief that she is around. Some philosophers argue that dreams lack the required affirmative character as well. Although, according to these philosophers, dreams have an immersive quality, they do not strictly possess an affirmative character. For this reason they cannot provide us with *genuine justification* for our beliefs about the world (see McGinn 2004: 96–112; Sosa 2007b).

Admittedly, this explanation might succeed in explaining why a belief cannot be empirically justified by a dream with the same content, and it does so without presupposing that justification requires reliability. But we can easily find another intuition in the vicinity of the OED*** intuition such that what has to be ruled out by good reasons is hallucination rather than dreaming. OED***+ reads as follows: *If you are justified in believing that you have acquired justified beliefs about the world on the basis of sense experience, you need to be justified in believing that you have not been hallucinating.* What might explain why dreams cannot provide us with justification for our beliefs about the world in non-reliabilist terms does not serve to also explain why hallucinations cannot provide us with such a justification. The alternative explanation does not apply to OED***+ since, for example, visual hallucinations are clearly sense-experiential states with an affirmative character.

Here is a *second* putative explanation of why we have to be justified in believing that the dreaming hypothesis is false in order to acquire empirical justification for our beliefs about the world. One might think that the dreaming hypothesis constitutes a certain type of defeater that removes one's *prima facie* empirical justification unless it is defeated itself. According to this view, the *dreaming hypothesis* would constitute an undercutting defeater (which conflicts directly with the efficaciousness of the *prima facie* justification), whereas the *skeptical hypothesis of global deception* would constitute a rebutting defeater (which conflicts with the truth of the *prima facie* justified beliefs). The nice thing about defeaters is that what they represent need not be true in order to make them epistemically efficacious. It will do if a defeater is simply *believed* or if there is some *evidence that suggests that the defeater is true*. But if defeaters need not actually be true in order to do their job, then even an

---

[20] McGinn (2004: 21): "Percepts supply (defeasible) reasons to believe; they insist on their own veracity. But images do not invite belief in this way; they do not purport to tell us how the world is ... The image is not evidence that things are presently thus-and-so in the external world... Percepts entitle you to form the corresponding belief, but images do not."

epistemic internalist who does not believe that justification requires objective reliability can make use of them.

However, considering the *mere possibility* of a scenario that would be in conflict with either the justificatory efficaciousness or the truth of a given belief does not suffice as a defeater.[21] Since considering the dreaming hypothesis does not generate any kind of defeater, it is not necessary to defeat this hypothesis in order to remain justified in one's beliefs about the world.

At this point, one might concede that there is no fully internalist explanation of the OED*** intuition. Somehow we must refer to external requirements for justification in order to explain why acquiring empirical justification and dreaming (or hallucinating) are incompatible. But there might still be an externalist account of this explanandum that does not involve a reliabilist condition.[22]

Something like the following *third* explanation suggests itself: empirical justification originates from factive mental states like perceptions of facts or knowledge.[23] Not every true mental representation automatically qualifies as a factive mental state. For this reason, true dreams or veridical hallucinations do not count as justifiers; something more is needed to constitute genuinely factive mental states. This account seems to motivate the claim that neither dreams nor hallucinations can provide justification, yet without being committed to the stronger view that justification involves reliability.

One might object that an account of factive reasons makes it impossible to account for justified false beliefs. But this is not correct. Even if the initial reasons must involve facts, their cognitive processing might still result in false beliefs if the beliefs do not perfectly correspond to the initial reasons' content. This may happen if what is perceived is falsely described or if one draws a content-extending inference, for example, an inference to the best explanation.[24] There is, however, a further, crucial objection. The proponents of factive reasons (such as Pritchard and Williamson) claim that factive mental states are more than just true representations. But what is the extra component that turns true representations into factive mental states? Both Pritchard and Williamson claim that the extra component of factive mental states is an epistemic one. Pritchard says: "Seeing that p, like knowing that p, expresses a rather robust epistemic relation that one bears to p." More specifically, Pritchard claims that "seeing that p could constitute one's

---

[21] This has already been argued above. See pages 92–3.
[22] This objection was suggested to me by Tim Kraft in personal conversation.
[23] For different versions of this account, see Williamson (2000) and Pritchard (2012).
[24] The latter alternative is endorsed by Williamson (2000).

epistemic basis for knowing that p" (2012: 21), and Williamson (2000) maintains that knowledge implies safety. On both accounts, the relevant factive mental state thus invokes an anti-luck condition that involves some kind of reliability constraint. We can now see more clearly that accounts of factive reasons are themselves presumably committed to a reliability requirement and therefore do not establish a genuine alternative to the explanation I have suggested.

Against the reliabilist explanation of the OED*** intuition, one might *finally* claim that the incompatibility of dreaming and hallucinating with acquiring empirical justification does not require any explanation at all. That is, one might argue that dreaming and hallucinating are simply paradigmatic cases of states that prevent epistemic agents from acquiring new pieces of evidence. An answer to the question *why* dreaming and hallucinating are in conflict with acquiring new justifiers would thus not be required. And if no explanation for OED** is required, then no *reliabilist* explanation is required either.[25]

However, it seems hard to believe that it is a brute and unexplainable fact that dreaming and hallucinating are incompatible with acquiring new justification. It is very natural to assume that both cases must have something in common by virtue of which they cannot provide empirical justification. To insist that no explanation is required or even available here seems like a fairly desperate move.

Finally, we have reached the desired result: there is an OED intuition, namely OED***, whose presumably best explanation requires us to assume that justification implies reliability. I must concede that I have not provided a conclusive defense of this claim. Rather, I have argued that all alternative explanations that I have considered here do not succeed. I take it that the burden of proof is now on my opponent's side.

7.2 Why the NED intuition does not suggest that justification is independent of reliability

If the results of Section 7.1 are basically correct, a plausible version of the Old Evil Demon intuition suggests that justification requires some kind of reliability. However, the OED intuitions are not the only kind of intuitions we have with respect to demonic worlds. There is also the New Evil Demon

---

[25] Something along these lines was independently suggested to me by Jochen Briesen, Jim Pryor, and Timothy Williamson in personal conversation.

intuition, that is, the intuition that victims of demonic deception can still have justified beliefs, which suggests, at least according to the received view, that justification is *independent* of reliability (see e.g. Foley 1985). Hence, we seem to have conflicting intuitions with respect to demon worlds. In the face of this worry, I will take a closer look at the NED intuition in this section.

To make some progress here, we should explicate the content of NED in more detail. According to a common view, the core of this intuition is that justificatory facts supervene on, or are determined by, facts about the non-factive mental perspective of the epistemic agent. Hence, we get as a first approximation:

NED*: The external world beliefs of our mental duplicate in the demon world would have the same justificatory status as our beliefs in a normal world.[26]

Spelled out in this way, NED does not entail that the beliefs of our mental duplicate in the demonic world are actually justified. This would clearly beg the question against the skeptic. It might turn out that *we*, although living in a normal world, don't possess justified beliefs about the world because we do not satisfy certain epistemic requirements. If this were true, our duplicate would also lack justified beliefs according to NED*. Now, our beliefs in the actual world are *ex hypothesi* formed by reliable processes such as perception that function unreliably in the demonic world. Since, according to NED*, there is no difference in justificatory properties between us and the demon's victim, being reliably produced may not be sufficient for justification. Hence, NED* may challenge simple versions of reliabilism that claim that a belief is justified *if* and only if it is based on a reliable process. But NED* neither shows that reliability is not necessary for justification nor does it establish mentalism as the correct view.

There are other versions of NED intuitions that might do better in calling into question the claim that reliability is necessary for justification. Consider this one:

NED**: The victim of demonic deception *can* be epistemically justified in her beliefs about the world.

For the sake of the argument, I will grant that NED** expresses an intuition about genuine *epistemic justification* rather than an intuition about having blameless, internally rational beliefs or about being the beliefs of a virtuous

---

[26] For a similar view, see Pritchard (2012: 38).

epistemic agent.[27] BonJour (2010: 228–9) clearly commits himself to something like NED**:

> The Evil Genius carefully controls their [the victims'] sensory and introspective experience, producing in them just the experiences they would have if they inhabited a particular material world, perhaps one exactly like our own, containing various specific sorts of objects and processes that interact and influence each other in a lawful way. The people in this position are, we may suppose, careful and thorough investigators. They accumulate large quantities of sensory evidence, formulate hypotheses and theories, *subject their beliefs to philosophical arguments ... for the likely truth of their resulting beliefs*. Are the beliefs about their apparent world that the people in such a Cartesian demon world arrive at in these ways justified? ... From an intuitive standpoint, it seems hard ... to deny that they are.[28]

BonJour not only claims that mental duplicates have the same justificatory status (as NED* claims), but also maintains that the victim of a demonic deception will have justified beliefs about the world if she fulfills all her epistemic obligations and possesses a philosophical meta-justification for her beliefs about the world as NED** requires.

In contrast to NED*, NED** seems to provide us with all that is needed to argue against the reliability condition of epistemic justification. Here is the corresponding *argument against reliability* in its standard form:

(P1) It is possible that an inhabitant of a demon world has epistemically justified beliefs about the world.

(P2) Necessarily, *all* belief-forming processes are unreliable in demon worlds.

Therefore,

(C) Epistemic justification does not depend on reliable belief-forming processes.

At first glance, this argument looks quite compelling. It is clearly valid, (P1) is one way of expressing the NED** intuition, and (P2) seems plausible given that the inhabitant of the demon world is a victim of an all-encompassing demonic deception.

---

[27] For weaker interpretations of the NED intuition, see Bach (1985), Engel (1992), and Weatherson (2008).
[28] My italics. See also Cohen (1984: 28).

In spite of its initial plausibility, however, (P2) is not correct. At least this is what I want to now argue. In order to see which processes will remain reliable in a demon world, one has to fill in more details about what goes on in such a world. According to the standard stipulation of the case, my demonic counterpart shares his non-factively individuated mental perspective with me. What differs between us are the contingent facts in the external world. All contingently existing external facts are completely removed in the demon world. My counterpart is living in a void. If this is an appropriate characterization of the demon world, then *perception* and *memory* of external states of affairs will function unreliably in the demon world. But there are other cognitive faculties whose reliable functioning would not be at all impaired by the demonic deception (see Grundmann 2003: 261–3; Lyons 2013). Consider, first, *introspection*. Since (i) *ex hypothesi* I share my mental perspective with my demon-world counterpart and (ii) the actual reliability of introspection is fully determined by my mental perspective, introspection must be reliable in the demon world as well. Secondly, consider *rational intuition*. Again, we start with the stipulation that rational intuition is reliable in the actual world. My demon-world counterpart has the same rational intuitions as I do, because this is implied by the sameness of our mental perspectives. Let us further assume that rational intuitions are only about *metaphysical* modalities. They represent what is *metaphysically* possible and what is *metaphysically* necessary. Metaphysical modalities are stable across all possible worlds. Hence, what is metaphysically possible in the actual world is metaphysically possible in any world, and what is metaphysically necessary in the actual world is metaphysically necessary in any world. This feature of metaphysical modalities is represented by unrestricted accessibility in modal logic. Together, these facts entail that rational intuitions are reliable in demon worlds as well. Even the Evil Demon cannot change the space of possible worlds, which are the truthmakers of my rational intuitions. Moreover, the rational intuitions in the demon world *ex hypothesi* represent the same modalities as in the actual world. But then, rational intuition must be reliable in the demon world if it is reliable in the actual world. Finally, consider *inference*. Deductive inferences are truth-preserving in all possible worlds. No matter what the world is like, a deductive inference leads one to a true conclusion if one's premises are true. Given that an inferential method is conditionally reliable if and only if it maps true inputs to mostly true outputs, deductive inferences are conditionally reliable even in the demon world. But what about *non-deductive* inferences? Not every non-deductively inferential method is conditionally reliable in demon worlds. Take, for example, inductive generalizations. If the demon world lacks the requisite uniformity of nature, inductive generalizations are not reliable in demon worlds. However, there are certain kinds of non-deductive inferences that are reliable even in demon worlds. Consider, for example, the following inference pattern (IP):

(P1)   I represent that p.
(P2)   Representations are reliable.

Therefore,

(C)   p.

Obviously, the conjunction of (P1) and (P2) does not deductively entail the truth of p. But in any world in which (P1) and (P2) are true, the truth of p is (objectively) probable. This is true even for the demon world. Here we have a case of a non-deductive inference that is conditionally reliable even in the demon world, although its premise (P2) is, of course, clearly false in the demon world. As we shall see below, this is exactly the type of inference that the demon victim can use to justify her beliefs about the external world.

Consider the victim of demonic deception. All her beliefs about the world are *ex hypothesi* false. Is she still equipped with reliable processes that result in beliefs about the world? Although this seems to be impossible at first glance – remember that the victim's beliefs about the world are all false – there is indeed a Cartesian route available to the victim to form beliefs about the world in a reliable manner. Note that, from a reliabilist point of view, it is sufficient for a belief to be inferentially justified if it is based on conditionally reliable inferences from reliably formed beliefs. But then our protagonist could use the following inferential method to arrive at beliefs about the world in a manner that is acceptable to the reliabilist:[29]

(P1)   I experience as if p.
(P2)   Experience is reliable in every possible world.

Therefore,

(C)   p.

Premise (P1) is based on introspection, which functions reliably even in the demon world, as I argued above. Premise (P2) is based on rational intuition, which also functions reliably in the demon world. Keep in mind that (P2) is

---

[29] For this argument, see Lyons (2013: 7–8). Surprisingly, Lyons's own attempt to square reliabilism with the NED intuition is not based on this argument.

actually false if we suppose that the cognizer is in fact living in a demon world, for experience does not function reliably in the demon world.[30] Therefore, there is at least one world in which experience does not function reliably, and this contradicts the claim that (P2) makes, namely, that experience is reliable in *every* possible world. But even if (P2) is false, it could still be based on a reliable process since reliability does not entail infallibility. You might wonder how (P2) can be justified on the basis of rational intuition. I don't want to defend a particular line of argument here, nor do I believe that there is any successful line of argument available. Since I grant that demon worlds are possible, there cannot be any *sound* argument supporting (P2).[31] But I do think that there are several rationalist attempts to give an *a priori* defense of something like (P2), for example, Descartes's proof of a benevolent God that supports the reliability of sense perception, or rationalist arguments from semantic externalism that support a minimal reliability of perceptual beliefs.[32] Finally, the inference from (P1) and (P2) to (C) is non-deductive. Since reliability does not guarantee truth, it is possible that a necessarily reliable process results in a false belief. Nevertheless, the non-deductive inference at hand guarantees that the conclusion is objectively probable in every world in which the premises are true. This will certainly satisfy reliabilist standards. Thus, we come to the surprising conclusion that, even in a world of demonic deception in which all beliefs about the external world are false, the epistemic agent could justify her beliefs about the world in a way that is acceptable to reliabilist standards. Hence, NED** does not conflict with reliabilism after all.

---

[30] In fact, (P2) is necessarily false, that is, false in all worlds, if the actual world is a demon world. Thanks to David Enoch for reminding me of this fact.

[31] As long as we stipulate that the inhabitant of the demon world possesses a mental perspective that exactly duplicates my own, this generates a devastating problem for my argument. For I have good reasons to doubt the soundness of the rationalist meta-justification. But if I have these reasons, my demonic counterpart, insofar as he duplicates my mental perspective, possesses them as well. Now, these reasons constitute defeaters for the rationalist meta-justification, so there is no mental duplicate of me in any demon world that has *ultima facie* justified beliefs about the world. But then my general argument seems to fail.

Notice, however, that it is not part of NED** that victims of demonic deception share my mental perspective. NED** only claims that there can be inhabitants of demon worlds that have justified beliefs about the world. In order to defend the view that these agents have reliable processes at their disposal, one must concede that I and my counterpart share our mental perspectives at least in part. Otherwise, the rational intuitions of my demonic counterpart could not be as reliable as my own. But the correspondence of perspectives can be restricted in order to avoid having my demonic counterpart inherit my defeaters for the rationalist meta-justification. Thanks to Joachim Horvath for making me aware of this complication.

[32] The locus classicus for this kind of semantic externalist argument is Davidson (1983). In Grundmann and Misselhorn (2003), we defend a rationalist understanding of semantic externalist arguments against external world skepticism.

So far, this is good news for the reliabilist. However, there is a further intuition about new Evil Demons that does conflict with reliabilism. Consider the following case:

NED***: The epistemic agents in the demon world base their beliefs about the world directly on sense experience, as we typically do. They also have *a priori* arguments that support the reliability of sense experience at their disposal. But in contrast to the case considered above, these arguments do not play a role in the formation of their beliefs about the world. Still, it is hard to deny that the agents arrive at justified beliefs in that world.

If this is what you intuit about the case, then according to your intuition, the relevant justification does not require reliability.

I agree that the reliabilist cannot fully explain NED***. But she can do something close to it.[33] She can explain how the victim of demonic deception can be justified in believing that her perceptual beliefs are justified – even if her justified second-order belief is false. Hence, the reliabilist can attribute meta-justification, but not first-order justification, to some inhabitants of demon worlds. This reliable meta-justification would be based on reliable rational intuition and conditionally reliable inference, as in the previous case. Now, what is established by NED***? One might want to say that reliabilism is refuted if one takes one's intuitions at face value. Alternatively, one might claim that reliabilism can explain almost all of our intuitions about the demon world. With respect to the unexplained rest, it seems rather unclear whether we really have the intuition that the victim's beliefs are first-order justified or whether what we really intuit is that the inhabitant of the demon world is justified in believing that she has justified first-order beliefs.

7.3 Conclusion

What role intuitions should play in analyzing epistemic categories is highly controversial in current meta-epistemology. Some people believe that surveys of intuitive responses to hypothetical cases suggest that intuition is in general too problematic to qualify as a trustworthy source of analysis.[34] Others think that analysis of our epistemic *concepts* is not a suitable method for discovering

---

[33] For this strategy, see also Grundmann (2003: 267–9).
[34] A paradigm of this experimental philosophy critique of epistemic intuitions is Weinberg, Nichols, and Stich (2001).

the metaphysical structure of epistemic categories.[35] I don't want to enter into this debate here. I will just note that I believe that intuitions about hypothetical cases are an important means to improve our understanding of, for example, the true nature of epistemic justification. For this reason, I take epistemic intuitions very seriously.[36]

I started out with the observation that we have different intuitions about justification with respect to different skeptical hypotheses. According to the New Evil Demon intuition, which has dominated the recent meta-epistemological debate, one can have justified beliefs about the world even if the skeptical hypothesis is true, that is, even if one is living in a demon world. According to the Old Evil Demon intuition, which is currently widely ignored within the meta-epistemological debate, one cannot possess justified beliefs about the world unless one is able to rule out relevant skeptical hypotheses. There is a strong tendency in current epistemology to regard the NED intuition as evidence for the internalist view that justification is independent of reliability and supervenes on the epistemic subject's non-factive mental perspective. At first glance, this view seems to be compatible with the OED intuition.

On closer inspection, we have found versions of the OED intuition, especially those requiring that we are justified in believing that the *dreaming hypothesis* is false, that cannot be explained on the basis of mentalism about justification but call instead for a robust connection between justification and reliability. This fits nicely with the observation that the NED intuition does not provide a compelling argument for mentalism but is in fact compatible with the view that justification requires reliability. Such a view may not fully explain all variants of NED intuitions: for example, it conflicts with NED***. But reliabilism is at least able to explain why inhabitants of demon worlds can be justified in believing that they have justified first-order beliefs, even if that second-order belief is not true. A general, systematic investigation of our intuitions about the relation between justification and skeptical hypotheses suggests that, all things considered, reliability is a necessary condition for justification after all.

---

[35] For this naturalistic challenge to conceptual analysis, see Kornblith (2002).
[36] For a defense of the use of intuitions as evidence, see Grundmann (2007, 2010).

8 BIVs, sensitivity, discrimination, and relevant alternatives

Kelly Becker

The central purpose of this chapter is to explore the implications of wedding the sensitivity principle in epistemology to the content externalism that serves as the engine of Putnam's brain-in-a-vat (BIV) argument. To a first approximation, the sensitivity principle says that S knows that p only if, were p false, S would not believe that p. Numerous criticisms of and counterexamples to sensitivity have appeared in the literature since it was first fully developed and defended by Nozick (1981).[1] Most of these problems are well known, opinions differ on which if any are devastating, and it would take the space of a lengthy essay just to describe the objections and possible replies, let alone elucidate and assess them. So I won't do that.[2] Instead, I aim to execute two tasks. In Section 8.1, I simply draw out the most direct anti-skeptical implications of sensitivity and content externalism, taken together. Many tangled questions arise about the cogency of arguments from content externalism and sensitivity to conclusions about knowledge of the external world. Particularly germane are questions about self-knowledge of thought contents. In Section 8.2, I focus on these questions. As we will see, on (what I shall call) the standard externalist view (Burge 1988), self-knowledge of content is possible even when one cannot distinguish one's actual thoughts from certain possible twin thoughts. Some philosophers are dubious, claiming that the standard view fails to account for the importance of a discriminating ability for self-

---

[1] Earlier close cousins of Nozickean sensitivity appear in Dretske (1971) and Goldman (1976). Note well that I follow contemporary usage in calling Nozick's *variation* condition 'sensitivity,' whereas Nozick thought of sensitivity as consisting of a variation condition and an adherence condition: If p were true, S would believe that p.

[2] But if you're not familiar with these issues, here are some of the thornier ones for sensitivity. (1) It implies that knowledge is not closed under known entailment. Nozick himself accepted this because he thought we could have ordinary empirical knowledge without being positioned to know that radical skeptical hypotheses are false. (2) Sensitivity seems incompatible with knowing that one knows. See Vogel (2000). See also Becker (2006) and Salerno (2010) for replies. (3) Sensitivity is incompatible with some cases of inductive knowledge. See Sosa (1999) and Vogel (1987, 2012). (4) Kripke (2011) counterexamples seem to show that sensitivity implies that S can know that both-p-and-q while not knowing that p.

knowledge of content. One might naturally think to turn to the sensitivity principle to illuminate self-knowledge of content, insofar as sensitivity appears both to imply a discrimination requirement on knowledge and to generate an account of the relevant alternatives that one's grounds for belief must be able to rule out in order for one's true belief to count as knowledge. I shall argue that this is a mistake. Sensitivity tells us no more about self-knowledge, and perhaps considerably less, than the standard externalist view.

Before moving on to the main program, let me elaborate on why one might think to turn to sensitivity in response to perceived deficiencies in the standard view of self-knowledge, which, again, and as I will explain below, accounts for non-empirical[3] knowledge of the contents of one's own thoughts without requiring the capacity to discriminate, for example, the thought *that water is wet* from the Twin Earth thought *that twater is wet*.[4] In my view, sensitivity offers an attractive necessary condition on perceptual knowledge precisely because (a) it typically requires an ability to discriminate the fact that p from what would be the case were p false, and (b) such an ability is crucial to achieving true beliefs that are not merely luckily true. In addition, sensitivity implies an account of relevant alternatives (Nozick 1981: 174f.). That is, sensitivity implies that S knows that p only if S's grounds for believing that p allow S to rule out relevant alternatives to p. Which ones are relevant? A relevant not-p alternative is one that would be the case were p false; it is one that holds in the closest world or worlds where p is false.

Thus an appeal to sensitivity might be thought to fill the bill if one were unsatisfied with the standard view of self-knowledge of content on the grounds that the standard view requires neither an ability to discriminate twin thoughts nor a way of determining which alternatives one must be able to rule out in order to achieve self-knowledge. The problem is that, when applied to self-knowledge rather than to perceptual knowledge, sensitivity implies no greater discriminatory capacity than does the standard view, and it is not a useful tool for determining which alternatives are in fact relevant.

As it turns out, however, sensitivity can be combined with Putnam's BIV argument to imply directly that we can know we're not BIVs. As we shall see, that result is only as satisfying as the character of non-empirical self-

---

[3] I frequently characterize self-knowledge of content as non-empirical, which I take to mean *a priori*. The nature and status of *a priori* knowledge is obviously controversial, however, hence the term 'non-empirical,' by which I mean *not essentially epistemically supported by perceptual experience of the external world*. Whether introspection qualifies as *a priori* or not, it is non-empirical in this sense.

[4] Where it serves to forestall confusion, I will put thought contents in italics.

knowledge available on a sensitivity account. Ultimately, sensitivity provides a pretty thin edifice on which to build Putnam's anti-skepticism.

One final preliminary. The sensitivity principle is only a necessary condition for knowledge. I do not want to get bogged down in questions concerning other necessary conditions, besides true belief. Our inquiry has to do with whether the sensitivity principle provides substantive illumination of Putnam's argument and of self-knowledge. This means that at times I will come very close to treating sensitivity, *arguendo*, as the crucial condition which, when satisfied together with true belief, constitutes knowledge. I hope this does not create any confusion about the central issues under discussion.

8.1 Sensitivity and knowing that I'm not a BIV

Do I know that I'm not a BIV who is hooked up to electrodes in such a way that I'm being fed illusory experiences as of (for example) typing on a computer?[5] Assume both that I believe that I'm not such a BIV and that my belief is true. Let us first answer the question according to the most basic version of sensitivity, call it S_0.

S_0:   S knows that p only if, were p false, S would not believe that p.

Take the BIV scenario as described above, a skeptical hypothesis, and call it SH_0.

SH_0:   I am a BIV, hooked up to electrodes in such a way that I'm being fed illusory experiences as of typing on a computer.

If SH_0 were true, I would nonetheless believe that I am not a BIV because I would have what seem to be normal experiences. Put differently, in the closest worlds where I am a BIV – those where everything else is held constant, hence those where I've only recently been envatted – I believe that I'm not a BIV. So my actual world belief that I'm not a BIV violates the sensitivity principle because my belief-grounding experience does not discriminate my actual situation from the BIV possibility. Therefore, I do not know that I'm not a BIV.

---

[5] As we explore the relations between Putnam's externalism and sensitivity, I presuppose that the reader is familiar with the basics of externalism and Putnam's anti-skeptical strategy. It is at least unclear whether Putnam's externalism was originally meant to apply beyond meaning and reference to thought content, since in his defense of the thesis (Putnam 1975) he also claimed that twins share psychological states. He later (Putnam 1996: xxi) explicitly claims to agree with Burge that thought contents are implicated in his externalism.

Of course, to this point I have not asked Putnam's question. Putnam's anti-skeptical argument was intended to defang a more radical skeptical hypothesis, namely, that all sentient beings are (and presumably always have been) inside the vat, whose machinery "is supposed to have come into existence by some kind of cosmic chance or coincidence" (Putnam 1981b: 12). Call this SH_1. Putnam's stipulations are in place to sever any causal link between brain states and everyday reality as we understand it.

I do not know that SH_0 is false because the closest world where it is true is one where I very recently became envatted. Up until then the world was more or less as I take it to be. My word meanings and thought contents are anchored to, among other things, brains and vats (and baseball bats and kitty cats). The content of the thought I express by 'I am not a BIV' is *I am not a BIV*. In the closest world where that's false, I believe it's true anyway. But Putnam's skeptical hypothesis is SH_1. (SH_1: I and all other sentient beings have always been BIVs with no salient connections to brains and vats (and bats and cats).) If SH_1 were true, then my words would mean something different and my thoughts would have different contents – they would be different thoughts whose contents are partly determined by different constitutive causal connections to radically different environmental features, presumably to features of the automatic machinery. Putnam concluded that my utterances and thought tokens of 'I am a BIV' (explicated as in SH_1) are false. They're obviously false if I'm not a BIV, and if I am a BIV, they are false because they mean something like *I am some specific state-type of some particular automated machinery*,[6] which I am not because I actually am a BIV. Hence in either case 'I'm not a BIV' is true.

If one accepts Putnam's claims about externalism, these results are fairly uncontroversial. But, even if Putnam is right, there are legitimate questions about the anti-skeptical force of this result.[7] As Brueckner notes: "The

---

[6] Putnam (1981b: 14) suggests other possibilities for the referents of a BIV's terms. I trust that my construal is clear enough for present purposes.

[7] Those sympathetic to Putnam might find the emphasis on BIV skepticism misplaced, given that his actual stalking horse is metaphysical realism and its associated magical theory of reference. My focus here is on the interplay between skepticism, Putnam's externalism, and sensitivity in large part because Putnam's argument has generated an ongoing discussion about skepticism. But I won't be too apologetic about shifting focus away from metaphysical realism because, even if Putnam's argument were successful in showing that we can know we're not BIVs, the question of metaphysical realism wouldn't be settled. If Putnam is right, a BIV thinks something true in tokening 'I am not a BIV,' because it cannot think *I am not a BIV*. This seems to demonstrate an impoverished cognitive perspective, such that certain truths are beyond the BIV's ability to entertain. In turn, we can wonder whether our perspective is also in some way deficient (Forbes 1995). If we don't know whether or how we might be deficient, then we don't know whether there are truths beyond our ability to grasp, and the specter of metaphysical realism reappears. Thanks to participants of the Southwest Epistemology Workshop (August 2014) for raising these larger issues.

anti-skeptical conclusion we desire is ... that I am not a BIV, not the conclusion that my sentence 'I am not a BIV' is true" (Brueckner 1992b: 204). Putnam promised to deliver the result that "the supposition that we are actually brains in a vat ... cannot possibly be true" (Putnam 1981b: 7). He later concludes, "In short, if we are brains in a vat, then 'We are brains in a vat' is false. So it is (necessarily) false" (Putnam 1981b: 15). The conclusion clearly does not support the claim that we could not possibly be BIVs. In fact, the way the conclusion is stated makes clear that it is possible that I am a BIV; it's just that if I were a BIV, my sentence 'I am a BIV' would be false.

The question is not merely whether what I say or think is true, but whether I *know* that I'm not a BIV. There are two relevant issues here. First, true belief is not sufficient for knowledge. Knowledge requires some non-accidental connection between the truth and what one believes. Second, and more importantly, if even an actual BIV would utter something true in saying 'I am not a BIV,' then unless I antecedently know which language I speak, English or BIVese, or somehow know independently that I'm not a BIV (in which case the appeal to content externalism does no work), it will be small comfort to know that my sentence is true.

The questions concerning the nature of self-knowledge consistent with content externalism and whether it suffices to generate Putnam's anti-skeptical conclusion have generated a massive literature.[8] Most take it as overwhelmingly plausible that we have privileged access to our own thoughts, which means (minimally) that we know their contents non-empirically and in an especially secure way. This presents a dilemma. Horn (1): Assume that self-knowledge of content requires an ability to discriminate thoughts expressed in English from those expressed in BIVese. We cannot discriminate those thoughts, so we don't actually know which thoughts we think, and therefore, for all we know, we could be BIVs thinking some other truth that we express by 'I am not a BIV.' Lacking the capacity to distinguish BIV thoughts from my own entails lack of self-knowledge.[9] Horn (2): Deny the assumption that self-knowledge of content requires the aforementioned discriminating capacity (Burge 1988; Falvey and Owens 1994). (I will say more later about how the standard view, explicated in Burge (1988), rejects the assumption.) If we deny the

---

[8] See Brueckner (2012) for a partial bibliography on Putnam's proof and Parent (2013) for a bibliography on self-knowledge and content externalism.

[9] Brown (2004: 50) gives a neat illustration of the kind of discriminative capacity lacking on the standard view. Someone is told she has been subject to slow-switching between Earth and Twin Earth and asked to press a button when she notices that her concepts shift.

assumption, it seems to imply that one could derive ordinary empirical knowledge from reflection on one's own thoughts. That is, if I really do know that by tokening 'I am not a BIV' I am thinking that *I am not a BIV*, then, together with my understanding of content externalism, in particular, of its implication that having thoughts about brains and vats requires at least having had some relevant causal contact with objects of those types, I can infer, just from knowledge of (through privileged access to) my own thoughts, that I exist (or have existed) in a world with brains and vats and not in some strange world where these objects never existed. Well, the second horn doesn't sound *bad* – it would be great if anti-skepticism were that easy – but it seems completely implausible.[10]

We could do an end-run around the self-knowledge controversy and generate Putnam's anti-skeptical result by appealing directly to the sensitivity principle. If my belief that not-SH_1 were false – if I and all sentient beings are and always have been BIVs – I would not believe that not-SH_1. I would have some other belief, such as *that I am not some specific state-type of some particular automated machinery*. Thus, according to sensitivity, I know (or can know) that not-SH_1 because if it were false I would not believe it. Perhaps this is close to what Putnam had in mind all along: "In short, if we are brains in a vat, then 'We are brains in a vat' is false" (Putnam 1981b: 15), precisely because it would mean something else and would express a different belief. I would not believe *that I am not a BIV* if I were a BIV.

The problem with this, as with all end-runs, is that they skirt the central issues. Unless I know that my thoughts are about brains and vats and not about machinery state-types, I don't know whether the belief that I express by 'I am not a BIV' is *that I am not a BIV*. It appears that the appeal to sensitivity has not in any way explained how I could know that SH_1 is false. The reason is that sensitivity is an attractive candidate epistemological principle when it implies a capacity to discriminate, not so much otherwise. Satisfying the principle for Putnam's purposes requires neither a capacity to distinguish in one's subjective experience the actual world from the BIV world, nor a capacity to distinguish thoughts expressed in English from those expressed in BIVese. We should not be tempted to take the by-pass offered by sensitivity without first investigating the question of self-knowledge of content and whether sensitivity illuminates its nature.

---

[10] Not everyone agrees that the strategy is implausible. See, for example, Warfield (1992, 1995). But most do. Boghossian (1997) argues that the strategy constitutes a *reductio* of content externalism.

8.2 Sensitivity and knowing that I think that I'm not a BIV

My main questions in this section are these: Can the sensitivity principle be employed to generate a condition on self-knowledge of content that captures some ability, not available on the standard view, to discriminate content? Does the sensitivity principle generate a set of relevant alternatives to one's actual thoughts, such that the ability to rule out those alternatives illuminates a kind of self-knowledge that is not implied by the standard view?

Whence these questions? (1) As mentioned at the outset, sensitivity is attractive when and because it implies both a discrimination requirement on knowledge and a criterion of relevant alternatives. So we might well investigate its implications for either a discriminatory component or relevant alternatives view of self-knowledge. (2) As suggested above, Putnam could be read as having made tacit appeal to sensitivity in his BIV argument, which was part of the impetus to our raising the question of self-knowledge. If we suppose that Putnam takes sensitivity to be a condition on knowledge in general, that also motivates our questions. (3) Some who argue that content externalism is compatible with non-empirical self-knowledge eschew the standard view in favor of a relevant alternatives view. Can sensitivity help with this? (3a) At least one philosopher (Sawyer 1999) characterizes the ability to rule out relevant alternatives in terms of satisfying conditionals such as sensitivity. Does that maneuver shed light on a kind of discriminatory self-knowledge that is more robust than what the standard view entails?

Let's begin by looking a bit more closely at what I've dubbed the standard view. On the standard anti-individualist view of self-knowledge of content (Burge 1988), second-order thoughts of the form 'I am thinking that p' and 'I hereby judge that p' are self-verifying.[11] This is partly because second-order thoughts presuppose satisfaction of the same conditions that determine first-order contents. To think *I am not a BIV* requires standing in some causal relationship with brains and vats. To think *I hereby judge that I am not a BIV* is to have a second-order thought part of whose content is the first-order thought, hence the second-order thought automatically inherits the first-order content.

Goldberg (2006a) points out that the epistemic status of one's second-order thoughts on the standard view is significantly stronger than on a reliabilist view. Given the self-verifying nature of second-order thoughts, their truth is

---

[11] The standard view works only as an account of knowledge of content, and for thoughts of this form. (Thus I could be wrong that I actually *judge* that p.) Whether in general one always knows what one is thinking, or what attitude one takes toward a thought, are separate issues.

guaranteed. (See also Brueckner (1992b) for similar 'guarantee' talk.) And given that one can know these facts *a priori*, one is *a priori* entitled to make second-order judgments. In contrast, reliabilism typically implies fallibilism. Because Brown (2004: 43) characterizes the standard view as a version of reliabilism, Goldberg claims that Brown's rejection of the standard view because it is merely reliabilist is not well motivated. On the other hand (and as Goldberg makes quite clear), what truly motivates Brown and others is the concern that the standard view is compatible with lack of discriminatory self-knowledge of content.

The concern can be illustrated by BIV thoughts. When I have the thought expressed by 'I judge that I am not a BIV,' my judgment inherits the content of the *BIV* thought, which is determined in part by causal relations between me and brains and vats in my environment. When a BIV thinks 'I judge that I am not a BIV,' its judgment inherits the content of its thought (*I am not some specific state-type of some particular automated machinery*). I never misjudge what I am thinking, nor does the BIV. Still, on the customary anti-individualist story, if I were to become envatted – for example, were my brain removed and put in a vat (and *cetera*) while I slept – once regular causal relationships were established between me and my new environment, my thoughts would change. Call this a slow switching case (because it takes a while to establish regular causal interactions). Those thoughts would be self-verifying, inheriting their first-order contents, which would ground self-knowledge (on the standard view). But it seems that no amount of armchair reflection or introspection would indicate to me that my thoughts have *changed*. I wouldn't be able to notice a difference. This is exactly the lack of discriminatory knowledge, which is undeniable, that some take to imply a lack of non-empirical knowledge of content altogether.

It is useful to be explicit about the common ground shared by principals to the debate. First, so far as I can see, nobody denies Burge's claims about the self-verifying nature of second-order thoughts. Second, everyone agrees that armchair reflection alone does not produce discriminatory self-knowledge. The question is whether self-knowledge requires the relevant discriminatory capacity.

Some are moved sufficiently by the call for a discrimination requirement to attempt to answer it, again, agreeing fully with the claim that one cannot discriminate thoughts in slow-switching cases. A strategy suggested by both Brown (2004) and Sawyer (1999) is to invoke a relevant alternatives theory of knowledge, according to which S knows that p only if S's true belief that p is based on grounds that would allow S to rule out all the relevant alternatives in which not-p. Some non-negligible level of discrimination is on offer here. S's thought that she is thinking she is not a BIV is based on introspection, which rules out the possibilities that she is thinking that roses smell nice, or that kittens are cute, or that she is not a television set, and other thoughts she would or might have had if she were not thinking that she is not a BIV. On the other hand, the possibility that S is a BIV thinking some thought that she could not distinguish from her actual thought is not a relevant alternative, hence she need not be able to rule it out in order to achieve self-knowledge of content.

Brown's and Sawyer's appeals to relevant alternatives constitute somewhat different strategies, so I will discuss them separately. Brown (2004) does not use subjunctive conditionals such as sensitivity to characterize self-knowledge. Instead, her claim is that whether one prefers a discrimination account of self-knowledge or a reliabilist account, under which she files Goldman's "global" (process) reliabilism, Nozick's "local" reliabilism (sensitivity), and the standard view, one should take seriously that self-knowledge requires ruling out relevant alternatives. Because possible twin thoughts are not relevant alternatives, self-knowledge does not require ruling out the possibility that one is thinking them.

Scrutinizing Brown's proposal does not much advance the inquiry into the questions guiding this section because she rightly claims that the self-verifying nature of second-order thoughts implies that the sensitivity principle is satisfied for them (Brown 2004: 122). Still, we might ask the obvious question: Why is the possibility that S is thinking some radically different thought that she expresses by 'I am not a BIV' not a relevant alternative? This will facilitate our discussion of Sawyer's similar view on this issue, and it will allow us to ask a related question: If introspectively indistinguishable "twin" thoughts are not *normally* (as Brown often puts it) relevant alternatives, then does the ability to rule out the alternatives that are relevant imply a kind of self-knowledge that is more robust than the standard view?

Why, then, does Brown think that twin thoughts are not relevant alternatives? She appeals to recognitional capacities that ground concept possession as a premise in her argument. To simplify, let's switch our example of a twin thought to *twater*. The possibility that some substance is twin water (XYZ) is not relevant to one's recognitional capacity to pick out water (H_2O) because Twin Earth is a distant planet that has no bearing on an Earthling's acquisition of the concept *water*. "Thus, there is no relevant alternative situation in which she encounters a duplicate instead of [water]. *A fortiori*, there is no relevant alternative situation in which [S] encounters a duplicate, develops a recognitional capacity for that duplicate, and so thinks a recognition-based thought about that duplicate" (Brown 2004: 144). Sawyer offers a similar argument (1999: 370f.).

The argument is too fast. It basically concludes that, because the alternatives that are relevant to obtaining a recognitional capacity that grounds concept possession are determined within an environmental context, so are the alternatives that are relevant to whether one knows what one is thinking. We can use the fake barns case (Goldman 1976), which is often used to illustrate relevant alternatives, to show that this is mistaken. Suppose that, along a stretch of country road, there are barn façades that Henry cannot distinguish from real barns. Henry sees the one and only real barn and forms the true belief that it is a barn. He does not know that it is a barn because he cannot rule out the possibility that it is a fake, which is a relevant alternative because there are so many fakes around. Does this mean that Henry does not have the concept of a barn because he lacks the requisite recognitional capacity? No. (Nobody even suggests this, which is in fact part of my point.) His ability to distinguish barns from other possible objects suffices as a concept-grounding recognitional capacity. But, in this environment, his ability to distinguish falls short.

My point here is not that there is no way to argue that twin situations are irrelevant alternatives; rather, it is just that the argument given is too quick. Henry has the concept of a barn even though there are environments that stymie the recognitional capacity that makes possible his possession of that concept. So why couldn't S have a recognitional capacity for water, thus grounding her possession of the concept *water*, and then "take" that concept to a twin environment in which the recognitional capacity is stymied?

My suggestion is that the environments in which concept acquisition and possession take hold determine the set of relevant alternatives that one must be able to rule out in order to have the required recognitional capacities, but there may be other environments that throw up other relevant alternatives which, lacking a capacity to rule them out, throws one's knowledge status into question. Think of Henry's travels to fake barn country as analogous to S's travels to Twin Earth.

One might argue that twin possibilities are irrelevant alternatives because Twin Earth scenarios and their ilk are outré. (But see Ludlow (1995) for a rebuttal.)[12] This is not the place to settle the issue. I'm content at this point to

---

[12] That slow-switching cases could present relevant alternatives seems more plausible for social externalism (or anti-individualism) as opposed to natural kind externalism.

have established that it is no simple task to show that twin possibilities are not relevant alternatives. If that is right, then the relevant alternatives account of self-knowledge might lead us right back to skepticism about knowledge of one's thought contents.

Whether twin possibilities are relevant alternatives is, for our narrower purposes, irrelevant. We are investigating the attempt to double down on the strategy of appealing to sensitivity to establish anti-skepticism – the first appeal to show that if SH_1 (I ... have always been a BIV) were false I would not believe it because I would believe something else, and the second to show that I know that I am thinking that I'm not a BIV because my second-order belief is also sensitive.

Sawyer appears to approach self-knowledge this way:

> In the actual situation, however, the possibility of duplicate thoughts is not relevant: there are no such duplicates. Once again, to put the point in terms of a conditional theory of knowledge: in the nearest possible world in which [S] doesn't believe that water is wet, she doesn't believe she has that belief. (Sawyer 1999: 370)

Sawyer claims that the relevant alternatives approach is more robust than the "deflationary" standard view. I think that it isn't and that it isn't. First, it might seem to be because it appears to imply some kind of discriminating capacity that the standard view does not. But if the relevant alternatives account is cashed in terms of something like sensitivity, this is an illusion.[13] If one's second-order judgments are self-verifying, then they always satisfy the sensitivity principle, even if twin cases *are* relevant alternatives. (If it were false that S is thinking that p, then she would not believe that she is thinking that p, because she would be thinking something else and her second-order belief would lock on to that content.) Second, the standard view implies no less a discriminating capacity than the relevant alternatives view – Brown's or Sawyer's. It's just that the standard view makes no explicit mention of relevant alternatives or discrimination. S knows that she is thinking that p rather than

---

[13] This should be obvious from the fact that there is no disagreement about our capacities to discriminate contents. Relevant alternatives strategies do not actually demonstrate some such capacity that is lacking on other views. Instead, they aim to give a general characterization of knowledge in terms of relevant alternatives, and then apply it to the case of self-knowledge. So to be fair, if this is *all* that appeals to sensitivity or relevant alternatives are meant to do, then fine – perhaps they achieve some success. My point throughout is that anyone who thinks the standard view does not establish genuine self-knowledge should be dubious about these other strategies. Sawyer (1999: 374) also claims that the standard view is too *strong*, implying self-knowledge where it is lacking. I shall set this issue aside.

some relevant alternative q because S's second-order belief is self-verifying: Again, then, if S were thinking something other than p, she would not believe that she is thinking that p.

The thought behind the relevant alternatives strategy is that the standard view fails to address the content skeptic's concern that self-knowledge of content requires some kind of discrimination capacity. It proceeds then to illuminate a kind of discrimination – the ability to distinguish actual thoughts from relevant alternatives – without sacrificing self-knowledge, because twin possibilities that one cannot distinguish are irrelevant. I've made the following points. First, the argument based on recognitional capacities that twin possibilities are irrelevant is at best inconclusive, which raises anew the threat of content skepticism. Second, it's useless to exploit the sensitivity principle to characterize the capacity, not already implied by the standard view, to discriminate thoughts. (But see again the somewhat concessive note 13.) Clearly, introspection alone does not suffice to discriminate the thought that *water is wet* from the thought that *twater is wet*. But if it were false that I am thinking that water is wet, say because unknown to me I was moved to Twin Earth a while ago, I would not believe that I am thinking that water is wet. Sensitivity is satisfied but I lack discriminating knowledge. (See also Falvey and Owens (1994: 117) on this point.) Nor does sensitivity, as applied to self-knowledge, shed light on the nature of the relevant alternatives. Suppose that slow-switching actually occurs (again, see Ludlow 1995). Then it might well be that if it were false that S is thinking that p, S would be thinking some indistinguishable twin thought, which would make the latter relevant. In order to determine which alternatives are relevant on a sensitivity account, we need to know independently what would be the case if p were false. This requires careful consideration of whether anything like slow switching actually occurs.

8.3 Concluding remarks and the second horn

Suppose that Putnam had something like sensitivity in mind when he argued that one can know that one is not a BIV. Critics complain that unless I know that my thoughts are expressed in English rather than BIVese, then for all I know I *am* a BIV tokening some other true thought that I express by 'I am not a BIV.' I have argued that a second appeal to sensitivity to establish self-knowledge of content is pointless. What makes sensitivity attractive as a condition on perceptual knowledge is that it implies a capacity to discriminate p from what would be the case were p false, and it determines which alternatives are relevant, namely, those that would be the case if p were false. But when applied to second-order beliefs about one's thoughts, sensitive beliefs are no more discriminative than the standard view's self-verifying ones. And we've seen that sensitivity does little to clarify relevant alternatives. One might as well accept the standard view.

Suppose one does accept the standard view of self-knowledge. Does that not impale us on the second horn of the dilemma from Section 8.1? Here is a version of the problem.

(1) I know (*a priori*) that I am thinking that I am not a BIV. (Standard view)
(2) I know (*a priori*) that if I am thinking that I am not a BIV, then brains and vats exist or have existed. (Content externalism)
(3) Therefore, I know (*a priori*) that brains and vats exist or have existed. (Deduction)

Reductio, for how in the world could I know *a priori* (or non-empirically; see note 3) that brains and vats have existed?

So much ink has been spilled on this issue that what I'm about to say is surely too brief, but here goes. (2) is misstated. It should be something more general:

(2*) I know (*a priori*) that if I am thinking that I am not a BIV, then there is or has been something external to my consciousness [namely brains and vats, whatever *those* are] which, having stood in relevant, systematic causal relations with my BIV thought tokens, makes possible my thought.

The conclusion this licenses is arguably *a priori* knowable. If one disagrees even with that, no matter. The point is that nothing so substantive as (3) is entailed by externalism and self-knowledge. (Cf. McLaughlin and Tye (1998b: 370) for similar deflation about what externalism implies.)

Boghossian's (1997) version of the *reductio* concerns the natural kind term 'water,' and the corresponding controversial premise is this: If I have the concept *water*, then water exists (or other speakers who have the concept *water* exist). I should like to recast that premise as well:

(2_W) I know (*a priori*) that if I have the concept *water*, then there is or has been something external to my consciousness [namely water,[14] whatever *that* is] which, having stood in relevant, systematic causal relations with my thought tokens, makes possible my having that concept.

---

[14] Or perhaps just components of water, from which one hypothesizes water.

On Earth, that "something external" is water (H_2O). On Twin Earth, where one's concept is *twater*, twin water (XYZ). What about Dry Earth, where inhabitants are systematically deceived by a mirage? Well, Dry Earth's inhabitants are indeed *systematically* deceived, and so if I am a Dry Earthling, there is 'something external to my conscious [namely dry water, whatever *that* is, (mirages)] which, having stood in relevant, systematic causal relations with my thought tokens, makes possible having the concept *dwater*.' Dry Earthlings make the empirical mistake of thinking dry water is actually a liquid. Their intention to name a natural kind may go begging. But they satisfy the basic externalist requirement on concept possession.

Or do they? Can one's beliefs about the natures of objects and properties to which one's words apply be that radically mistaken, consistently with possessing a concept? Sure. For one thing, many of their central beliefs are *not* mistaken. Dry water *looks* like a liquid, and it is colorless and odorless. For another, Dry Earthlings reliably perceive the mirages. Insofar as Dry Earthlings reliably apply their term 'water' to the mirages, and insofar as their *dwater* thoughts are anchored to dry water, I see no reason to think they could not have a *dwater* concept.

Clearly I haven't attempted to come to grips with Boghossian's nuanced presentation of the *reductio*, nor do I aim to. In my view, the nature of what one can know *a priori* according to externalism is too frequently overstated in the literature. All content externalism tells us is that, to possess any empirical concept, there must be some systematic connections between something external to consciousness to which it applies and one's thought tokens involving that concept. Appeals to natural kinds and concepts individuated by social factors are meant only to illustrate the sorts of conditions that are typically at work, assuming, of course, that the world is a lot like how we philosophers take it to be.[15] We could be wrong about all of that – about their

---

[15] Can one afford to be so careless about the distinction between natural kind concepts and others? Isn't it the case that if 'water' turns out not to name a natural kind, thereby flouting our intentions, then by default its semantics are descriptive, where the concept *water* is the concept of a colorless, odorless, etc. liquid? I don't see why. Time and again Burge has shown how non-natural kind concepts are individuated by reference to factors that outstrip an individual's descriptive resources or explicational abilities. (Burge (2007) offers a nice selection of articles on this. See esp. chapters 4–6 and 10–14.) The false dichotomy appears to be: For any expression intended as a natural kind term, it either succeeds in picking out a natural kind and therefore expresses a natural kind concept, or it fails to pick out a natural kind, and therefore the concept is individuated in terms of some description. If *dwater* is anchored to mirages, Dry Earthians have a concept individuated partly by its correct applications to mirages, but about the nature of the stuff to which it applies they are very wrong. Suppose a Dry Earthian scientist finds this out, and at the same time discovers a rare colorless, odorless, liquid. Here is how she reports her findings: "Water is not even a liquid! But we have discovered a substance that answers to our description of water!"

really being natural kinds, about their being other people – but we, or, to be safe, *I*, cannot be wrong in thinking that my consciousness is not the only thing that has ever existed.[16] And that is a far cry from Putnam's conclusion.

Appendix: Methods

S_0 is, of course, not Nozick's considered formulation of sensitivity because he thought that application of the sensitivity condition should be indexed to S's actual method of belief formation. His grandmother case illustrates the rationale. Grandma is sick in the hospital and her family comes to visit, whereby she comes to see that her grandson is well. Were he not well, the rest of the family would lie and say that he's fine, and she would believe it. Thus while intuitively she knows that her grandson is well, if that were false, she would believe it anyway, thus apparently violating sensitivity (Nozick 1981: 179). But if we hold fixed the grandmother's actual method of forming belief, which crucially involves perception and not testimony, we can say that grandmother knows her grandson is well. Nozick amends sensitivity thus:

S_I: If p weren't true and S were to use [method] M to arrive at a belief whether (or not) p, then S wouldn't believe, via M, that p. (Nozick 1981: 179)

How best to individuate Nozickean methods is a vexed issue. How finely are they individuated? Are they individuated by reference to phenomenal features of experience? By reference to external causes? This last suggestion surely is not in the spirit of Nozick's idea: "any method experientially the same, the same *'from the inside'*, will not count as the same method" (Nozick 1981: 185, my italics).[17] A related question is whether Nozick's basic statement, above, is even correct. Luper-Foy (1987b) points out that Nozick's method-relative sensitivity cannot handle one-sided methods, namely, those that are capable of yielding the belief that p is true but not the belief that p is false (e.g. *Whenever perceiving Junior's rosy cheeks, believe that he is well*). If satisfying Nozick's antecedent requires application of one's actual method, for example requires that one witnesses Junior's rosy cheeks, one's actual belief will not

---

[16] McLaughlin and Tye (1998b: §12) conclude their paper with interesting speculations about whether content externalism and self-knowledge can ground *a priori* knowledge that solipsism is false.

[17] In Becker (2012), I explicate a way of individuating methods that I claim is both Nozickean and independently attractive.

satisfy the consequent. Luper-Foy's suggestion is to move reference to method out of the antecedent entirely, thus:

S_2: If p weren't true, then S wouldn't believe, via M, that p. (Luper-Foy 1987b: 225)

If her grandson were not well, Granny would not believe that he is well, using her "*Whenever perceiving Junior's rosy cheeks, believe that he is well*" method.

Fortunately, the question of how to characterize method-relative sensitivity need not be settled for our purposes. Whatever my method in coming to believe that SH_1 is false, I would not believe via that method that I am not a BIV. If SH_1 were true – if I and all sentient beings are and always have been BIVs whose experiential inputs are generated by a computer whose existence is a cosmic accident – I would not believe that I am not a BIV because there is no explanation of how I could even entertain such thoughts. Thus sensitivity implies that I (can) know that I am not a BIV.

Does the same result, namely that the question of how to characterize method-relative sensitivity need not detain us, hold for self-knowledge of content? Recall that the premises of the standard externalist view of self-knowledge are not at issue. Rather, the controversy is whether the self-verifying nature of second-order beliefs involving first-order thought contents is sufficient for knowledge. Our question, then, is whether our various formulations of method-relative sensitivity generate differential results when coupled with the standard view. S_0: If it were false that I am thinking that I'm not a BIV, I would not believe that I am. S_0 is satisfied because in the closest worlds where I am not thinking that I am not a BIV, I am thinking about something else or not thinking at all, and therefore do not believe that I am thinking that I'm not a BIV. S_1: If it were false that I am thinking that I'm not a BIV and I used introspection to form a belief about what I am thinking, I would not believe that I am thinking I'm not a BIV. Given the standard view, S_1 is satisfied even if my method involves introspecting a token of the expression 'I am not a BIV,' for if I were a BIV, I would thereby introspect an expression with some other content, and hence the first-order content of the self-verifying second-order thought would not be *that I am not a BIV*. S_2: If it were false that I am thinking I'm not a BIV, then I would not believe that I am thinking that I'm not a BIV via my introspective method. S_2 is also satisfied. In the closest worlds where it's false that I am thinking I'm not a BIV, I'm thinking something else, and therefore would not believe via introspection that I am thinking that I'm not a BIV. If BIVese thoughts are relevant alternatives – if, owing to slow-switching, one of the closest worlds in which it's false that I am thinking that I'm not a BIV is a world where I am a BIV and introspect 'I'm not a BIV' – I do not believe that I am thinking that I'm not a BIV. Through these results one catches a glimpse of one of my central conclusions in Section 8.2 – that sensitivity adds nothing to the standard view. There is nothing surprising about this, given that if second-order thoughts are self-verifying, they're also sensitive. I trust that my more specific conclusions are less self-evident: (1) that, even though sensitivity seems to imply a discrimination requirement, it is hopeless to use sensitivity to characterize any discriminating features of self-knowledge beyond those already implicit in the standard view; (2) that, even though sensitivity seems to generate a criterion of relevant alternatives, (a) whether it does so is controversial, and (b) even if it does, this is of no consequence because *whatever* alternatives are relevant, given the standard view, the sensitivity principle is satisfied.

Part III
Metaphysics

9 Brains in vats and model theory

Tim Button

Hilary Putnam's anti-skeptical BIV argument first occurred to him when "thinking about a theorem in modern logic, the 'Skolem–Löwenheim Theorem'" (Putnam 1981b: 7). One of my aims in this chapter – following Putnam, Thomas Tymoczko, and Adrian Moore – is to explore the connection between the argument and the Theorem. But I also want to show that Putnam's BIV argument provides us with an impressively versatile template for dealing with skeptical challenges.

The template I have in mind was most clearly set out in a remarkable – and remarkably brief – passage:

> Suppose we (and all other sentient beings) are and always were 'brains in a vat'. Then how does it come about that *our* word 'vat' refers to *noumenal* vats and not to vats in the image? (Putnam 1977: 487, original italics)

Two points leap out from this passage. First, the intended refutation of skepticism turns on *semantic* considerations. Second, the refutation involves an accusation of *self-refutation*:[1] if the skeptical scenario actually obtained, then the skeptic would be unable to formulate her skeptical scenario. These two points allow us to unify some of Putnam's most enduring contributions to the realism/antirealism debate: his discussions of brains-in-vats, of Skolem's Paradox, and of permutations.

After considering some general questions about our engagement with skepticism (Section 9.1), I shall present and defend my favorite version of Putnam's BIV argument (Section 9.2). My aim is not to offer a complete defense of the argument, but to highlight its working parts, and also to explain why the argument is significant. The key point is that, having answered the BIV skeptic, we must jettison any philosophical picture which treats BIV skepticism as *unanswerable*.

For correspondence and discussion, I thank Tim Bays, Jane Heal, Adrian Moore, Michael Potter, Hilary Putnam, Tim Sundell, Trevor Teitel, Joshua Thorpe, and Rob Trueman.

[1] The 'self-refuting' nature is emphasized by Putnam (1981b: 7–8).

I then apply the same considerations against two further varieties of skepticism. In particular, I first show how to answer skolemism (Section 9.3), and then show how to answer the kinds of semantic skepticism that arise during Putnam's model-theoretic arguments (Section 9.4). In all three cases, the antiskeptical argument does not merely defeat the skeptic; it also shows us that we must reject some *prima facie* plausible philosophical picture.

9.1 Why to engage with skepticism, and how

If a skeptic is any good, then she will present us with an *unanswerable* challenge. One might reasonably wonder, then, why we should even bother to engage with skepticism. Perhaps the right response is simply to dismiss unanswerable challenges as *uninteresting*,[2] maybe even just *because* they are unanswerable.

With Putnam, I think that this is wrongheaded. There are at least three good reasons for engaging with skepticism, and understanding those reasons will also help us to understand how we ought to engage with it.

Reason 1. Even if we fail to answer the skeptic, we can learn from engaging with her. If the skeptic is any good, then she raises questions concerning concepts that are central to our way of thinking. Dialogues with skeptics therefore potentially provide us with a means for profound philosophical investigations.

This thought supplies a criterion for when it is worth engaging with skepticism. Suppose the skeptic starts by employing "assumptions which we ourselves hold" (Putnam 1994a: 284), and so raises a challenge which seems to arise from *within* our own worldview. Then, if she argues well, she will "confront us with an antinomy" from within our own worldview, "and one always learns from an antinomy" (Putnam 1994a: 284). Call the skeptic who raises an antinomy from within our own worldview an *internal skeptic*. It is worth engaging seriously with such a skeptic, since we may learn about our own worldview, or even about the world itself.

Conversely, if the skeptic does not use our own tools against us – if she is not an internal skeptic – then her skeptical scenarios will be *genuinely* uninteresting. In that case, we are free simply to walk away.

Reason 2. To concede that the skeptical challenge is unanswerable is to capitulate too easily. As we shall see, some skeptical challenges *are* answerable.

Saying this, of course, raises the question of what it takes to *answer* the skeptic. After all, a really irritating skeptic might refuse to accept any premise in any argument we present against her; or she might refuse to accept any

---

[2] Something like this is suggested by Devitt (1984: 64, 75).

rules of inference; or whatever. Such a skeptic cannot be *answered*, in the sense that nothing we can say will stop her from pestering us. This, however, should not bother us. For if the skeptic refuses to accept *anything*, then she will have ceased to be an internal skeptic, in the sense outlined above. She will no longer be outlining an antinomy that arises from within our own worldview. And, as such, we will be free to ignore her.

Consequently, when we engage with some skeptical challenge, our strategy for answering will always be to show that it is not an *internal* skepticism.[3]

Reason 3. When a skeptical challenge is answerable, those philosophers who have declared it to be unanswerable may be guilty of more than mere hastiness. The *unanswerability* of certain skeptical challenges is central to certain philosophical pictures. In such cases, if we discover that we can answer the skeptical challenge after all, then we also discover that we must jettison the associated philosophical picture.

I have presented three reasons for engaging with skepticism, reasons which also suggest how we should set the terms of that engagement. At the moment, though, these are just abstract reasons-in-principle. To make them concrete, we must start engaging with particular versions of skepticism.

9.2 BIV skepticism

I shall begin with BIV skepticism, and Putnam's refutation of it. Much has been written about Putnam's argument, and I have done my best to defend it fully elsewhere (Button 2013: chapters 12–14). Consequently, my main aim in this section is not to offer a complete defense of the BIV argument. It is simply to have a plausible argument against BIV skepticism, which can serve as a blueprint for further anti-skeptical arguments in subsequent sections.

Introducing the skeptic. Say that someone is a BIV just in case, for the entire duration of their lives – past, present and future – they and all of their worldmates are brains in vats. The BIV scenario is then the scenario in which everyone is a BIV. And anyone who thinks that the BIV scenario actually obtains is a BIV *skeptic*.[4]

---

[3] This is emphasized by Putnam (1994a: 284–5) and Button (2013: 121–3).
[4] It is probably more normal to use 'the BIV skeptic' for someone who maintains that we do not know whether the BIV scenario obtains. I avoid this for two reasons: first, it is best to avoid epistemological notions at the outset (see pages 138–9 for more); second, though nothing ultimately turns on it, the discussion is easier to follow if the skeptic is actually *advancing* a position. Exactly similar comments apply to the other skeptical positions I discuss in this chapter.

BIV skepticism can be motivated by the following apparently natural line of thought:

> Obviously, all the information that we obtain about the empirical world is obtained through our sense organs. Suppose, now, that those organs have been replaced with a computer, which is wired into our brain, but which feeds us exactly the same electronic signals as our sense organs typically do. We would obviously be unable to tell the difference. So: we cannot tell whether things are as they seem, or whether we are BIVs.

The challenge raised here is (at least initially) a variety of radical *Cartesian* skepticism. We are being threatened with the thought that appearances might be radically, nightmarishly deceptive, so that (almost) all of our beliefs are false. Indeed, the BIV scenario is not much more than a sci-fi reworking of the nightmare skeptical scenario discussed in Descartes's First Meditation. However, precisely this sci-fi gloss allows the BIV skeptic to maintain that she is using her own principles against us; that she is raising an antinomy from within our worldview. As such, the BIV skeptic purports (I stress, *purports*) to present radical Cartesian skepticism as an *internal* skepticism.

A Moorean response. Since BIV skepticism purports to be an internal skepticism, we can reasonably hope to learn something from engaging with it. However, before I consider Putnam's response to BIV skepticism, I wish to consider a *Moorean* response to BIV skepticism. To be clear: I do not want to argue for or against this Moorean response. Instead, I introduce it for two reasons. First, it will help me to flesh out the idea of *internal skepticism*, as discussed in Section 9.1. Second, this Moorean response usefully contrasts with Putnam's own BIV argument.

Here is the Moorean response to the BIV skeptic (G. E. Moore 1939):

(iB)   BIVs have no hands.
(iiB) I have two hands.
(iiiB) So: I am not a BIV.

Both of the premises in this Moorean argument sit well within my worldview: by definition, BIVs have no hands; whereas my best theory of the world tells me, among other things, that I have hands. Accordingly, the BIV skeptic must deny some claim that sits well within my worldview. And this might suggest that the Moorean response satisfactorily answers BIV skepticism, in the sense that it shows that BIV skepticism cannot be an *internal* skepticism.

That thought, however, is too quick. The BIV skeptic claims to motivate the BIV scenario by focusing on a central aspect of our empirical theorizing.

In particular, she focuses on our beliefs concerning how we receive information about the empirical world through our senses. She then uses this particular aspect of our theorizing to throw shade on the remainder of our theorizing. Her point is that, if I *am* a BIV, then it will falsely *seem* to me that I have hands; so that *even by my own lights* I cannot take for granted that I have hands. And it is not too difficult to get into the state of worrying that the Moorean anti-skeptical argument is no more suasive than the BIV skeptic's initial challenge:

(iB)   BIVs have no hands.
(¬iiiB) I am a BIV.
(¬iiB)   So: I have no hands.

To repeat: I am not siding here with the skeptic against the Moorean. My point is just that an internal skepticism need not offer a challenge which is compatible with literally *all* of our beliefs. (Indeed, anything that was so compatible would scarcely constitute a *challenge*.) Rather: an internal skepticism need only invoke some of our most central principles of reasoning, in order to undercut our ability to appeal to certain other beliefs – often beliefs which we hold very dear – in our attempt to answer the skeptical challenge.

Now, since the internal skeptic uses only *some* of our principles against us, and since the centrality of such principles comes by degree, one might well expect that there is not always a sharp answer to the question of whether a particular version of skepticism counts as *internal*. Similarly, we might well expect that there is not always a sharp answer as to whether a particular anti-skeptical argument counts as *Moorean*. I am very sympathetic to these ideas, but I cannot explore them properly here.[5] For now, it suffices to note the following: there is at least a workable distinction (if not a sharp dichotomy) between internal and non-internal skepticism, and between Moorean and non-Moorean responses to skepticism.

The BIV argument. Putnam's BIV argument is not a Moorean response. Instead, it aims to show that BIV skepticism is *self-refuting* when considered as an *internal* skepticism. Here is the argument, as I understand it:[6]

(1B)   A BIV's word 'brain' does not refer to brains.
(2B)   My word 'brain' refers to brains.
(3B)   So: I am not a BIV.

---

[5] They fit extremely well with what I say in Button (2013: chapters 15–16).
[6] I offer this version of the argument in Button (2013: 118, 125). It draws from Tymoczko (1989a: 285), Wright (1992: 74), Brueckner (1992a: 127), and Putnam (1992: 369).

The two premises establish that my language is not the language of a BIV, from which (3b) follows. For the remainder of this section, I shall sketch defenses of both premises, and then explain why the conclusion is so significant.

The language of BIVs. Premise (1B) is to be justified by rejecting all *magical* theories of reference. In slightly more detail, here is a sketched defense of (1B):[7]

> Consider Brian, a BIV. Because Brian is a BIV, no one in Brian's world has ever tokened the word 'brain' whilst interacting appropriately with a brain. So, on a naïve causal theory of reference, Brian's word 'brain' cannot refer to brains. And we will be led to the same conclusion, even if we offer a more subtle theory of reference, provided that the theory retains some plausible causal constraint on reference. Indeed, in order for Brian's word 'brain' to refer to brains, there would need to be some *magical* connection between words and objects, such that there was (for example) an intrinsic connection between the letters *b–r–a–i–n* and brains.

To offer a full defense of (1B), more would need to be said. But my main aim here is not to defend the BIV argument itself in great detail. So I shall simply take it as established that (1B) holds if we reject all magical theories of reference.

One point, however, deserves comment. A magical theory of reference is not *formally* inconsistent. Consequently, the BIV skeptic could resist the BIV argument, without falling into formal inconsistency, by embracing magic. But, in so doing, she would have given up on the idea of employing our own tools against us. She would have given up on the idea of showing that, *by our own lights*, we cannot simply ignore the BIV scenario; for our own lights tell us not to countenance magic. In sum: if BIV skepticism must rely upon a magical theory of reference, then it is no longer an *internal* skepticism, and so, for reasons explained in Section 9.1, we have earned the right to ignore it. Contraposing: since the BIV skeptic wants to be taken seriously, she must accept premise (1B).

My language. Premise (2B) is to be justified by defending disquotation in the mother-tongue. In slightly more detail, here is a sketched defense of (2B):

> When I present a semantics *for* my own language, I must *use* my own language. Consequently, I have no option but to offer disquotational semantic clauses. And (2B) is just such a disquotational clause.

---

[7] This sort of justification is given by Putnam (1981b: 16–17; 1992: 369) and Wright (1992: 219). See also Button (2013: 118–23).

In any other context, no further justification for (2B) would be required. But we are in the strange situation of arguing with a skeptic; and the skeptic is likely to push back on this point.

In particular, the BIV skeptic will probably complain that the argument (1B)–(3B) is nothing more than a *Moorean* response to her skeptical challenge. Since she thinks that we are BIVs, she denies that we have hands; similarly, since she thinks that we are BIVs, and has just agreed with (1B), she denies that our word 'brain' refers to brains. Her skeptical challenge then renews itself, as follows:

(1B) A BIV's word 'brain' does not refer to brains.
(¬3B) I am a BIV.
(¬2B) So: My word 'brain' does not refer to brains.

However, affirming (¬2B) undercuts the BIV skeptic's ability to formulate her own skeptical challenge, as I shall now explain.

The BIV skeptic attempts to present her challenge by talking us through the BIV scenario. That is, in saying 'everyone is a BIV,' she hopes to present us with the worry *that* everyone is a BIV, that is, with the worry *that* everyone ever is always an envatted *brain*. However, given (¬2B), saying 'everyone is a BIV' would simply fail to present us with any thought *about* brains. It is unclear what thought (if any) it would present us with; but that need not concern us. The point is just that she would simply have *failed* to confront us with the worry *that* we are brains in vats. Thus, premise (2B) is implicitly required by the BIV skeptic herself in the very *formulation* of her skeptical challenge.[8] For similar reasons, premise (2B) is required by the BIV skeptic even in order for her vocalization of (¬2B) to present us with the thought *that* my word 'brain' does not refer to brains. In short: to deny (2B) is *self-refuting*.[9]

At the very least, then, the BIV skeptic needs to accept that the word 'brain', as it occurs in the formulation of the BIV scenario, somehow does refer to brains after all. In desperation, then, the BIV skeptic might suggest that the BIV argument is too crude; she might maintain that it ignores the fact that reference depends upon *context*. More specifically, she might abandon (1B) and (2B) in favour of the following:

---

[8] Compare Tymoczko (1989a: 284–6).
[9] Importantly, this is not the kind of self-refutation involved in the Moorean contradiction 'it is raining and I believe it is not raining.' Whether the Moorean contradiction is true or false, I can represent the scenario it describes. By contrast, if the BIV scenario obtained, the skeptic would be unable even to represent that scenario. See Brueckner (1996: 277) and Button (2013: 126–7).

(aB)   In *ordinary* contexts, my (i.e. a BIV's) word 'brain' does not refer to brains.
(bB)   In *philosophical* contexts, my (i.e. a BIV's) word 'brain' refers to brains.

This will allow her to formulate the BIV scenario, at least in philosophical contexts. Unfortunately, (bB) invokes a magical theory of reference, every bit as much as the denial of (1B). Granted, it is magic which is *local* to the philosophy classroom – or, rather, to the *appearance* of the philosophy classroom, since there are not *really* any philosophy classrooms in the BIV world – but it is magic nonetheless. We have already rejected magic in general, and we should equally well reject local magic.[10]

The debate surrounding the BIV argument continues beyond this point, but I shall not pursue it any further.[11] We have arrived at the following. The BIV skeptic must accept (1B), because the alternative involves invoking magic, and she wants to be an internal skeptic. The BIV skeptic must accept (2B), because she relies upon it in formulating her own skeptical scenario. We have therefore established the following: *if BIV is an internal skepticism, it is self-refuting*. The BIV skeptic is answered.

I shall now explain why this matters.

Epistemological versus semantic externalism. Sometimes the challenge posed by the BIV scenario is explicitly framed in terms of knowledge: *you cannot know that you are not a BIV*. In response to this challenge, we might try to unpack the concept of knowledge along externalist lines. We might then respond in something like the following fashion:

> If we are not BIVs, then we have appropriately safe and sensitive true beliefs (which entail) that we are not BIVs. So, given our account of knowledge, we *know* that we are not BIVs (assuming that, in fact, we are not BIVs). Hence we have answered the challenge of how we *know* that we are not BIVs.[12]

Whatever the merits of this kind of argument, it cannot help to address the root anxiety induced by the BIV scenario. The skeptic might phrase her challenge in terms of knowledge, but she need not. She can instead say: *you*

---

[10] Compare Ebbs's (1996: 514–18) argument that content skepticism vacillates between a 'subjective' and an 'objective' point of view.

[11] A particularly interesting suggestion is that the BIV argument answers the initial skeptical challenge, but leaves us with a lingering, ineffable, anxiety. For more, see Wright (1992: 93) and Button (2013: 137ff.).

[12] Zalabardo (2009: 80–2) presents a detailed development of this kind of strategy (although this indented paragraph is not a quote from Zalabardo). See also Williamson (2000: chapter 8).

cannot be certain that you are not a BIV; or: *you cannot be justified-from-within that you are not a BIV*; or: *nothing guarantees that you are not a BIV*. Most simply, she can just ask: *might you be a BIV?*[13]

Putnam's BIV argument invokes *semantic* externalism, rather than *epistemological* externalism. And this makes his anti-skeptical argument more robust, in at least one clear sense. Semantic externalism allows us to establish that a BIV cannot entertain certain thoughts. In particular, Brian the BIV cannot even ask himself whether he *is* a BIV, let alone entertain whether he might be one, or affirm *that* he is not one. Consequently, Putnam's anti-skeptical argument guarantees that I am not a BIV, *because I can so much as ask whether I am one.*[14]

Even then, of course, the BIV argument has its limitations. It tells me that I am not a BIV, but it does not straightforwardly allow me to conclude that my brain was not scooped from my skull last night and plunged into a vat. (In that scenario, my word 'brain' presumably *would* still refer to brains.)[15] So the question still remains: Why should we *care* that we can answer the BIV skeptic?

Why this matters. At the start of this section, I said that we should engage with BIV skepticism because it purports to be an *internal* skepticism. It can just seem obvious that we cannot rule out the BIV scenario; obvious, that is, that we might actually be BIVs. So it can just seem to be a philosophically neutral starting point that a theory which gives every appearance of being true might really be radically false. This last principle is characteristic of *external realism*; the realist position whose "favourite point of view is a God's Eye point of view," as Putnam puts it.[16] So: it might just seem obvious that what external realism presents is the neutral starting point to begin one's philosophizing.

In these terms, the BIV argument shows us that this philosophical picture is *not* a neutral starting point. In fact, so far from being neutral, it is *disastrous*. For if the external realist picture were correct, then BIV skepticism would be unanswerable. Since BIV skepticism *is* answerable, the picture is fatally flawed. More specifically: the picture must either rely upon a tacit assumption of magic, as per the discussion of (1B); or it must be self-refuting, as per the discussion of premise (2B).

---

[13] So Zalabardo (2009: 82) caveats his argument by saying 'Of course we might be wrong about this', that is, about our assumption that we are *not* BIVs. The skeptic can walk away from issues concerning knowledge; this 'might' is all she needs to get a foot in the door.
[14] Tymoczko (1989a: 281, 284) puts the point this way.
[15] For extensive discussion of vat-variations and their significance, see Button (2013: chapters 15–16).
[16] Putnam (1981c: 49). In Button (2013: esp. chapter 8), I argue that this principle (which I call the Cartesianism Principle) is the *distinctive* feature of external realism.

In short: the BIV argument teaches us that external realism is either incoherent or magical. That is why the BIV argument matters.

9.3 Skolemism

I now want to consider a skeptical challenge which arises in the context of mathematics. It falls out of reflections on Skolem's Paradox, in something like the way that BIV skepticism falls out of reflections on apparently mundane thoughts concerning how we find out about the world around us. It can be refuted via a similar argument, which I believe was first formulated explicitly by Thomas Tymoczko and Adrian Moore.

Skolem's Paradox. Consider the following result:[17]

The Löwenheim–Skolem–Mostowski (LSM) Theorem. For every transitive model $\mathcal{F}$ of ZF, there is a countable, transitive model $\mathcal{H}$ which is elementary equivalent to $\mathcal{F}$.

Presumably, ZF has a transitive model. So, ZF has a countable, transitive model, $\mathcal{H}$, by the LSM Theorem. Now, ZF proves 'there is an uncountable set,' so $\mathcal{H}$ must make this sentence true. Formalizing this slightly, we say:

$$\mathcal{H} \models \exists x \neg \exists y(y \text{ is an enumeration of } x)$$

Hence, for some b in $\mathcal{H}$'s domain:

$$\mathcal{H} \models \neg \exists y(y \text{ is an enumeration of } b)$$

But, because $\mathcal{H}$ is both countable and transitive, every member of $\mathcal{H}$'s domain is countable. So in particular:

$$\exists y \, (y \text{ is an enumeration of } b)$$

---

[17] To say that a model, $\mathcal{M}$, is *countable* is to say that its domain, M, is countable. In general, to say that x is *countable* is to say that there is an enumeration of x (i.e. an injection from x to the natural numbers), and x is *uncountable* iff x is not countable.

To say that a model, $\mathcal{M}$, is *transitive* is to say the following: If $a \in b \in M$, then $a \in b$ iff $\mathcal{M} \models a \in b$. The effect of this stipulation is that what $\mathcal{M}$ takes to be membership *really is* membership.

To say that $\mathcal{M}$ is *elementary equivalent* to $\mathcal{N}$ is to say that they satisfy (i.e. make true) exactly the same (first-order) sentences.

Mostowski certainly deserves mention in the statement of the LSM Theorem (which is Theorem 3.8 of Mostowski (1969)), since its proof involves Mostowski's Collapsing Lemma. It is well known that Skolem-style results (such as the LSM Theorem) can be avoided by moving from first-order logic to second-order logic with a full semantics. For a full survey of this point and its dialectical significance, see Button and Walsh (MS: §§5–6).

This is (one version of) Skolem's Paradox. And, whilst it might initially be surprising, it is readily explained. There is an enumeration of b. However, this enumeration lies outside $\mathcal{H}$'s domain, and so beyond the range of the quantifier '$\exists y$' as interpreted *within* $\mathcal{H}$. In a slogan: to be countable-in-$\mathcal{H}$ is not to be countable *simpliciter*. Paradox dissolved.[18]

Introducing the skeptic. Nonetheless, this version of Skolem's Paradox naturally gives rise to a skeptical line of thought (see A. W. Moore 2001: 160–4).

> Mathematical entities are abstract entities, in Platonic Heaven. Given their abstractness, it is obvious that we could only refer to them *directly* if we had some kind of supernatural, magical powers. We have no such powers, so the best hope of our picking them out is by employing formal theories. So: we pick out the sets, for example, as the entities satisfying some particular formal set theory, such as (some extension of) ZF.
>
> But suppose, now, that we do not live in a universe with any uncountable sets, but instead live in a countable, transitive universe built along the lines of $\mathcal{H}$.[19] Then we would surely be unable to tell the difference. Every sentence of our set theory that 'ought' to be true would be true; every description in the language of set theory that 'ought' to be uniquely satisfied would be uniquely satisfied; and so forth. So: we cannot tell whether there really are uncountable sets, or merely seem to be.

In short, we have been led to the worry that every set is countable. This is the *skolemist scenario*. For brevity, I shall refer to the denizens of the skolemist scenario as *smallworlders*, and anyone who thinks that the skolemist scenario actually obtains is a *skolemist*.

Like the BIV scenario, the skolemist scenario seems to arise in a fairly mundane way. We begin with some fairly pedestrian reflections – not this time upon how our senses inform us about the world, but on incontestable results from model theory – and we are swiftly confronted with a foundational challenge. Like BIV skepticism, then, skolemism presents itself as an *internal* skepticism. This is why skolemism initially commands our attention.

This is the first of several similarities between skolemism and BIV skepticism. However, before I explore other similarities, it is worth

---

[18] For more on the mathematics of Skolem's Paradox, see Bays (2009: §2).
[19] This step is surprisingly contentious. The implicit idea seems to be that we can simply input 'the universe' into the LSM Theorem, generating $\mathcal{H}$. However, presumably 'the universe' is class-sized, and so does not form a model that can be plugged into the LSM Theorem. This point is pursued by Velleman (1998), Bays (2001: 335–40; 2007: 119–23), and Button (2011).

highlighting an important disanalogy. As mentioned in Section 9.2, the BIV scenario is primarily a vehicle for Cartesian angst. The initial worry that it generates is that appearances might be radically deceptive, so that (almost) all of our beliefs are false. By contrast, the skolemist scenario does not ask us to consider a situation in which (almost) all of our mathematical beliefs seem to be true but are really false. On the contrary, the skolemist deliberately places us in a scenario which is tailor-made to make our favourite mathematical theory true. Her skeptical challenge is that our theory is true for 'unintended' reasons; because Platonic Heaven is much smaller than usually thought. Skolemism is therefore not a version of *Cartesian* skepticism, but of something rather different, which I shall call *metaphysical* skepticism.[20]

BIV skepticism and skolemism consequently begin life as different varieties of skepticism. However, they need not remain that way permanently. After some reflection, we might come to decide that Brian the BIV has mostly true beliefs, but is simply deceived about the nature of his world. In this case, the BIV scenario will equally have become a vehicle for *metaphysical* skepticism.[21] None of this, of course, affects the success of the BIV argument, since all the argument requires of Brian is that he fails to refer to brains. But it will be important, in what follows, to recall that the skolemist scenario is *never* a vehicle for Cartesian angst.

Moorean responses. I now want to return to the similarities between BIV skepticism and skolemism. First among them is that they are both presented as *internal* skepticisms. Now, when I considered BIV skepticism, I probed what this amounted to by considering a Moorean response. It is worth considering a Moorean response to skolemism:

(iS)   If I am a smallworlder, then there are there are no uncountable sets.
(iiS)   There are uncountable sets.
(iiiS)   So: I am not a smallworlder.

Here, (iS) is true by definition. And (iiS) is surely as central to our mathematical practice as anything else. So: we have a Moorean response to the skolemist.

This kind of Moorean response seems to underpin arguments against skolemism which make appeal to 'naïve' or 'informal' mathematics; in such cases, 'naïvety' is introduced in order to defend (iiS). The skolemist will claim,

---

[20] Compare A. W. Moore's (2011: §3) discussion of Georg.
[21] See A. W. Moore (2011: §3) and Button (2013: 141–8).

though, that (iiS) simply begs the question against her. She will point out that, if I am a smallworlder, then I simply *cannot* take mathematical practice at face value, and so cannot infer much from the fact that all mathematicians are happy to claim that there are uncountable sets. Indeed, the skolemist will say that it is just as question-begging to take mathematical *utterances* at face value as it is to respond to BIV skepticism by taking *appearances* at face value.

As in the discussion of BIVs, I have not mentioned this Moorean response because I think it is good or bad. Instead, I have raised it as a contrast with the kind of response I want to offer, and also to emphasize the sense in which skolemism presents itself as an internal skepticism. Skolemism picks up on (what it takes to be) a central aspect of our philosophical picture: that our only access to mathematical objects is through the truth of certain mathematical sentences. And, on the basis of this principle, it purports (*purports*) to establish that *even by our own lights* we cannot take for granted that there are uncountable sets.

The anti-skolemist argument. The aim of the anti-skolemist argument, then, is to show that this is mistaken. In particular, it aims to show that if skolemism is an internal skepticism, then it is self-refuting. Consequently, we will be forced to reject the picture according to which our only access to mathematical objects is through the truth of certain mathematical sentences.

To offer the anti-skeptical argument, it will help to recap how skolemism arose in the first place. The LSM Theorem convinced us of the existence of a countable, transitive model, $\mathcal{H}$, of ZF. No paradox ensued, since being uncountable-in-$\mathcal{H}$ is not to be uncountable *simpliciter*. However, skolemism was driven by considering the skeptical thought that, metaphorically, we might be 'trapped within' $\mathcal{H}$. Stipulating that a set is *countable*$^{\mathcal{H}}$ just in case it is countable-in-$\mathcal{H}$, here is the anti-skolemist argument:

(1S) A smallworlder's word 'countable' applies only to countable$^{\mathcal{H}}$ sets.
(2S) My word 'countable' applies only to countable$^{\mathcal{H}}$ sets.
(3S) So: I am not a smallworlder.

The argument is due to Tymoczko and Moore, both of whom are explicitly inspired by Putnam's BIV argument.[22]

---

[22] Tymoczko (1989a: 287–90) and A. W. Moore (2001: 165–7). The argument is also similar to A. W. Moore's (2011: §3) discussion of set-skepticism, and to Einheuser's (2010: 243–6) discussion of skepticism about absolutely general quantification. It is worth, though, highlighting some slight differences between all of these arguments.
  First: my immediate aim is only to show that the skolemist is incoherently committed to both premises. By contrast, Moore and Tymoczko *themselves* embrace (analogues of) both premises.
  Second: Moore's analogue of (2S) is something like: *My word 'countable' refers to (i.e. applies to all and only the) countable sets*. This is stronger than my (2S). To argue that the skolemist is committed

The language of smallworlders. It is easy to see that the skolemist is committed to (1S). The motivating thought behind skolemism is the following: *If* our world is like $\mathcal{H}$ in containing only countable sets, and *if* our words are interpreted along the lines suggested by $\mathcal{H}$, *then* all of our mathematical claims will come out true (just as true as before). But to interpret our words along the lines suggested by $\mathcal{H}$ is precisely to say that the word 'countable' should apply only to countable$^\mathcal{H}$ sets. The entire skolemist challenge, then, is built around acceptance of (1S).

To be clear, this defense of (1S) is explicitly *ad hominem*, and rather different from the defense of premise (1B) of the BIV argument. I make no claim to have defended (1S) from all possible challenges. On the contrary, (1S) is extremely vulnerable to attack. The skolemist line of thought began by reflecting on the difficulties of referring to mathematical objects, given their abstractness. But these difficulties might well push us, not towards skolemism, but towards the idea that it is just impossible that our mathematical vocabulary to apply to *anything*. Maybe, indeed, mathematics is just so much *symbol-shuffling*.[23]

The anti-skolemist argument will not help us to refute this pessimistic thought. But it is not meant to: it is meant only to refute *skolemism*. And it can do that easily enough, since the idea that we cannot refer to mathematical objects *at all* is just as problematic for the skolemist as for the ordinary mathematical platonist. At the risk of repetition: the skolemist *herself* is committed to (1S), since it is presupposed in her attempt to motivate her skeptical scenario.

My language. I now turn to premise (2S) of the anti-skolemist argument. The defense of this premise closely mirrors the defense of premise (2B).

The skolemist is likely to complain that the argument (1S)–(3S) is nothing more than a *Moorean* response to her challenge. Indeed, since she thinks that we are smallworlders, (2S) is precisely what she contests. Her skeptical challenge then renews itself, as follows:

(1S)   A smallworlder's word 'countable' applies only to countable$^\mathcal{H}$ sets.
(¬3S)   I am a smallworlder.
(¬2S)   So: my word 'countable' applies only to countable$^\mathcal{H}$ sets.

---

to (2S) would raise issues concerning the skolemist's commitment to *absolute generality*, and I would prefer to avoid such issues here. (This also explains why I have deviated slightly from the template laid down by the BIV argument.) I discuss a third difference in footnote 30, below.

For a survey of some related anti-skeptical arguments in the philosophy of mathematics, see Button and Walsh (MS: §7).

[23] Indeed Klenk (1976: 485–7) suggests that reflecting on skolemism should lead us to formalism.

Affirming (¬2S), however, undercuts the skolemist's ability to formulate her own skeptical challenge. The skolemist presents her challenge via the skolemist scenario. That is, in saying 'every set is countable', she hopes to present us with the worry *that* every set is countable. However, given (¬2S), what she has said simply does not present us with that thought. Instead, it presents us with the thought *that* every set is countable$^{\mathcal{H}}$. And the skolemist denies this *herself*. She wants to say:

> There are countable$^{\mathcal{H}}$ sets and uncountable$^{\mathcal{H}}$ sets; but even the uncountable$^{\mathcal{H}}$ sets are countable.

However, if this speech is to mean what the skolemist wants it to mean, then the last word in her speech cannot apply *only* to countable$^{\mathcal{H}}$ sets. In short, if the skolemist is going to be able to articulate, motivate, or defend her skeptical challenge, she needs to *accept* (2S).

At the very least, then, the skolemist needs to accept that the word 'countable,' as it occurs in the formulation of the skolemist scenario, somehow does apply beyond the countable$^{\mathcal{H}}$ sets. In desperation, then, the skolemist might suggest that the anti-skolemist argument is too crude; she might maintain that it ignores the fact that application depends upon context. More specifically, she might suggest abandoning (1S) and (2S) in favour of the following:

(aS)   In *mathematical* contexts, my (i.e. a smallworlder's) word 'countable' applies only to countable$^{\mathcal{H}}$ sets.

(bS)   In *philosophical* contexts, my (i.e. a smallworlder's) word 'countable' does not apply only to countable^{H} sets.

When I considered this kind of response in the case of BIV skepticism, I maintained that (bB) invoked a magical theory of reference. A similar point holds here. In order for the skolemist to defend (aS) and (bS), she needs to carve out a distinction between distinctively *mathematical* uses of the word 'countable' – as when she opens her set theory textbook and works through its contents – and distinctively *philosophical* uses of that word – as when she formulates the skolemist scenario. The difficulty she faces is that her scenario is formulated using entirely *mathematical* vocabulary ('countable sets') and is motivated entirely by the consideration of *mathematical* results (the LSM Theorem). What, then, can be meant by the idea that the statement of the skolemist scenario is *philosophical rather than mathematical*?[24] Otherwise put: if the skolemist severs the connection between mathematical language

---

[24] This is very close to parts of Tymoczko (1989a: 290); but see footnote 30, below.

and the formulation of her skeptical scenario, then skolemism ceases to be an *internal* skepticism.

As a final effort, the skolemist might maintain that context affects application-conditions in the following, more sophisticated, way.

> I spend some time as an active mathematician. Then I stand back and reflect upon what I have done. I realise that I could be interpreted – without loss – as having failed to talk about any uncountable sets. Of course, even as I assert this, I must acknowledge that I am not now failing to talk about any uncountable sets; that is what the anti-skolemist argument teaches me. Skolemism is, indeed, refuted.
>
> But now I stand back and reflect on what I just did in 'refuting skolemism'. And I realise that everything I said could be interpreted – without loss – as having failed to talk about any uncountable sets, even when I reached the conclusion 'I am not *now* failing to talk about any uncountable sets.' Of course, even as I assert this, I must acknowledge that it would be wrong for me to say (in the same breath) that every set is countable, for the anti-skolemist argument can be repeated at this level.
>
> But now I stand back and reflect . . .
>
> And so it goes. Whenever I run the anti-skolemist argument, a new sceptical hypothesis immediately pops up. I can answer every such challenge. But at no stage am I stably convinced that I was talking about any uncountable sets. So, whilst I cannot ever say 'every set is countable,' on pain of the anti-skolemist argument, I worry that no set is *absolutely uncountable*, as it were.[25]

This line of thought is ultimately, though, 'sophisticated' only in the sense that it is sophistry. It fails to express a serious skeptical challenge, for two reasons.

First: The skolemist keeps raising the same skeptical challenge, over and over again. However, she also acknowledges that the skeptical challenge can be answered whenever it arises. Moreover, the answer that we offer is *exactly* the same answer, every time. Despite this, the skolemist suggests that the skeptical challenge nevertheless remains unanswered, in some profound sense. But why should we not think that the challenge has been straightforwardly *answered*, over and over and over again, until we simply tired of repeating ourselves?[26]

---

[25] Skolem uses the expression "absolutely uncountable" in a number of places (1929: 272; 1941: 468; 1958: 635). And this use of the word 'absolutely' has *some* affinity with the purely technical notion of *absoluteness*.

[26] Compare Lewis (1984: 225–6) on the Respondent/Challenger dialectic, and Putnam (1992: 284–5) on infinitely regressive skepticism.

Second: The skolemist seems to be suggesting that, for every set, there is some perspective – the *absolute perspective*, as it were – from which that set appears countable. However, the skolemist also grants that, for any perspective that we *can* adopt, we can successfully run the anti-skolemist within that perspective. As such, the skolemist faces a straightforward dilemma. To the extent that I *can* make sense of the idea of the absolute perspective, I can also grasp that one could present the anti-skolemist argument from within that perspective. To the extent that I *cannot* make sense of the idea of the absolute perspective – to the extent that it is ineffable – I cannot make sense of the supposed skeptical challenge.

Why this matters. We could spend more time chasing down further skolemist-epicycles. Nonetheless, I think we have answered the skolemist. More precisely, and as in the case of BIV skepticism, we have shown the following: *if skolemism is an internal skepticism, it is self-refuting*. And, just as in the case of BIV skepticism, this discovery teaches us that a particular philosophical picture is either incoherent or magical.

The picture in question was characterized by Putnam as *moderate realism* about mathematical entities. It is *realist*, because it pictures mathematical entities as bona fide entities in Platonic Heaven. It is *moderate*, because it does not allow that humans have supernatural, magical powers which enable them to refer directly to these mathematical entities; indeed, the moderate realist admits that we can pick out mathematical entities only by employing formal theories (if at all). But such moderate realism is all that is required to take us from Skolem's Paradox to the skolemist scenario – just re-read the skeptical speech on page 141 – and for skolemism to emerge as an *unanswerable* skepticism.

Our ability to answer the skolemist, then, shows us that moderate realism is a fatally flawed picture. Far from being a plausible starting point for mathematical philosophizing, it is either incoherent or reliant upon magic. We learn, in other words, that we must abandon the picture whereby mathematical entities are "lost noumenal waifs looking for someone to name them" (Putnam 1980: 482).

This last line is the conclusion which Putnam himself draws, after arguing at length against moderate realism. However, Putnam criticizes moderate realism by deploying his *model-theoretic arguments*. By contrast, I have tried – following Tymoczko and Moore – to translate Putnam's attack on external realism, via the BIV *argument*, into an attack on moderate realism. This suggests a pleasing convergence between Putnam's model-theoretic arguments and the BIV-style of argumentation. I shall explore that convergence in the next section.

A brief digression on indeterminate language. Before that, for the sake of completeness I wish to compare the BIV-style argument against skolemism with a related, but flawed, anti-skeptical argument.

Let us introduce a new kind of skeptic, the *set-indeterminist*. Noting that the 'intended' model and the countable model $\mathcal{H}$ make exactly the same sentences true, the set-indeterminist maintains that they present equally good reference candidates for my set-theoretic vocabulary. In particular, she maintains that there are two equally good reference candidates for my word 'countable': the countable sets on the one hand, and the countable$^{\mathcal{H}}$ sets on the other. She therefore maintains that set-theoretic vocabulary has indeterminate conditions of application.

Someone might try to offer a purely disquotational argument against the set-indeterminist, as follows:

> The word 'countable' applies to all and only the countable sets.
> So: the word 'countable' has determinate conditions of application.

Harry Field describes this argument as "a clearer version" of the argument-strategy that Putnam pursues in his 1980. However, Field immediately notes that the word 'bald' applies to all and only the bald things, even though the word 'bald' has *vague* (and hence indeterminate) conditions of application (Field 1994b: 398–9). This simple observation elegantly undermines the purely disquotational argument.

Fortunately, Field's observation does not affect my BIV-style argument (which I regard as the 'clearer' reconstruction of Putnam's aims in his 1980). Indeed, set-indeterminism is just as vulnerable to a BIV-style argument as skolemism. I shall briefly explain why.

I can coherently say that the people with fewer than n hairs and the people with fewer than $n + 1$ hairs are equally good reference candidates for my word 'bald.' This makes it easy to see why 'bald' has vague conditions of application. But the key feature of $\mathcal{H}$ is that some uncountable$^{\mathcal{H}}$ sets are countable. So I cannot coherently say, as the set-indeterminist wants to, that the countable sets and the countable$^{\mathcal{H}}$ sets are equally good reference candidates for my word 'countable.' That would be like saying that the bald people and the non-bald people are equally good reference candidates for my word 'bald.' It would contradict the disquotational platitude that the word 'bald' (respectively, 'countable') applies to all and only the bald (respectively, countable) things, which is needed to formulate the skeptical challenge. Otherwise put: the skeptical challenge would be unformulable if it were true, which is just the point of the BIV-style argument.

9.4 Semantic skepticism and the model-theoretic arguments

Semantic skepticism. Skolemism was motivated by a result from model theory. We can motivate an alternative kind of skepticism via a much simpler result:[27]

> *The Permutation Theorem.* For any non-trivial structure, there is a distinct, isomorphic structure.

We can understand the main idea behind this result without invoking any fancy model theory. It simply requires a two-step imaginary exercise. First: imagine laying out all the objects in the world, together with various labels (names) for them, and with other labels (predicates) for collections of them (perhaps under a certain ordering). Second: imagine shuffling the objects around, willy nilly, without disturbing the labels (so the labels do not 'follow' the objects during the shuffling, but end up applying to new objects). After a moment's reflection, it should be clear that this process will not affect the truth-values of any sentence. (And after another moment's reflection, it should be clear that the same process would have worked, even if we had started with objects which were *intrinsically featureless*.)

There are plenty of ways to turn the Permutation Theorem into a skeptical challenge. Here is a simple one. Suppose we start by believing that our word 'cat' refers to cats. We then apply the Permutation Theorem, shuffling the entities around. Say that *cats** are the entities which we shuffle into the slots which were formerly occupied by cats. (Putnam makes this idea vivid, by pointing out that the *cats** might all just be *cherries*, provided that there are at least as many cherries as cats.) Then the *permutation scenario* is the skeptical scenario that our word 'cat' refers to *cats**, and the *permutation-skeptic* is the skeptic who thinks that the permutation scenario is actual.

Permutation-skepticism is not a version of Cartesian skepticism. Far from threatening us with the worry that (almost) all of our beliefs are false, the whole process of permutation is deliberately designed to preserve the truth-values of our sentences. In that sense, permutation-skepticism is more like skolemism than like BIV skepticism. However, unlike skolemism, it need not even threaten us with the idea that we are ignorant as to the 'nature' of the world. Rather, the worry is *just* that our words do not refer as they are

---

[27] For a brief technical discussion of the result, see Putnam (1981a: 33–5, 217–18), Button (2013: 14–16, 225–31; 'non-trivial' is defined there), or Button and Walsh (MS: §§2–3). To say that two structures are isomorphic is to say that there is a structure-preserving one-to-one map between them; it follows that they are elementary equivalent (in the sense explained in footnote 17, above).

(intuitively) supposed to. Consequently, permutation-skepticism is a third kind of skepticism: a purely *semantic* skepticism.

I have not yet said anything to indicate *why* we might take permutation-skepticism seriously. I shall say a little more on that towards the end of this section. But of course, once we have opened the door to considering one 'deviant' permutation of our vocabulary, we should not stop there. Any permutation – and hence any interpretation – will be on the table as a way that our words might refer. And if there is nothing to tell between the rival interpretations, then we are likely to be pushed, from regarding permutation-skepticism as unanswerable, to treating as unanswerable the thought that each of our words refers equally to every thing. Call this last thought *complete semantic skepticism*.

Some philosophers have claimed to learn to live with the unanswerability of complete semantic skepticism. For example, in response to considerations like those above, J. J. C. Smart suggested:

> I do not much mind the idea that reference slides freely over the surface of noumenal waters, except that I do not think of the noumenal waters as consisting of unknowable things in themselves: there are just the electrons, protons, stars, cats, cabbages and other perfectly knowable objects.[28]

Unfortunately, this is literally unintelligible. Smart wants to tell us something about cabbages and cats. Well, which things are the cabbages, and which are the cats? If complete semantic skepticism is true, then Smart says of each thing 'it is a cabbage' and 'it is not a cabbage,' to the same extent. Admittedly, nothing is both 'a cabbage' and 'not a cabbage' relative to the same interpretation at the same time; but so what? If complete semantic skepticism is right then, when Smart says that the world is made up of 'electrons, protons, stars, cats and cabbages,' if he makes any assertion at all, he asserts only *that there are some objects*.

An anti-skeptical argument. Evidently we are once again in the territory of self-refutation. To make this even clearer, we can present an anti-skeptical argument – in the spirit of the BIV argument – against the permutation-skeptic. The argument has a familiar form:

(1P) If the permutation scenario obtains, my word 'cat' does not refer to cats.
(2P) My word 'cat' refers to cats.
(3P) So: I am not in the permutation scenario.

[28] Smart (1995: 309); see also Lewis (1984: 231).

Premise (1P) is true by definition, so all of the action is with premise (2P).

One might try to defend (2P) on the grounds that it is as certain as anything. And, of course, (2P) *is* as certain as anything. But to stress *that* point would be to present the argument (1P)–(3P) as a *Moorean* response to the permutation-skeptic. And to do that would be to miss what is really interesting about Putnam's model-theoretic arguments.

In keeping with the BIV argument and the anti-skolemist arguments, the point is that (2P) is required by the permutation-skeptic herself, in order to formulate her skeptical scenario. She attempts to raise a skeptical concern by saying "our word 'cat' does not refer to cats." This presents us with the worry *that* our word 'cat' does not refer to cats, only if the last word in the formulation of the worry refers to cats. That is, the very intelligibility of the skeptical challenge requires that our word 'cat' *does* refer to cats after all.

Similar moves and counter-moves are likely to be made here, as were made in the discussion of BIV skepticism and skolemism. However, they are no more convincing in this new setting. We thus conclude as follows: *If permutation-skepticism is internal, it is self-refuting.*

Why this matters. The question arises, though, of why we should ever have thought that permutation-skepticism – or, indeed, any kind of semantic skepticism – was worth taking seriously. The answer is that the two philosophical pictures that have already been attacked in this chapter – (general) external realism and (mathematical) moderate realism – treat some form of semantic skepticism as *unanswerable*.

It is easy to see that moderate realists must find (some kind of) semantic skepticism unanswerable. Recall that the moderate realist grants no tools for picking out entities, beyond the use of formal theories. But the Permutation Theorem then teaches us that, if we can find any model of a formal theory, we can find many different models. So the moderate realist is left with no tools for picking out any *particular* entities with her mathematical words. Consequently, the moderate realist will find complete semantic skepticism (restricted to mathematical objects) wholly *unanswerable*.

It is rather less obvious that external realists will find some kind of semantic skepticism unanswerable. Indeed, to explain why this is so is a significant project in its own right.[29] Here, though, is a very brief pointer in the right direction. Towards the end of Section 9.2, I explained that external realism is characterized by a commitment to the view that even an ideal theory might be radically, hopelessly false. Suppose that we have adopted this picture. Then,

---

[29] Interested parties should see Putnam (2000) and Button (2013: part A).

intuitively, hypotheses about what my words refer to should be just as amenable to skeptical concerns as hypotheses about what is around me. And this opens the door to various versions of semantic skepticism, including permutation-skepticism.

However, using a BIV-style argument, we have shown that *if permutation-skepticism is internal, it is self-refuting*. And our ability to answer the skeptic therefore shows us that certain pictures – those which treated the skepticism in question as unanswerable – are fatally flawed. More precisely: we have another demonstration that both external realism and moderate realism are either incoherent or magical. That, of course, is the moral which Putnam himself draws from his model-theoretic arguments.

To be clear: Putnam does not explicitly present the refutation of permutation-skepticism (and hence of external realism, for example) in the form of the BIV-style argument (1P)–(3P). However, Putnam evidently regards the external realist's inability to answer the (semantic) skeptical challenges raised by the permutation-skeptic as a *reductio* of external realism. I have argued that this reductio is successful. But more than that: I have argued that it is successful for the same reasons as the BIV argument and the anti-skolemist argument, for all three arguments can be accommodated within a single template.

9.5 Skepticism and philosophical pictures

In this chapter, I have defended three related anti-skeptical arguments. I now want to comment on the general structure, not merely of the anti-skeptical arguments, but of the broad dialectic that I have employed.

At a fairly high-level of abstraction, Putnam gave us a step-by-step process for criticizing certain philosophical pictures:

Step 1. Isolate a particular philosophical picture.
Step 2. Observe that some skeptical challenge is unanswerable, given this picture.
Step 3. Show that the skepticism in question is actually self-refuting (or reliant on magic).
Step 4. Conclude by rejecting the original picture as incoherent (or reliant on magic).

This process unifies some of Putnam's most famous contributions to the realism/anti-realism debate from the late 1970s and early 1980s: his discussions of brains in vats, of Skolem's Paradox, and of cats and cherries. (And, in passing, it may help to correct a common misreading of Putnam. No one thinks that Putnam ever embraced BIV skepticism. By exact parity of reasoning, no one should think that Putnam ever embraced skolemism, or radical semantic skepticism.)

In order for the anti-skeptical arguments to figure in Step 3 of this four-step process, it is crucial that the arguments themselves should not depend upon any very substantial philosophical picture. To make this point clear, consider again the way in which the external realist must treat BIV skepticism as unanswerable. Suppose, now, that we could show that BIV skepticism is self-refuting (or magical), but *only* given the additional assumption of some *constructivist* metaphysical picture (say). Then we would not have shown that external realism *itself* is incoherent (or magical). Rather, we would have shown that external realism cannot coherently be combined with constructivism. That would be rather unsurprising, and rather uninteresting.

Fortunately, the anti-skeptical arguments do *not* require that we should adopt any particular philosophical picture. Rather, our anti-skeptical arguments all operate on skepticism *from within*. The lynchpin of all of the anti-skeptical arguments is just that, if the skeptical scenario were actual, then we would be unable to articulate this (barring magic). No particular ontological approach is required to establish this point.[30]

In using the anti-skeptical arguments during our four-step rebuttal of a certain philosophical picture, we do not, then, need to invoke some *alternative* philosophical picture. Moreover, having overthrown one philosophical picture, we should perhaps pause before putting any alternative picture in its place. Maybe the best way to prevent seemingly-unanswerable-but-actually-self-refuting skeptical challenges from arising is simply to learn how to philosophize in the *absence* of comforting pictures. (That is the lesson I try to draw in Button (2013).)

---

[30] In this respect, my treatment of the anti-skeptical arguments differs significantly from Tymoczko's. Whilst defending the second premises of the BIV argument and the anti-skolemist argument, Tymoczko (1989a: 289–90, 296n3) makes several contentious philosophical claims which seem distinctly *constructivist*. He refers to this constructivism as "internal realism," citing the closing image of Putnam (1980: 482); he might equally have cited the extremely constructivist imagery of Putnam (1981c: 52, 54). Tymoczko then acknowledges that the official conclusion of his argument is: "if internal realism is presupposed by Putnam's [BIV] argument, it is also presupposed by the standard resolution of Skolem's paradox" (Tymoczko 1989b: 296n3). For my purposes, Tymoczko's conditional conclusion is much too weak. However, this is not to deny something which I hope is obvious: I have benefited hugely from Tymoczko's paper, in my understanding of both the BIV argument and the anti-skolemist argument.

For now, though, we have seen a deep connection between Putnam's thoughts on BIVs, on Skolem's Paradox, and on permutations. A simple argumentative template shows us how to defeat certain versions of skepticism and, in so doing, how to overthrow certain philosophical pictures. That is why Putnam's BIV argument matters.

10   Realism, skepticism, and the brain in a vat

Janet Folina

Could a skeptical hypothesis be true? Could we all be brains in a vat? It is conceivable that someone is a brain in a vat. It thus seems conceivable that I am a brain in a vat, and it may seem conceivable that we are all brains in a vat. But that is an illusion, argues Putnam – at least for certain ways of constraining the thought experiment (Putnam 1981b). In a nutshell, I can't conceive that I am a brain in a vat because in order to do so I have to be a non-envatted brain. If I am envatted, my concepts are also envatted, and so I am not able to think my hypothetical situation. Since I can come to know this by reading Putnam's paper (or seeming to read it), I come to realize that, like Cartesian skepticism about my own existence, brain-in-a-vat skepticism about myself is not really conceivable if true. Moreover, since we can conceive of brain-in-a-vat skepticism, it cannot possibly be true.

Now, I am no skeptic. I don't regard it as a worthy philosophical position. But I also don't think it is refutable. My non-skepticism is more like an axiom than the result of an argument. Similar broad principles include naturalism and induction. They all seem like good first principles, even though attempts to justify them appear circular. Moreover, I am convinced by Wittgenstein's arguments in *On Certainty* both that the skeptic's demands are unreasonable and (thus) that they cannot be met. The skeptic's does not engage in the ordinary language "game" of asking for and providing justification, though he seems to. So although one cannot meet the skeptic's demand we can reject those demands as unreasonable.

Having been convinced by Wittgenstein that skepticism is not refutable, any argument that presents itself as refuting skepticism awakens my – well – skepticism. Now Putnam's more general target is "metaphysical realism" – the approach to truth that seems to imply that global skepticism presents us with a real possibility. Since a view can be possible but false, the mere falsity of a skeptical hypothesis does not undermine realism. For that Putnam needs to show that skepticism *cannot possibly* be true.

Did Putnam do the impossible? Did he refute skepticism? I will argue that what Putnam shows is the unthinkability of BIV skepticism (if it is true). But this shows neither that BIV skepticism is false nor that it is necessarily false – which is what he needs to show in order to refute either skepticism or metaphysical realism. So he refutes neither skepticism nor metaphysical realism.

10.1 Background

Descartes's skepticism begins with the thought experiment of an individual person, sitting by a fire, wondering what is real, or true. We are each deceived at times; could someone, could I, be deceived about everything? Is it possible? Descartes's answer is "no" of course, for if I am thinking then I, the subject of these thoughts, must exist.

Nevertheless, even if I (the subject of this thinking) exist it still seems possible that every *other* belief I have about what is real or true, turns out to be false – at least for my beliefs about the external world. Despite Descartes's claim to rescue us from this skeptical predicament, it seems a consequence of the Evil Deceiver hypothesis that I could be deceived about the color of the apparent trees outside my window, the existence of my family, and possibly even the truth of 2 + 3 = 5. That is, if I can (seem to) think at all, then I exist; if I have the *experience* of thinking then I exist. But my experience of (or as of) thinking might be so confused or unstable that even my simple arithmetic judgments turn out false. Further, my conceptual framework might not be as it seems, so even beliefs that are ordinarily considered analytic could turn out false.

Now Descartes doesn't go this far, focusing only on the content of our judgments and not also on their form – our conceptual framework. His concern with arithmetic is over the *application* of the rules, the possibility of always erring; he does not doubt the rules themselves.[1] But Putnam does go this far. He captures what we all probably thought in reading Meditation I: how can Descartes know that he is making any sense at all under the Evil Genius hypothesis?

Thus, Putnam's brain-in-a-vat (hereafter BIV) thought experiment reinvents and extends Descartes's skeptical dilemma; in so doing he aims to confound it. Rather than Descartes's disembodied mind, we are brains with brain states, but in a vat rather than human bodies. Rather than the Evil

---

[1] Thanks to Geoff Gorham for this.

Deceiver, there are machines controlling our brain states. And – crucially – rather than a solitary meditation, we are to envision everyone – every thinking being – existing as individual brains in a communal vat. So, the world is a bunch of brains in a large vat with some machinery; the machinery both causes experiences and unifies, or synchronizes, the experiences across the brains. (The vision is reminiscent of Leibniz's "windowless," synchronized monads; it also seems to have inspired the movie *The Matrix* (Warner Bros., 1999).)

The main purpose of the BIV thought experiment is somewhat unclear. Certainly one target is skepticism. "I am claiming that there is an argument we can give that shows we are not brains in a vat" (Putnam 1981b: 8). Another target is metaphysical realism; Putnam also advances theses regarding semantics. The aims are intertwined; for example, a problem with metaphysical realism is that it enables global skepticism. In contrast with metaphysical realism, Putnam supports "internal realism," which provides a different concept of truth. For the "metaphysical" realist truth is transcendent, that is, largely independent of epistemological factors. For the "internal" realist truth is immanent; it is tied to epistemology; it is "internal" to our epistemic situation. Putnam often describes truth as "idealized justification" (Putnam 1977: xvii) or rational justification under ideal epistemic conditions (Putnam 1981b: 55).

I am unconvinced that one can both refute skepticism and show it to be incoherent (in order to undermine metaphysical realism). If skepticism can be refuted must it not be intelligible? In any case I will argue that he neither refutes skepticism nor undermines metaphysical realism. External world skepticism is not refutable – not non-circularly at least. And the argument against metaphysical realism, via the *incoherence* of BIV skepticism, fails too. Though it is more interesting, I will argue that it, too, relies on a kind of circular reasoning. That is, the conclusion that global skepticism is either incoherent or false presupposes the falsity of metaphysical realism.

10.2 The argument

Putnam's anti-skeptical claims occur in several slightly different forms:

I. If it were true that we were brains in a vat we could not "*say* or *think* that we were" (Putnam 1981b: 7).
II. "*It* [the supposition that we are all brains in a vat] *cannot possibly be true*, because it is, in a certain way, self-refuting" (7).

III. "If we can consider whether it is true or false, then it is not true... Hence it is not true" (8).
IV. "In short, if we are brains in a vat, then 'We are brains in a vat' is false. So it is (necessarily) false" (15).

The last two provide the main inference in the argument against skepticism.

Though its conclusion seems epistemological, the argument is semantic; its key assumption is a causal theory of reference. A reason to favor a causal account of reference is that it supports Putnam's conception of meaning as not "in the head." Terms neither magically refer nor intrinsically have meaning, and concepts are not 'mental objects' (Putnam 1981b: 21). This is an anti-Cartesian view of meaning associated with the work of the later Wittgenstein. As I find Wittgenstein's views on language persuasive, as well as Kripke's arguments for the role of causality in (some) reference, I'm sympathetic to this aspect of Putnam's argument. One should aim for non-magical theories of reference and meaning; a causal theory of reference is one such view. Furthermore, the status of the world *does* play a role in the reference of certain terms. How does this function in the argument?

To briefly review the argument I will begin with a single envatted brain. Suppose A is a brain in a vat. Putnam asks, what does A refer to by terms like "tree"? If she is envatted, and always has been envatted, can she refer to Real World (RW) earth trees by her "tree"? By hypothesis she lacks any causal connection to RW trees, since – we are to suppose – she has always been in the vat. What's causing the "tree" mental state is the evil scientist turning a knob rather than a RW tree. So what can A denote by "tree"?

There are at least three options.

1. Nothing. A *feels* that she uses language to refer to things like trees, but this is an illusion.
2. RW trees. Despite the absence of a direct causal connection between A and RW trees, she somehow refers to them (perhaps via the evil scientist's causal connection to trees and his desire to dupe her).
3. Vat trees. If A is using language in coherent patterns (not worrying about private rule following for now), then her term "tree" refers to something causally connected to her tree-ish mental states. This could be the patterns of phenomena associated with the vat-tree concept, the type of electrical stimuli used by the evil scientist to cause mental tree-ish states, or the evil scientist himself. If "tree" does *not* refer to RW trees, yet refers to *something*, then let's call whatever it *does* refer to: BIV trees (Putnam 1981b: 14).

10.3 Three suspicions

Before moving on to my central point, I will address three aspects of Putnam's argument that seem immediately suspicious. First, there is an apparent reference-shift in the conditional that Putnam sometimes uses (e.g. in statement I above) to convince us that the BIV scenario is not thinkable. This seems suspicious because it seems similar to equivocation. Second, the semantic analysis of the skeptical sentence relies on a kind of self-reference that, as Putnam urges, is similar to the liar paradox. This seems suspicious because it is not clear how to draw valid conclusions from paradoxical sentences or groups of sentences. Third, there is a potential for infinite regress that Putnam blocks by a stipulation. This seems suspicious because the stipulation has an *ad hoc* feel.

10.3.1 A shift in reference

The basic argument – that BIV skepticism can't be *expressed* by anyone for whom it is true – depends on a reference-shift. We start with a sentence P, such as "A is a brain in a vat" or "We are brains in a vat." This is a sentence about the way the world is. It depends on who A is, what brains and vats are, and their RW factual relationships. Putnam argues, however, that the terms in the sentence P *when uttered or thought* only co-refer with the original P, if P is in fact false. If P is true (e.g. when uttered by vat outsiders about A), then its utterance by someone in the vat refers to BIV vats, BIV brains, etc. The reference-shift is more apparent in the first version of Putnam's anti-skeptical claims above: If it were true that we were brains in a vat we could not "*say* or *think* that we were." The antecedent is about RW brains and vats; the consequent is about what *cannot be expressed* by those in the vat.

Of course, as Putnam goes on to argue, the consequent (We could not "*say* or *think* that we were") is not exactly accurate. A can *sort of* think that she is a brain in a vat even if she is, but the vat she would be thinking of is the vat-vat, the BIV vat, rather than the RW vat. The referents of A's terms have shifted to BIV things (if they refer at all). A can experience something very close to the thought that she is a brain in a vat, but – Putnam argues – she cannot have the very same thought that we have (the one that refers to RW vats).

If reference and thoughts shift in this way, then meanings in the vat must also shift from their cognates out of the vat. Thus if A is a brain in a vat, then when A appears to ask or consider whether P is true (where P = "A is a brain in a vat"), she is really considering P*, the vat version of P.² In addition, since her referents are different from ours, P is true for us, but P* can be false for her (provided that in the vat she is not in a vat*).

The shift is caused by conceiving of P as an utterance (thus indexed to a certain person or set of persons) rather than as an abstract sentence. The antecedent of our conditional (A is a brain in a vat) is not an utterance; it is a sentence about a state of affairs. In contrast, the consequent that A cannot think P is not an empirical state of affairs but a *modal* claim about an *intensional* context – about the *possibility* of the *thought* or *utterance* of P by A. It is about whether or not we, or A, "can say or think" P.

For Putnam, owing to a causal theory of reference and its implications for the meaning of the relevant language, the envatted do not really speak the same language as the non-envatted. If P is true of A, then A can't think P, she can only think the envatted version of P: P*. For any of us, if it were true that we were brains in a vat we could not "*say* or *think* that we were" (Putnam 1981b: 7). This is because anyone in a vat cannot "think herself out of" the vat.

Of course, Putnam does not limit himself to considering the solitary tortured A. Putnam's version of the BIV nightmare endeavors to remove the context of the RW entirely by dumping everyone else into the vat with A. This avoids some problems associated with the private language argument; it also aims to eliminate the contrast between the matter of fact P and the utterances by the envatted of P*. In the global vat there are no thoughts of P anywhere in the universe, just thoughts of P*. What does this mean for skepticism?

In this predicament nobody would be able to think, no less know, his or her actual ontological situation. Perhaps this shows that some ways of attempting to think the skeptical worry are incoherent. What are we really thinking when we consider whether we are living in the communal, synchronized vat? Putnam shows that it cannot be assumed that those thoughts are actually coherent.

Our worry was over the reference shift in the conditional of statement I. But there is no simple equivocation. Putnam does not *equate* P with P*; his point here is that in either case – whether we are thinking P or P* – our thought is either false or it fails to express the skeptical situation it aims to express.

10.3.2 Paradox?

Let's say we accept Putnam's claim I, that if P is true of A then A can't utter or say "P" and similarly for the group version. Putnam is not content with this

---

² Following common practice, asterisks will indicate BIV concepts and sentences.

and wants to proceed to claim II. "*It* [i.e. the supposition that we are all brains in a vat] *cannot possibly be true*, because it is, in a certain way, self-refuting." Is P false just because A cannot say or utter it? No. A dog can't say or think "I am a dog in a cage," though it may be true of that dog. Nor is P false even if *nobody* could say or utter it: surely not all sentences were false before humans *spoke*. So inferring that P is (necessarily) false from the fact that A can't say P requires more argument.³

The reference to self-refutation is intended to remind us of the liar paradox. Just as a sentence cannot truthfully say of itself "I am false", so – Putnam argues – an envatted person cannot truthfully think of herself "I am a brain in a vat." If she seems to be thinking that, what she is really thinking is "I am a brain* in a vat*." So if A is envatted, there is a true sentence about A that A cannot think. Putnam compares the BIV assertion to the liar paradox, arguing that the attempt to make the self-referential assertion yields its negation – if it is true (Putnam 1981b: 7).

However, which sentence is supposedly negated? As we saw above, unlike the liar sentence, we have two sentences here: P and P*. Does the attempt to assert P result in its negation? No. The reference shift argument entails only that "P" can't be said or thought. The attempt to say "P" in the vat fails, so A only says "P*." Even if we stipulate (as Putnam goes on to do) that P* is false (in the vat) we don't have a paradox like that of the liar. The liar sentence entails Q if and only if not-Q, a contradiction. In contrast, Putnam's scenario entails if P then "P" is not sayable; and (with his later stipulation) if P then not-P*. Neither of these is a paradox.

The group BIV predicament is analogous, in that it depends on self-referential features of the skeptical statement. If we are all envatted, none of our concepts can "escape" the vat. So any attempt to think the (by hypothesis) true thought fails for us, just as they failed for A, because the hypothesized true thought can only "occur" outside the vat. Since we cannot think the RW

---

³ Note, however, that Putnam avoids saying here that P is necessarily *false*; rather, he says it "*cannot possibly be true*." Does this matter? If a sentence cannot possibly be true, it is necessarily either false or meaningless. Is his point not that P is false but that P is meaningless in the vat – and that is why it cannot be true? It is hard to tell. Sometimes Putnam just says such claims are "not true" and sometimes that they are outright "false." ("In short, if we are brains in a vat, then 'We are brains in a vat' is false. So it is (necessarily) false" (Putnam 1981b: 15).) Furthermore, P is not meaningless in any ordinary way in the vat. Sentences can be meaningless from the perspective of some language if when considered or thought in that language they don't make sense. But as Putnam tells us, P cannot be considered, uttered or thought in the vat; so the problem is not *just* that the vat language fails, say, to assign truth conditions to it. The attempt to consider P leads to P*. So it is not meaningless in our ordinary sense. It might be more accurate to think of P as *transcendent* in the vat, rather than meaningless.

true thought, what we actually think is P*. But, again, even if P* is false, the conditional, if P then not-P*, is not a paradox. Nor is: if P is true of a group of beings then they can't think it.

There are questions over the use of ordinary rules of logic when reasoning about or from the semantic paradoxes (see e.g. Hofweber 2007). Putnam presents the BIV argument as resulting in a (kind of) paradox. So one worry was over whether his reasoning was legitimate. However, since there is no genuine paradox here, the special concerns about reasoning from the semantic paradoxes are moot. Nevertheless, Putnam does seem wrong in thinking that P is self-refuting. A further question: can P possibly be true?

10.3.3 Infinite regress?

Putnam thinks P, the expression of BIV skepticism, is necessarily false. But to be necessarily false, P would have to be self-refuting or simply inconsistent. However, as I argued above, though P shares with other self-refuting sentences the property of self-reference, unlike the liar sentence, P does not entail an actual contradiction. What about P*? Does Putnam think that P* is necessarily false? Does he think P entails the falsity of P*? Even if P is true, whether or not P* is false depends on whether A, or we, are in a vat* in the vat. This suggests that the skeptical utterance could spiral into an infinite regress of nested utterances rather than falsity.

When the envatted A thinks, "I wonder if I'm in a vat," we can grant that she isn't thinking about our RW vats. What vats is she thinking of? Putnam's answer is the BIV vat – the referent as caused by the mad scientist or mad computer. Her thought about being possibly envatted is a thought about a vat, *from in the vat*. Since she doesn't know she is in the RW vat, or vat-0 (let's call this the object level vat), her thought that she might be in a vat appears to her to be about vat-0 but it is really (from our non-envatted, vat-0, perspective) about vat-1. (As when fictional characters wonder if they are in a virtual or fictional reality.)

This seems to lead to an infinite regress rather than to the negation P*. That is, if I am in the vat my thought that "I am in the vat" does not refer to the vat I am in; so it – we grant – is *not true of the vat I am in*. But it doesn't follow that my thought is thereby *false in the vat*; for it could be true *in* the vat *of* the vat I am thinking about. And it *would* be true, if I am in a vat (vat-1) in the vat (vat-0). This of course will regress along the following lines. If I am in a vat in a vat then when I wonder if I am in a vat I am really wondering about a vat in a vat in a vat (a vat-2) – since I can reason this way. And so on.

Putnam blocks this infinite regress by a brute stipulation that the beings in the vat are not in a deeper vat, or a vat*. But this seems like cheating. It gets him the falsity of P*, rather than the consideration of P**, P***, etc., but merely by stipulation. To stipulate "the vat stops here" does not feel like a part of a genuine solution to the skeptical puzzle.

Nevertheless this is Putnam's thought experiment and it is clever. By making the vat communal he avoids violating the private language argument; by stipulating that the sequences of mental states are synchronized we – like Leibnizian monads – are living in a quasi-interactive, virtual reality to which our terms somehow (purportedly) refer; and by stipulating that in the vat we are not in a further vat the infinite regress is blocked so that P* (at least) turns out to be false. Although the form of argument is not *if P then* not-P, Putnam seems to have shown that, in his very specific skeptical thought experiment, whichever version of it I am thinking – whether it is P or P* – must be false.

To reiterate, consider the BIV thought experiment, P. If I am not in the vat, then I can think P, but it is by hypothesis false. On the other hand, if I am in the vat, then my attempt to think P results in P*. But then it is false too, owing to Putnam's (semi *ad hoc*) stipulation. Thus the conclusion is that whatever the semantic content of this skeptical thought experiment, whether it is P or P*, *it* – my thought – must be false.[4]

10.4 Externalism (about reference) and internalism (about truth)?

The causal theory of reference is the hinge on which Putnam's argument turns (Hickey 2005: section 2). Should the metaphysical realist, or skeptic, accept it? Is Putnam's use of it fair? Does Putnam actually accept it? Moreover, what exactly is a causal theory of reference?

Roughly, it is the view that successful reference involves some causal connection between a term and its referent (Putnam 1981b: 16). Why would this be? One reason, noted above, is to avoid "magical" theories of both reference and meaning. "Thought words and mental pictures do not intrinsically represent what they are about" (5). So something extrinsic is also required because "meanings just aren't in the head" (19). Neither reference nor meaning is in the head, Putnam argues; there is more to both reference

---

[4] In reconstructing Putnam's argument for this chapter I consulted several resources, including Brueckner (2012) and Hickey (2005); I wanted to re-read Putnam, thinking through the arguments for myself, but I have probably borrowed more than I realized. The literature is too large for someone outside the field to come to grips with it quickly; my attempt in this chapter is simply to bring a fresh eye to the issues and to Putnam's philosophy more generally.

and meaning than what goes on "inside." This is why, for Putnam, machines running programs cannot refer to things in the external world (10). It is not that there is something lacking in the running of the program; rather, there is no proper connection between the terms as used by the computer and the outside world.

Of course, causal connectedness is not sufficient for reference; it is only necessary. Communal usage is also necessary.[5] So, understanding a language requires understanding meanings, which requires use *and* successful reference, which requires "causal interaction" with things – either the things themselves to which we refer, or other "things in terms of which they can be described" (Putnam 1981b: 16–17).

This theory is *prima facie* congenial to an ordinary realist. To say that what we pick out by natural kind terms depends on *the way the world is* seems almost the definition of realism. This theory supports (as it is meant to) the scientific realist belief that progress is possible. When we determine that there is a difference between "fool's gold" and genuine gold we are making a *discovery* about gold rather than narrowing the meaning of the term "gold" (since its extension was narrowed). That is, such changes constitute empirical discoveries rather than analytic shifts. Putnam cites Kripke as holding: "that *the natural kinds themselves* play a role in determining the extensions of the terms that refer to them" (Putnam 1977: 74). On such a view, "the *contribution of the environment*" plays a role in determining the reference of our terms. If the environment were different, reference would be different (75).

Putnam endorses the causal theory of reference because it opposes the idea of meanings as "in the head." But he also criticizes the view, citing electrons (where my causal connection is really to textbooks) and extra-terrestrials (where there presumably is no causal connection) as concepts that challenge the view (Putnam 1981b: 51, 52). He goes on to say that the theory "is not so much false as otiose" (53). So – although he appeals to a causal account of reference in the BIV argument, his views about it are rather unclear and more complicated than they might at first seem.

In the following I will discuss two problems with the way Putnam deploys the causal theory of reference in his BIV argument. First, the fact that contingent facts play a role in reference does not entail that *whatever* it is that causes our ideas *is* the referent of the relevant terms. Indeed, elsewhere Putnam makes just this point (about 'electron' as just mentioned). Yet Putnam's BIV argument seems to rely on just this view of the role of causality

---

[5] Putnam adheres to a Wittgensteinian account of meaning.

in reference. Second, Putnam repudiates the idea of a "ready made world" (Putnam 1977: 211), which he associates with metaphysical realism. But can *the way the world is* determine reference if there isn't a way the world is apart from our conceptual schemes? I'll elaborate on each of these two points.

10.4.1 Reference in the vat?

First, why should the metaphysical realist be concerned about Putnam's use of the causal theory of reference? Because it may seem that he takes it to imply that by "tree" the BIV refers to *whatever it is* that causes her tree-ish mental states. Now, the causal theory says reference is causally connected to the objects to which I *successfully* refer. Where there is no connection there is no reference – whether it's the Turing test, or the ant's accidental drawing of Winston Churchill (Putnam 1981b: 10, 1). In each of these cases reference, and/or depiction, fails owing to the lack of an appropriate connection.

Crucially, Putnam draws a contrast between the BIV's reference to trees* and the ant's (accidental) drawing of Winston Churchill. However, where Putnam sees a contrast the realist may instead see a similarity. That is, for the realist, the BIV's tree-ish mental states may no more represent trees* than the ant's path represents Winston Churchill^{ant}. We don't say of the ant that since it doesn't represent Winston Churchill it must represent something else – the ant's version of WC; similarly, the realist may decide that the BIV's failure to refer to RW trees means "tree*" simply fails to refer. Putnam's mistake (the realist may say) is to infer that since the BIV is not referring to RW trees she must be referring to something else, that is, trees*. The question is, why consider BIV reference as successful? What differentiates the BIV from the ant?

Well, given the thought experiment as construed – with the experiences synchronized in the communal vat – it is hard to resist the view that BIV "speech" is meaningful. So if there is meaningful communication (via speech*), and reference is an ingredient in meaning, then the BIV must mean *something* by "tree" other than RW trees. Putnam argues: there must be something in virtue of which "the brain is *right*, not *wrong* in thinking 'There is a tree in front of me'" (Putnam 1981b: 14). The three options Putnam suggests are "trees in the image," "electronic impulses that cause tree experiences," or "features of the program" that cause those electronic impulses (14). This creates an internal vat world where both "vat" and "tree" refer to vats and trees "in the image in vat-English, or something related . . . but certainly not to real vats" or real trees (14). So Putnam is non-committal about what the BIV refers to by "tree" but he thinks that she refers to something.

To reiterate, though "tree" in the vat doesn't refer to RW trees, it is essential to Putnam's argument that it does refer to *something*. If terms in the vat simply failed to refer,[6] then the sentences containing them could not be true or false in the vat; and so his anti-skeptical argument would not work. The argument depends on the general success of vat-communication, and that most sentences are either true or false (in the vat).

However, to say that by "tree" the BIV refers to *whatever* causes her tree-ish mental states seems too permissive. What if the BIVs evolved from being merely brains in a vat their whole lives to brains in a vat that after a certain number of years grew individual bodies? They would then be able to "step out" of the vat.[7] What would a newly embodied person think? Surveying the still-envatted brains, with the machines, electricity and computers, would she think, "oh, so this is what 'trees', 'brains', etc. really look like"? No. She would say, "Gosh, the world is nothing like I thought it was. There are no trees here." She would realize that her term tree was generated by a grand hallucination. We can be mistaken about reference even if our referential language has a systematic use.[8] Since there are no trees in the vat world, "tree" failed to refer despite the coherence of her conceptual scheme while in the vat.

In other words, the realist might view all empirical claims (perhaps all claims) made in the vat as simply false. There is some appeal to this. It resembles how we think of fiction and virtual reality. Though it may be "true in" a virtual reality that I am a spy, it is literally false that I am a spy. Though it may be "true in" the Harry Potter stories that Hogwarts is a school, it is literally false. Similarly, just because sentences are "true in" the vat does not mean they are literally true.

To agree that the reference of "tree" depends on the real, contingent nature of trees views natural kinds as having a nature; it supports the idea of scientific discovery over change in conceptual scheme, or in meaning. These are some of the reasons Putnam gives on behalf of a causal theory of reference, which would make it congenial to a metaphysical realist. It is not to say that "tree" refers to whatever causes the "tree-ish" mental state. The view that terms refer to *whatever* is systematically, causally connected to their use essentially presumes a coherence, internal realist, conception of reference and thus truth. It presumes that coherence entails successful reference. It thus seems to beg the question against the metaphysical realist, who should therefore not accept it.

---

[6] In general – of course some terms can still fail to refer in the vat.
[7] Come on, it's not much more crazy than the original thought experiment.
[8] This may remind us of Plato's point about language in the cave: "And if they could talk to one another, don't you think they'd *suppose* that the names they used applied to the things they see passing before them?" (*Republic*, Book VII, 515b, my italics)

10.4.2 Internal realism and reference?

Another question is whether the causal theory of reference can be sensibly conjoined with Putnam's view that there is no "ready made" world. One problem along these lines is the cartoon, straw man construal of the metaphysical realist as believing not in a roughly ready-made world, one with some natural kinds carved out, but with all of its details "fixed" (forever?). Putnam's metaphysical realist believes that there is

> some fixed totality of mind-independent objects. There is exactly one true and complete description of "the way the world is". Truth involves some sort of correspondence . . . its favorite point of view is a God's Eye point of view. (Putnam 1981b: 49)

Pace some correspondence account of truth, I don't think a realist needs to be saddled with the rest, especially the commitments to a Completely Fixed world of which there is only One True Description.

Leaving the straw man problem aside, what is the alternative to realism? Coherence, or idealized rational acceptability, over a correspondence theory of truth, the mind-dependence of objects over the God's eye perspective, etc. For Putnam, "'Objects' do not exist independently of conceptual schemes" (Putnam 1981b: 53). My question now is, how does this fit with a causal theory of reference?

On its natural interpretation, the causal theory of reference implies a commitment to there being a way the world, or environment, is independent of and prior to reference and thus meaning. "Just as the objective nature of the environment contributes to fixing the reference of terms, so it also contributes to fixing the objective truth conditions for sentences" (Putnam 1977: 86). This is the version the realist may find congenial.

However, Putnam does not advocate this version of the causal theory of reference, which has thus been used as a kind of bait and switch in the BIV argument. It seems congenial to the realist to say that what we end up picking out by our terms depends on the world, at least for natural kind terms and other rigid designators. Why? It implies that *there is a way the world is* prior to our attempts to designate objects and kinds via concepts. But Putnam does not believe this. Instead, he endorses a view of the world and language as inter-dependent, as developed together via some kind of dialectical process perhaps. This is because "'objects' do not exist independently of conceptual schemes." So his appeal to the causal theory of reference is misleading.

To reiterate, the causal theory of reference as supported in the BIV argument appears congenial to the realist. But Putnam's appeal to it is not realist – as he makes clear in the last clause (formerly omitted) of the passage quoted above: "Just as the objective nature of the environment contributes to fixing the reference of terms, so it also contributes to fixing the objective truth conditions for sentences, although not in the metaphysical realist way" (Putnam 1977: 86). So insofar as Putnam does adopt a casual account of reference it is not the realist version it at first seems.

In addition to being misleading, Putnam's appeal to causality for reference seems circular. The causal account of reference makes the nature of the world, including the natural kinds, an *ingredient* in reference and thus meaning. Part of the point of invoking causality is to explain how reference can succeed even when description fails, or needs to be corrected. For example, false or incomplete descriptions – such as the famous "man with champagne" who is drinking cider, or the yellow metal for the natural kind gold – can succeed in picking out a person or a natural kind (Kripke 1980: 25). Ostension can succeed, science can correct use, only if there are things and kinds "out there" to which to point. So, on an ordinary understanding of how this works, the things and kinds cannot depend on meaning, or concepts – on pain of circularity. But this apparently circular view is precisely what Putnam endorses. Not only the way the world is carved up, but the existence of objects too, depend on conceptual schemes. So: concepts depend on reference (because reference is an ingredient in meaning); reference depends on objects (the causal theory of reference); and objects depend on concepts. This certainly seems circular.

How can we understand Putnam's view? What exactly is the connection between conceptual schemes and objects that he endorses? There is no "ready-made" world, and "'Objects' do not exist independently of conceptual schemes" (Putnam 1981b: 53). Note the single quotes. Of course there are no *concepts* of objects independently of conceptual schemes. That is trivial. Are there also no objects? Is his claim epistemological or ontological?

Clearly the necessity of concepts for objects cannot reduce to the very concepts we are attempting to acquire by ostension. This would contradict the causal theory of reference appealed to by Putnam and it is certainly circular. (The concept of 'tree' cannot be grounded in reference to trees if trees don't exist prior to the concept of 'tree.') What about the necessity of *some* surrounding concepts for the acquisition of new referential concepts? As an epistemic thesis this seems empirically false. Language must start somewhere; infants enter a language via crude associations.[9] But as an ontological thesis it is unclear what it means. It involves the view that the world is not fully formed, that different conceptual frameworks carve up the world in different ways. Whether or not this view is consistent with a causal account of reference depends on how amorphous the "world" is supposed to be independent of concepts;[10] but it may not be as circular as it first seemed.

10.5 Last worries

Before concluding I will develop a worry regarding the last point above. My worry is that the internal realist vision may be implicitly presupposed in the anti-skeptical argument. So if Putnam's main target is metaphysical realism, rather than the skepticism it enables, then there is a different kind of circularity in the BIV argument.

Putnam's third statement of the anti-skeptical argument is: III. "If we can consider whether it is true or false, then it is not true ... Hence it is not true." The fourth is: "if we are brains in a vat, then 'We are brains in a vat' is false. So it is (necessarily) false." There are two ways to understand his reasoning. One is that it is a *modus ponens* inference, as follows. We accepted the conditional based on the reference-shift argument; so if we can consider whether it is true or false, then whatever we are considering (P or P*) is not true. We should accept the antecedent, "we can consider whether it is true or false," because we

---

[9] Initial language learning may require some instincts about objects and their permanence; but this instinct is no full-blown conceptual scheme. Later of course I may acquire new referential concepts by "slotting" them into what I already know. But as a thesis about our ability to acquire referential concepts in general it seems wrong.

[10] And this is not at all clear. Putnam both endorses and criticizes the assumption of independent objects (Putnam 1981b: 53–4). To avoid radical indeterminacy, reference needs a way "in" other than via truth-values of whole sentences. (This is the lesson from model-theoretic argument.) But the rejection of a way the world is makes it unclear how such relationships can be built. The realist version of the causal theory of reference "is not so much false as otiose" (53). This is because it requires the world to be sorted into kinds and objects independent of our "lassoing them." Yet:

> In a sense, I would say, the world *does* consist of 'Self-Identifying Objects' – but not in a sense available to the externalist. If, as I maintain, 'objects' themselves are as much made as discovered, as much products of our conceptual invention as of the 'objective' factor in experience, ... then of course objects intrinsically belong under certain labels; because those labels are the tools we used to construct a version of the world with such objects in the first place. But *this* kind of 'Self-Identifying Object' is not mind-independent ... (Putnam 1981b: 53–4)

Again, the single quotes in the above passage are confusing, and the view quite unclear. 'Self-identifying objects' *exist*, but only because we *think* that way?

are doing just that by reading his chapter. And thus the consequent of the conditional follows.

But how can we know that we are considering P rather than P*? How can we know we are reading his chapter on "Brains in a Vat" rather than reading* Putnam*'s chapter* ... ? Obviously we can't – not if we are seriously engaging the skeptic. Indeed this inference has been criticized as harboring an epistemic circle (see Brueckner 2012: section 2). So if the reasoning is a simple *modus ponens* then it seems circular.

Another alternative is that Putnam's reasoning is closer to disjunctive elimination. We are either brains in a vat or not. If we are *not* brains in a vat, then we *can* consider this possibility; but then it is (by hypothesis) false. And if we *are* brains in a vat, then such a thought is – *for us* – unavailable because our concepts are blocked from expressing the (by hypothesis) truth. But what can we conclude from the inexpressibility of P? When Putnam says "it is not true," what does he mean?

As argued above, the inaccessibility of a thought to a group of sentient beings – that in the vat P is inaccessible to rational consideration[11] – does not entail that it is false – that the fact it expresses fails to obtain. At least, it does not entail this for the metaphysical realist. It may do so if we assume an internal realist conception of truth and facts: that what cannot be "true for" the BIVs is not true. Is Putnam presupposing internal realism in his argument against metaphysical realism? Is he begging the question? Perhaps.

Putnam encourages us to reason as follows. We are either in the vat or not. If we are, then our skeptical thought is of P*; if we aren't then our skeptical thought is of P. If we are thinking P*, our thought is false (by stipulation) and if we are thinking P, our thought is false since I can only consider "P" if P is false. Either way, it – the skeptical thought – is false. So it is false.

This would be valid if there were a single "it." But there isn't. The skeptical thought in one disjunct is P*, while in the other it is P. By hypothesis they are phenomenologically identical, and we suppose an isomorphism of linguistic relations too. (That is, "skepticism" is an epistemological position both in and out of the vat, "brain" is the thinking matter of a human person both in and out of the vat, "vat" is a container in which fluid can be stored both in and out of the vat, etc.) But their referents are different; thus *what* is false is different on the two alternatives. Referring to both as "it" encourages us to unite the two possibilities, to see them as utterances (that occur "within" an epistemic situation) rather than as different sentences (in different languages)

---

[11] For example, in Roy Cook's sense (2013: chapter 6).

articulating different states of affairs. Perhaps here is where the assumption of internal realism slips in: in the assumption that the only relevant situation is the view from within: what can be asserted, or true, "for us" on either of the alternatives.

Either Putnam thinks that P and P* can be identified so that both are "it," the BIV skeptical hypothesis, or he thinks that the difference between P and P* doesn't matter for the significance of the argument. But to identify the two skeptical thoughts violates the causal theory of reference that the argument depends on; and the idea that the differences between them don't matter is to assume that the falsity of P* is just as effective against skepticism as the falsity of P. But to assume this is to assume internal realism.

That is, to assume that the falsity of P* is as close as that of P for refuting skepticism takes neither skepticism nor metaphysical realism seriously. It assumes that skepticism* being *false for us* (in the vat) is just as good as skepticism being false in the RW. It assumes that, because the epistemic situations seem identical, the differences between the facts underlying not-P and those underlying not-P* are irrelevant. It assumes that if ideal knowers* in the vat decide we are not in the vat then we are not in the vat. So it assumes that truth is idealized justification (Putnam 1977: xvii).

The metaphysical realist denies each of these assumptions. For her, "true" is not the same as "*true for*" no matter how ideal the epistemic conditions are. The same goes for "false" and "*false for*." The metaphysical realist denies that the epistemic and semantic limitations of life in the vat entail any ontological conclusions. For her, all we can conclude from Putnam's BIV scenario is either not-P (we are not brains in a vat) or not-P* (we* are not brains* in a vat*). *But we don't know which, and which matters.* It matters, because, for her, the falsity of P* does not entail the falsity of BIV skepticism.[12] The thought that it does, because it doesn't matter which alternative (P or P*) is false, is to presume internal realism in the argument against metaphysical realism.

Another way to put the point is as follows. Putnam focuses on utterances, and thoughts, rather than facts, or states of affairs. And if we accept his assumptions about the causal theory of reference,[13] it seems to follow that in the vat I cannot think "I am a brain in a vat." I cannot think that because I cannot think *of* or *about* RW brains and RW vats.

---

[12] In fact, the conclusion that P* is false depends on the assumption that the second disjunct, P, is true. But this is the original skeptical hypothesis!
[13] Which I have argued above is itself problematic.

But it doesn't follow from this inability that I cannot have thoughts *that* are epistemically identical to the BIV thought (or nearly so). Nagel makes this point about the significance of Putnam's argument.

> Only that I can't express my skepticism by saying "Perhaps I'm a brain in a vat." Instead I must say, "Perhaps I can't even think the truth about what I am, because I lack the necessary concepts and my circumstances make it impossible for me to acquire them!" If this doesn't qualify as skepticism, I don't know what does. (Nagel 1986: 73)

Even if I can't think *of* RW vats and brains, I can have the thought *that* the world may be fundamentally different from how it seems. I just may not be able to say, utter, know, or imagine the precise conditions that yield my situation of ignorance. But as Nagel points out, rather than disproving skepticism, this only extends, or strengthens it. At least this is how a realist would see it.

My point is that to see the inability of expressing P as undermining rather than strengthening skepticism presupposes the internal realist picture of truth (as something like ideal justifiability). Putnam wishes us to respond to the unavailability of P for the BIV by shifting to the thought that is available, P*. In contrast, the realist is interested less in thoughts or utterances and more in facts, states of affairs. For the realist, the unavailability of P for the BIV does not make the sentence untrue. For her, though the BIV's *utterance* "I am a brain in a vat" can be false, the BIV can still – in fact – be a brain in a vat.[14]

10.6 Conclusion

There were two ways to construe Putnam's target. One is that he attempts to disprove skepticism. There appears to be a problematic epistemic circularity in this argument; and I am unconvinced that there is a way around it.[15] The other way to see Putnam's point is that it aims to undermine metaphysical realism. It does this not by showing skepticism false but by showing it to be incoherent. I have argued that this also fails for two related reasons.

First our inability to clearly articulate the exact conditions under which we may be deluded – our inability to think *of* or *about* them – fails to make the

---

[14] This is pointed out in Brueckner (2012: section 2).
[15] See Brueckner (2012: sections 3–5); see also Wright's attempt (1994).

thought *that* we are so deluded incoherent. The skeptical thought simply lacks specificity.[16]

Second, framing the problem in terms of specific utterances, shifts our focus to what can be *true for* a group; but this begs the question against metaphysical realism. Moreover, the vague attitude that it doesn't matter which of P or P* is false – since whichever we can utter is false – also begs the question, for it also presupposes internal realism.

Putnam has shown something important. He has shown that when we attempt to think "we could all be in a giant vat" we may not be thinking what we think we are thinking. Though neither a refutation of skepticism nor of metaphysical realism, that such a thought is either false or it fails to express what we intend it to express[17] is itself significant and surprising. It provides an important clarification of Meditation I, where Descartes stops short of doubting his conceptual framework, doubting only the content of his beliefs, not their form. Putnam has shown that skeptical uncertainty can *and should* extend to facts about language, restricting what can be *a priori* inferred about, and from, the very contents of our thoughts.

But this does not undermine skepticism for the metaphysical realist; it exacerbates it. Not only may we be brains in a vat; if we are, we cannot precisely, coherently think this basic fact! For a realist who does not presuppose *internal* realism, and for whom ignorance is not bliss, there is simply no solace to be found in the BIV argument.

---

[16] This was Nagel's point. The standard response to Berkeley is similar: the conception *that* there is an unconceived tree (perhaps somewhere in some deep forest) lacks a certain specificity, and so avoids Berkeley's attempt at a similar paradox.

[17] If we accept that reference is causal along Putnam's lines.

11 Rethinking semantic naturalism

Igor Douven

In Putnam's characterization of metaphysical realism, this position is committed to a correspondence conception of truth as well as to the claim that truth outstrips empirical adequacy. Putnam's model-theoretic argument seeks to refute metaphysical realism by arguing that, on this conception of truth, truth and empirical adequacy must coincide. It has been noted in the literature that the argument involves as an auxiliary premise a thesis sometimes called "semantic naturalism," according to which semantics is an empirical science like any other. At the time when the model-theoretic argument was presented, semantic naturalism was taken to imply, among other things, that if truth is indeed to be defined in terms of a correspondence relation, then that relation ought to be characterizable in physical terms. This chapter argues that metaphysical realists should reject semantic naturalism as a fundamentally physicalist-reductionist program. It does not follow that they must abandon the view that semantics is to be pursued as an empirical science. This chapter points to some promising approaches to semantics that are scientific without being physicalist and that do not support Putnam's model-theoretic argument.

11.1 The model-theoretic argument

Hilary Putnam's (1978, 1980) widely discussed model-theoretic argument (MTA) is directed against metaphysical realism, two key tenets of which – in Putnam's statement of the position – are correspondence truth

(CT)   Truth is a matter of correspondence to the facts.

and methodological fallibism

I am grateful to Christopher von Bülow for valuable comments on an earlier version of this chapter. This paper was presented at the Ludwig Maximilians University, Munich. I thank the audience on that occasion for their stimulating questions.

(MF)   Even an empirically adequate theory – a theory that is predictively accurate and that satisfies any theoretical virtue one may like – may still be false.

The conclusion of the MTA is that MF is false: an epistemically ideal theory is guaranteed to be true.

Despite its somewhat intimidating name, the core of the MTA is quite straightforward, and involves no model theory beyond what is commonly covered in an intermediate logic course. The argument can be usefully split into three parts. The first part starts by assuming that the world is infinite, and then considers an empirically adequate theory that has (also) infinite models but that is otherwise arbitrary.[1] On some interpretations of this theory's language, the theory will no longer be empirically adequate. (For instance, if the theory entails the sentence "All ravens are black," then an interpretation of its language that assigns the set of white things to the predicate "black" will render the theory empirically inadequate, because all or most ravens are outside that set.) But it follows from standard model-theoretic results that the theory has models of every infinite cardinality that render the theory empirically adequate. So whatever the exact (infinite) cardinality of the world, the theory will have a model of the same cardinality as the world on which it still gets all predictions right and satisfies every desirable theoretical virtue.

In the second part, we are asked to pick some model of this kind and define a one-to-one mapping from its domain onto the world in such a way that empirical adequacy is preserved. (Putnam shows that this can always be accomplished.) We are next asked to suppose truth to be defined in terms of this one-to-one mapping. That makes truth a matter of correspondence – so justice is done to CT – but it also renders the empirically adequate theory true. Given that this theory was picked arbitrarily among empirically adequate theories that have an infinite model, it follows that any such theory must be true.[2]

In the final part of the MTA – often referred to as the "just-more-theory move" – Putnam anticipates that metaphysical realists will protest that the mapping that is supposed to be defined in the argument may well not

---

[1] Putnam actually considers an empirically adequate theory that is also *complete* in that, for every sentence in the language of the theory, the theory entails either that sentence or its negation. But this feature of the theory is inessential to the argument.

[2] Strictly speaking, an empirically adequate theory may still be false even if everything so far is granted, to wit, by declaring the world to have a certain finite cardinality. Surely, however, the intent of MF was not to express that an empirically adequate theory may err in declaring the world to be finite; MF is to be read more generally as stating that an empirically adequate theory may be false even if it has infinite models.

coincide with the correspondence relation in terms of which truth is to be defined, which is *special* and singled out by the existence of particular causal connections between our words and parts of the world. However, according to Putnam, metaphysical realists lack the resources to discredit the mapping – or, for that matter, any other mapping on which the theory comes out as true – as being somehow unintended. Whatever the exact story about the causal connections allegedly forging relations between our words and the world, this story is just more theory and can as such be added to the empirically adequate theory we are considering, after which the thus extended theory can again be subjected to the above model-theoretic procedure. On the standard reading of the relevant passages in Putnam's writings, Putnam is claiming that the just-more-theory move cannot be convicted of treating the metaphysical realist unfairly, given that, after all, the story about causal connections comes out *true* in the end. What more could the metaphysical realist ask or hope for?

This is the MTA in a nutshell, glossing over the finer dialectical points. Consideration of these points in the next section will show that the MTA, and specifically the just-more-theory move, is open to a seemingly fatal objection unless the argument is assumed to rely on the auxiliary premise

(SN)   Semantics is an empirical science like any other.

From a modern perspective, SN appears entirely innocuous. However, at the time when the MTA was conceived, it was common to think that a semantics, or any other purportedly empirical theory, could not be scientifically acceptable if its key concepts could not, in the end, be accounted for in strictly physicalist terms. So, when combined with CT, SN was thought to imply that the correspondence relation in terms of which truth must be understood is ultimately characterizable in the vocabulary of modern physics.

In this chapter, I will argue that the combination of CT and SN, understood as jointly being part of a physicalist-reductionist program, can, and should, be given up by the metaphysical realist. I will further argue that the metaphysical realist can give up these theses without having to abandon the view that semantics is to be pursued as an empirical science. As will be pointed out, there are promising approaches to semantics that are scientific without being physicalist and that do not support Putnam's model-theoretic argument.

Sections 11.2 and 11.3 are aimed at bringing out more clearly the point of the MTA, with Section 11.3, especially, highlighting the important role that SN plays in that argument. I then argue that the metaphysical realist is committed neither to CT nor to SN-read-as-a-physicalist-thesis (Section 11.4), and that giving up these theses leaves enough room for holding that semantics is answerable to the highest scientific standards (Section 11.5).

11.2 Methodological fallibilism and correspondence truth

Putnam presented his model-theoretic argument as an important motivation for his turning away from metaphysical realism and moving to a position he termed interchangeably "pragmatic realism" and "internal realism." As the former name suggests, he saw his new position as a continuation of sorts of the American pragmatist tradition. This tradition has always had an anti-skeptical motivation (Hookway 2010), which makes it tempting to read the MTA as straightforwardly aiming to establish its conclusion that an empirically adequate theory cannot be false, which is an anti-skeptical claim.[3] This interpretation may obtain further support from the fact that the MTA is often seen as a formal counterpart of the brains-in-a-vat argument in Putnam (1981a: chapter 2), which in turn is generally regarded as an anti-skeptical argument.

But if the point of the MTA were really to establish the falsity of MF, the argument would overshoot the mark. For while Putnam is not as explicit on this issue as he might have been, it seems clear enough that an empirically adequate theory is not guaranteed to be true from a pragmatic realist perspective either. The main characteristic of this position is that the world does not force upon us the concepts with which to describe it. The world does not come prepackaged, with a built-in structure or, to put it another way, equipped with natural kinds, which our concepts must then try to latch on to. Rather, we impose structure on the world by selecting a conceptual scheme by means of which we talk and think about the world. This "conceptual relativity," the dependence of what the world is like on our conceptual apparatus, goes so deep as to make even such seemingly fundamental questions as which objects there are in the world depend on conceptual choices we make. Still, Putnam (1989) says:

---

[3] To say that the negation of MF is anti-skeptical is just to say that it goes against what certain brands of skeptics – in particular, scientific anti-realists – hold. By itself, MF does not give rise to skepticism: one may hold that an empirically adequate theory is not *guaranteed* to be true while at the same time holding that we would be *justified in believing* such a theory; and the latter claim is generally held to be incompatible with skepticism.

> Once we make clear how we are using "object" (or "exist"), the question "How many objects exist?" has an answer that is not at all a matter of "convention." Our concepts may be culturally relative, but it does not follow that the truth or falsity of everything we say using those concepts is simply "decided" by the culture. (20)
>
> Our conceptual space restricts the "space" of descriptions available to us; but it does not predetermine the answers to our questions. (39)

Thus, in Putnam's view, conceptual relativity has no tendency to secure the truth of our theories.

It might be thought that at least the truth of an *empirically adequate* theory follows from, or is at least strongly suggested by, Putnam's (sometimes) equating truth with justification (or rational acceptability) under epistemically ideal circumstances (see e.g. Putnam 1981c: 55). But on no interesting interpretation of the term does "empirical adequacy" refer to epistemically ideal circumstances. If empirical adequacy were a property that a theory has only if each prediction it makes is borne out under epistemically ideal circumstances, where such circumstances are understood as being ideal for determining the prediction's truth-value (Putnam 1994a: 258), then probably few metaphysical realists would deem MF a thesis worth fighting for. If, on the other hand, an empirically adequate theory is one whose predictions are borne out under the kind of circumstances in which scientists typically operate, then an empirically adequate theory may still be false even if truth is understood as justification under epistemically ideal circumstances. After all, while the circumstances that scientists normally work in tend to be epistemically very good, they often fall short of being epistemically ideal in Putnam's sense.

And although Putnam changed his mind about truth several times after his pragmatist turn, at least in his early days as a pragmatic realist – which is when he devised the MTA – he seems to have had no qualms about CT *per se*. According to Putnam (1979: 228),

> internal realism is a first order theory about the relation of a language to the speaker's environment. From *within* [a conceptual scheme] the notion of "correspondence" between words and sets of things is as legitimate and meaningful as the notion of a chair or a pain.

The notion of correspondence might even play a role in a conception of truth as justification under epistemically ideal circumstances, where these might be circumscribed as circumstances that are ideal for determining the correspondence of the sentence whose truth is at issue with the world, thereby possibly avoiding an apparent circularity in how Putnam tends to describe epistemically ideal circumstances.[4]

Even though, in my view, CT *per se* is not the target of the MTA, I do believe that the *combination* of CT and SN is. More precisely, the target seems to be CT as understood by a proponent of SN, who holds that the correspondence relation that is fundamental to truth (according to CT) is to be conceived as a relation characterizable in scientifically respectable language. Shortly, I will want to be still more precise about what the combination of CT and SN amounts to in the eyes of the opponent that Putnam envisions. First, however, I should like to say more about why I believe SN to play a central role in the argument. Indeed, given that SN receives no explicit mention in Putnam's various presentations of the MTA, and given also that most commentators on the argument have ignored SN, the contention that the thesis is central to the MTA may *prima facie* appear implausible.

To appreciate the role of SN in the MTA, we must have a closer look at the just-more-theory move that, according to most commentators on the MTA, invalidates this argument.

11.3 The just-more-theory move and semantic naturalism

In Section 11.1, I presented a truncated version of the MTA, skipping the finer dialectical points. In fact, Putnam's own presentations of the MTA have left many readers wondering how exactly, at certain junctures, the dialectic is to go. Especially the move from "an empirically adequate theory is guaranteed to come out true under some one-to-one mapping from the domain of one of its models to the world" to "an empirically adequate theory is guaranteed to be true" has puzzled commentators. How is this move supposed to be justified?

As was briefly mentioned in the introduction, Putnam anticipates, in the relevant part of the argument, that the metaphysical realist will insist that one cannot just *stipulate* the one-to-one mapping that we are asked to consider as the correspondence relation in terms of which truth is defined; that correspondence relation – the reference relation – stands out by

---

[4] See Alston (1996: 204ff.). In fairness to Putnam, it is to be noted that he never pretended to offer more than an "informal elucidation" of truth (Putnam 1981c: 56). In fairness to his critics, however, that Putnam never offered more than an informal elucidation is certainly grounds for complaints, given the centrality of the notion of truth in both the critical and the constructive parts of his writings. See Douven, Horsten, and Romeijn (2010) for an attempt to provide a formal definition of truth in the spirit of Putnam's pragmatic realism.

obtaining in virtue of how our words are causally connected to the world. In the standard way of spelling out this part of the argument, Putnam dismisses the (supposed) metaphysical realist's reply as being just more theory, that is, by arguing that causal relations talk – typically dressed as the "Causal Theory of Reference" (CTR) – can simply be added to the empirically adequate theory at issue, yielding a new theory which can be subjected to the same model-theoretic treatment as the old one.[5]

Metaphysical realists complained about this just-more-theory move – a lot![6] And they seemed to have a strong rejoinder to it. They argued that if causality fixes the reference of our words, and thereby fixes the correspondence relation that is supposed to go into the definition of the truth predicate, it will fix the reference of the causal talk vocabulary as well. But then that settles the issue. In particular, Putnam has no right to assume that the CTR is false and so can be subjected to his model-theoretic tricks.[7]

In Douven (1999a), I offered a different reading of the MTA, in particular of Putnam's dismissal of the CTR as being just more theory. Whereas SN plays no role in the MTA as it is customarily read, in the reconstruction of the argument that I proposed it occupies center stage. In the reconstructed argument, the just-more-theory move does not amount to claiming the right to assume that the CTR is false, but rather to claiming the right to assume that the CTR *may* be false. That right comes from the fact that, by SN, CTR will be an *empirical* theory so that, by MF, it may be false like any other empirical theory. Obviously, we may then consider what follows from the supposition that this possibility obtains. And, on the reconstructed argument, that is enough for Putnam to reduce metaphysical realism to absurdity. To put the gist of the reconstruction a bit more schematically, Putnam supposes a certain possibility (by the metaphysical realist's lights) and shows this possibility to have a particular consequence. While the metaphysical realist is not committed to the *actual* truth of that consequence, she *is* committed to the *possible* truth of that consequence. And – the reconstruction shows – already

---

[5] This presupposes that the CTR is consistent with the empirically adequate theory that we start with, but that is something that metaphysical realists who advocate the CTR must hope to be the case anyway.

[6] See, for example, Glymour (1982), Devitt (1983, 1991), Lewis (1984), Field (1994b), Alston (1996: 141), Hale and Wright (1997b), and Bays (2001).

[7] Even if their reading of the just-more-theory move is granted, some care is needed in stating where the mistake lies. For instance, Devitt (1984: 228) concludes his critique of the just-more-theory move by saying that Putnam "is not entitled to assume that the [CTR] is false in order to show that it is false." I do not see any reasonable way of reading the argument on which Putnam commits this error. At most, the argument can be read in such a way that Putnam assumes CTR to be false in order to show that it is *true*.

that possibility conflicts with the metaphysical realist's further commitments. Importantly, the putative possibility from which Putnam starts (on this reading) follows from MF in conjunction with SN, but not from MF alone or from MF in conjunction with CT.

The reconstructed MTA is not beyond dispute. For instance, it still relies on Global Descriptivism (GD), according to which the vocabulary of our language should be interpreted so as to make the theories we hold come out true. Without GD, there is no reason in the first place to believe that the one-to-one mapping that is defined in the MTA is the one that goes into the definition of truth. In Douven (1999b), I distinguished between two interpretations of GD: one on which GD sounds *prima facie* plausible, rooted in the widely endorsed Principle of Charity (Wilson 1959), and one on which GD sounds dubitable at best. I argued that only on the second, dubitable interpretation does GD help to establish the conclusion of the MTA. There is no need to go into the details of this objection, or to query whether there are still further reasons for objecting to the MTA, whether or not in reconstructed form, for what Putnam seems to find so deeply problematic about the conjunction of the metaphysical realist premises introduced so far can be brought out without any reliance on questionable assumptions.

One way to do this is suggested by Bas van Fraassen (1992). In that paper, in the context of a broader discussion of what the (supposed) demise of foundationalism means for science, van Fraassen addresses the question of how to relate scientific models to the world.[8] In his paper, van Fraassen does not discuss, or even refer to, the MTA. Nonetheless, the question about nonfoundationalism and models and the question raised by the MTA fall under the same broader question of how to relate purported representations of the world (theories, models, maps) to the world itself. Van Fraassen contends that we relate a representation to the world through a linguistic act but then goes on to note that the same question of representation can be asked about the interpretation of the language involved in the linguistic act. That interpretation, after all, is itself a model – a model of the language we speak and use to relate models to the world. How do we relate *that* model to the world, specifically, to the language we speak? A regress looms!

According to van Fraassen, the problem we seem to face here really springs from a mistaken conception of language. In preparation of his diagnosis of

---

[8] Models in the sense at issue in van Fraassen's paper are not the models that figure in the MTA; see Giere (1988: chapter 3) or van Fraassen (1989: chapter 9).

the problem, he presents a story in which he imagines being lost in Taxco (van Fraassen 1992: 10f.). He asks a local citizen for directions, and the citizen is so kind as to draw a very detailed and very accurate map of Taxco. Van Fraassen takes the map back home when he leaves, and in the next year he searches in various atlases for areas in the world that are exactly as the map depicts. He finds 27 such areas. Using a photocopier, scissors, and paste, he produces 27 maps, one of each of these areas. When he returns to Taxco, van Fraassen shows these maps to the citizen who had so kindly drawn the map of Taxco for him, asking him on which of these maps of 27 different areas they are located. The maps look all the same, so the citizen cannot answer the question. Thus – van Fraassen concludes – now the citizen is lost; he does not know where he is.

Van Fraassen uses this story to illustrate his claim that the view according to which understanding a language involves knowledge of an interpretation of that language – the view that underlies the aforementioned threatening regress – is defective and must be rejected in favor of the view that we *live* in a language. Unfortunately, he does not elaborate on the notion of living in a language and does not explain how that circumvents the supposed need for an interpretation of the language. But for present purposes, it is enough to note that van Fraassen's little story also serves to illustrate why the view of language and thought that flows from the conjunction of CT and SN is incoherent. On that view of language, the citizen confronted with the 27 maps is lost indeed, given that only one of the maps stands in the right causal relation to Taxco needed for being a truthful representation of it, and the citizen cannot tell which map that is. By contrast – van Fraassen points out – on the intuitive way of thinking about the matter, each of the 27 maps is a perfectly fine and useful map of Taxco, and the citizen is not lost at all. A view that forces us to deny either claim is to be rejected.

To make the point in still more general terms, note that, given the conjunction of CT and SN, what our words refer to is determined by causal connections that are "out there in the world." As with all worldly facts, we may be mistaken about which word is connected to which part of the world. In itself, it is not at all absurd to think that we make this kind of mistake. Some people may use the word "carmine" believing that it refers to certain shades of blue, whereas in reality it refers to certain shades of red. In fact, when we are acquiring a new language, we will probably make many such mistakes. But even in that kind of situation, these mistakes tend to be isolated. By contrast, in the present picture of semantics, it is a real possibility that we are collectively and systematically deluded about the reference of literally *every* referential term in our language. Worse yet, given MF, this possibility may obtain even if we have arrived at an empirically adequate theory of the world.⁹ In that case, neither empirical facts nor theoretical considerations could ever alert us that all is not right with what our theory says about the reference-determining facts. We might thus be stuck forever in a predicament similar to that in which the unfortunate brains in a vat in Putnam (1981a: chapter 1) find themselves: like these brains, we might forever communicate in a language that we do not understand and we might forever think thoughts whose content is unknown to us.¹⁰ This is too much to believe; it does not take any model theory to appreciate that!

11.4 The commitments of metaphysical realism

How damaging the argument so far is for metaphysical realists depends on how strongly committed they are to the picture of language that emanates from the combination of CT and SN. Metaphysical realism is, above all, a *metaphysical* thesis, a thesis about what there is. According to a recent description of it, metaphysical realism is the thesis that

> the world is as it is independently of how humans take it to be. The objects the world contains, together with their properties and the relations they enter into, fix the world's nature and these objects exist independently of our ability to discover they do. (Khlentzos 2011)

---

⁹ Strictly speaking, a metaphysical realist could try to argue that, although even an empirically adequate theory may fall short of the truth, some parts of such a theory – for instance, parts concerned with the reference of our words – *are* guaranteed to be true. It is hard to see how this claim could be successfully argued for, however.

¹⁰ It might be denied that the brains in a vat do not know the contents of their assertions and thoughts. Supposing the CTR, they are *right* to endorse each instance of "'X' refers to Xs." For instance, "'Cat' refers to cats," thought of as a sentence in their language, is a truth about the word "cat" as it occurs in that language: the word may be supposed to refer to certain parts of the computer program that feeds the brains with inputs, which, in *their* language, is precisely what "'Cat' refers to cats" says. All that this shows, however, is that the brains in a vat cannot coherently express the concern that they are in the situation in which they actually are by wondering whether "cat" really refers to cats. However, "from the outside" we have no difficulty stating the problem. We can simply say that their assertions and thoughts have the same narrow content they would have were the brains embodied instead of envatted so that it seemed to them that they were making assertions and thinking thoughts about brains, vats, cats, and so on – where "brain," "vat," "cat," and so on, are words in *our* language – and not about lines of computer code (cf. Putnam 2000); in *this* sense, the brains are deluded about their assertions and thoughts. Obviously, this way of putting the problem presupposes that we ourselves are *not* brains in a vat or deluded about *our* language for other reasons. However, although some commentators have missed this point (most have not), Putnam never claimed that it is a real possibility that we are mistaken about the content of our assertions and thoughts in the way the brains are. He takes it for granted that we know our language and, from that given, argues against a certain conception of language.

Other common ways of characterizing metaphysical realism refer to the world's having a built-in structure that we aim our concepts to latch onto, but that is not shaped, not even partly, by which concepts we use to talk and think about the world. And Richard Boyd (1992) seems to point to the same realist sentiment when he urges that, while we contribute to reality by interacting causally with it – by cutting trees, digging canals, building bridges, and so on – we do not contribute to it conceptually.

So, was it unfair by Putnam to ascribe CT and SN – which are *semantic* theses – to the metaphysical realist? Not really, I think, for although at the time when the model-theoretic argument was conceived there were no internet surveys polling philosophers' opinions on various profession-related matters, I strongly suspect that, had such a survey been held in those days, it would have shown that by far most who were attracted to the metaphysical idea of a mind-independent, prepackaged world also subscribed to both CT and SN.

Note, though, that this does not necessarily mean that the metaphysical realist is *committed* to these theses. David Bourget and David Chalmers (2014) recently conducted a survey among (analytic) philosophers and found that a small majority – 50.8 percent, to be precise – of their respondents endorse CT. This finding may well be due to the fact that, for over fifty years, CT has tended to be presented as the default theory of truth in introductory courses in the philosophy of language, philosophical logic, and epistemology, rather than revealing much about the commitments of the respondents; in particular, it reveals nothing about how readily they would abandon CT if it were shown to conflict with some thesis they have been actively advocating in their writings. Much the same may be true of the philosophers who, in the 1970s, identified themselves, or would have identified themselves, as metaphysical realists. Reductive physicalism was a broadly shared background assumption in the analytic philosophy community of those days, and from the perspective of reductive physicalism, a semantics that seeks to reduce reference to causality[11] and to then define truth in terms of reference seemed the only viable option.

Still, the metaphysical and the semantic issue must be kept separate.[12] While the independence thesis, which is also part of what Putnam presented under the header of metaphysical realism, is still very prominent in current

---

[11] Or that seeks to reduce reference to some other relation acceptable to the physicalist, but causality is considered to be the only serious candidate here; see Devitt (1991: chapter 3).

[12] As Devitt – a card-carrying metaphysical realist – also insists in his (1991: chapter 1).

metaphysics,[13] the same cannot be said of CT. Even if, as emerged from Bourget and Chalmers's survey, in our profession in general CT is still favored by many, logicians and other specialists working on truth are nowadays more inclined toward some version of deflationism.[14] All versions of deflationism share the view that truth is a "lightweight," insubstantial notion which lacks an essence like, most notably, correspondence. Our language possesses a truth predicate not because there is some important property that sentences (or propositions, or whatever one's favorite truth-bearers are) may have and that we want to be able to refer to, but because the truth predicate adds expressive power to the language: with the predicate, we can say (and, in mathematics, prove) things that go non-trivially beyond what we could otherwise say (and prove).[15]

While it may thus seem that metaphysical realists can abandon CT, some will say that this would be too quick, and that unless metaphysical realists are willing to also abandon SN, CT in particular is indispensable. According to Michael Devitt (1991: chapter 3), for instance, truth plays a key explanatory role in naturalized semantics, specifically in articulating sentence meanings, and a deflated notion of truth just cannot play that role.[16] Moreover – Devitt thinks – of the substantive notions of truth, CT is the only plausible candidate. Hence, a metaphysical realist who wants to keep on board SN is committed to CT.

But *must* the metaphysical realist want to stick to SN? One might think so, given that abandoning SN might seem to amount to admitting spooky meaning-conferring properties, or in any case to holding that scientific findings are irrelevant to semantics and semantics is not answerable to the usual scientific standards. Probably no modern philosopher would want to subscribe to any of this. What I will argue, however, is that although metaphysical realists should certainly want to commit themselves to the pursuit of semantics in a scientific spirit, it does not follow that they must stick to SN in the form assumed by Devitt and others. In fact, in that form SN makes little contact with what is going on in science insofar as this bears on semantic questions.

---

[13] See, for example, Sider (2011) for a recent defense.
[14] See, for example, Horwich (1990), Field (2008), Halbach (2011), and Horsten (2011). It is to be noted that this development also seems to have had some effect on the philosophical community at large: 25 percent of Bourget and Chalmers's respondents reported that they subscribed to deflationism. Horsten (2011: 59) and Fischer (2012: 403) will have the specialists in mind when they assert that deflationism is currently the most popular conception of truth.
[15] How much expressive power the truth predicate adds differs for different versions of deflationism; see Horsten (2011).
[16] See, in the same vein, Davidson (1996), though see also Fischer (2008).

11.5 Semantic naturalism – new style

In making his case for the indispensability of CT, Devitt (1991: chapter 3) assumes a Davidsonian account of sentence meaning, according to which sentence meaning is to be explained in terms of truth; specifically, in this account the meaning of a sentence is given by the conditions under which the sentence is true (cf. Davidson 1984). For truth to serve this purpose – Devitt argues – it must be substantive, which means that, in the absence of serious alternative candidates, truth must be understood as correspondence with the facts. As a further part of his semantics, Devitt insists that the correspondence (or reference) relation is to be analyzed in physical terms, specifically, in terms of causation, as sketched in Devitt (1981) and Devitt and Sterelny (1987). This is probably the most articulate example of a naturalized semantics program of the kind that, in my analysis, constitutes the real target of Putnam's MTA. But, I will argue, a naturalized semantics need not take this form. In fact, apart from its appeal to physics, there is little in Devitt's proposal that warrants calling it "naturalist."

To begin with, the semantics starts from a model of sentence meaning ("sentence meaning = truth conditions") that – as I have argued in Douven (1998) – rests on a tenuous empirical footing. To be sure, the model is simple, especially in view of the fact that it is meant to apply uniformly across our language; and simplicity counts as a theoretical virtue. Be this as it may, simplicity on its own offers little reason to accept a theory. Early Hippocratic medicine, which sought to explain all ailments by reference to four bodily fluids, was in a clear sense *much* simpler than modern medicine is, which links some diseases to genetic disorders, others to viral or bacterial infections, again others to lifestyle, and so on, often without there being any deep theoretical connections between these different categories of possible causes. Still, the empirical evidence strongly favors modern medicine over the simpler Hippocratic medicine.

Ironically, the assumption of physicalism adds another aprioristic aspect to Devitt's proposal. For, contrary to what its name may suggest, physicalism is at bottom a *metaphysical* thesis: there is simply no empirical evidence suggesting that any concept from the special sciences that is not reducible to physical concepts is to be rejected as being unscientific, and similarly for hypotheses from the special sciences.[17] It was mentioned above that, when the

---

[17] One may think of physicalism as requiring only supervenience on the physical, specifically as requiring that nothing happens in reality without something happening in physical reality. Thus conceived, the thesis is extremely weak, and in any event too weak to guarantee that reference can be *characterized* in physical terms.

MTA was published, physicalism was the received doctrine: the accomplishments of twentieth-century physics – impressive by any standard, and before which everything accomplished in the special sciences pales – had led philosophers to regard physicalism as beyond serious dispute. But that was then. In the meantime, much of physicalism's erstwhile status has eroded. For example, many philosophers nowadays regard empirical psychology as a field in excellent scientific standing, and few seem to care anymore about whether the concepts central to this field can ultimately be accounted for by physics.

These remarks have little critical force in the absence of at least the outline of an alternative approach to semantics that is more recognizably naturalist. Of course, there exist alternative approaches to semantics that seek to explicate sentence meaning in terms of some key concept other than truth, like verifiability, or warranted assertability, or rational acceptability, or what have you. Even if such proposals aim to spell out their preferred key concepts in scientific terms, that does not make them less aprioristic than Devitt's. On the other hand, it may not be clear whether there could be any more thoroughly naturalistic approach to semantics than Devitt's, or than ones like it that replace truth by some other concept that is supposed to carry the explanatory load.

As a matter of fact, much interesting work is already going on in psychology and cognitive science showing that a naturalized semantics need not start from an *a priori* conception of sentence meaning or an *a priori* commitment to physicalism. Particularly relevant here is work currently done in cognitive semantics, which is explicitly meant as an alternative to truth-conditional semantics.[18] In cognitive semantics, meaning is ultimately rooted in bodily experiences and discriminatory capacities. For instance, in Peter Gärdenfors's (2000, 2014) semantics, meanings are regions in conceptual spaces, where these spaces are constructed on the basis of similarity judgments, and the regions result from locating prototypes in these spaces.

In a different approach to cognitive semantics, Terry Regier (1996) studies the interpretation and acquisition of spatial relation terms (such as prepositions like "in," "outside," "between," and "next to") from a connectionist perspective. His analysis is entirely in cognitive and neural terms and at no point relies on something like a truth-conditional account of meaning. Of course, it remains to be seen whether this approach generalizes to other parts of our language.

[18] See, for example, Gärdenfors (2000: chapter 5; 2014), and Langacker (2008: 28).

A very different but equally naturalist approach to meaning, intentionality, and, more generally, human communication is to be found in Michael Tomasello's work.[19] Specifically, Tomasello studies these broadly semantic phenomena from the combined perspective of developmental psychology and evolutionary biology. In his account, meanings are grounded in basic skills that humans share with non-human primates. These skills – like pointing, gesturing, and pantomiming – are partly unlearned, genetically hard-wired capabilities, which came to serve as the basis of meaningful communication in groups of human primates that shared common goals and interests. The details of the account have been partly filled in through refined experimental work, involving human participants as well as apes. Again, nothing has so far emerged that resembles the *a priori* model of meaning that has dominated much of semantical theorizing by philosophers.

Further examples of naturalized approaches to semantics carried out in a new style are to be found in an area closer to home for philosophers, to wit, research concerning natural language conditionals, which involves both philosophers and experimental psychologists, often engaging in joint projects. Researchers are investigating questions such as how people evaluate conditionals – in terms of probability, acceptability, credibility, and so on – how they interpret conditionals – for example, which paraphrases they are willing to accept – how interpretation may depend on someone's cognitive abilities, which inference patterns involving conditionals people subscribe to, how people adapt their beliefs or degrees of belief when they learn a conditional, and many more questions. Little of this work relies on an *a priori* view of the meaning of conditionals. This is not so much because the researchers active in this area are concerned about any possible aprioristic aspects of semantics, but simply because – as even the staunchest defenders of the kind of program that Devitt advocates will admit – no semantics for conditionals hitherto proposed looks at all promising, if only because literally all of them violate some or other seemingly non-negotiable adequacy constraint.[20]

Not everyone may be equally impressed by the semantic projects mentioned here or by other current semantic research in psychology and cognitive science. Nevertheless, I believe that this research at least shows that semantics can be pursued in a scientific spirit without necessarily being part of a reductionist–physicalist research program. Because, for all we currently

---

[19] See, for example, Tomasello (2003, 2008).

[20] For an overview of the main results of this program so far, see Douven (2013, 2015). See also Pfeifer and Douven (2014).

know, CT is not essential to that pursuit, metaphysical realists can jettison CT without necessarily being unscientific about semantics.

In summary, I have argued that, contrary to what a first encounter with the MTA might suggest, the real target of that argument is not MF but rather the picture of how language and thought relate to the world that emerges from the conjunction of CT and SN, supposing the latter is seen as forming part of a larger physicalist program. But a change of view about physicalism in general, and recent developments in psychology and cognitive science concerned with semantic questions in particular, warrant a rethinking of what SN must amount to. And this suggests a view of this thesis under which it no longer helps to establish the conclusion of the MTA.

12 Internal to what? Contemporary naturalism and Putnam's model-theoretic argument

Patricia Marino

In *Reason, Truth, and History* (Putnam 1981a), Hilary Putnam deploys the model-theoretic argument (MTA) against metaphysical realism, arguing for an "internalist" alternative and applying his thoughts to a wide range of philosophical problems. This chapter examines some of Putnam's ideas from the point of view of contemporary naturalism. Naturalism shares with internalism some central elements, such as rejection of a God's eye point of view, yet there are deep methodological differences. Here, I discuss some of these differences through consideration of various matters such as theories of reference and truth, the existence of mathematical objects, and brain-in-a-vat type skepticism. I argue that, though the internalist and naturalist share an interest in "our" methods, one point of divergence is over what this comes to, with particular disagreement over the question of whether the methods we associate with science have special epistemic status. Toward the end I explore some practical implications of this difference.

12.1 Internalism and naturalism

In a (1993) paper, Putnam expresses his pleasure that "most" of the readers of *Reason, Truth, and History* have correctly interpreted its argument as a *reductio*. The position being reduced to absurdity is, of course, metaphysical realism. On the metaphysical realist perspective, "the world consists of some fixed totality of mind-independent objects. There is exactly one true and complete description of 'the way the world is.' Truth involves some sort of correspondence between words or thought-signs and external things and sets of things" (Putnam 1981a: 49). Putnam dubs this perspective "the externalist perspective," because "its favorite point of view is a God's Eye point of view" (49).

I am grateful to Jonathan Dewald, Heather Douglas, Tim Kenyon, and Penelope Maddy, for discussion and comments on previous drafts of this chapter.

One of Putnam's strategies for reducing metaphysical realism to absurdity is through the model-theoretic argument. That argument assumes that there is a reference relation R attaching words to things, and draws the conclusion that, even while keeping the truth values of all of our sentences fixed, there are infinitely many relations that R could be. From this, Putnam says, it follows that "there are always infinitely many different interpretations of the predicates of a language which assign the 'correct' truth-values to the sentences in all possible worlds, no matter how those 'correct' truth-values are singled out" – a conclusion, he suggests, that we cannot accept (Putnam 1981a: 35).

This problem with reference purportedly dooms the correspondence theory of truth, because there is no way to fix a particular relation between our sentences, thoughts, and theories on the one hand and the world of mind-independent objects on the other. In response to the idea that truth might involve some sort of abstract mapping of concepts onto things, Putnam says, "The trouble with this suggestion is not that correspondences between words or concepts and other entities don't exist, but that too many correspondences exist. To pick out just one . . . we would have already to have referential access to mind-independent things" (Putnam 1981a: 72–3).

But his solution is not a turn to idealism or relativism. One of Putnam's central claims in the book is that to assume a rejection of metaphysical realism leads one into forms of anti-realism is a mistake – this is a false dilemma. The way out is instead to reject metaphysical realism in favor of internalism. Internalism holds that "what objects does the world consist of is a question that it only makes sense to ask within a theory or description" (Putnam 1981a: 49). "'Truth,' in an internalist view, is some sort of (idealized) rational acceptability – some sort of ideal coherence of our beliefs with each other and with our experiences *as those experiences are themselves represented in our belief system* – and not correspondence with mind-independent or discourse-independent 'states of affairs'" (50). Putnam emphasizes that the kind of rationality central to internalism is a part of our conception of "human flourishing": because the fact–value distinction is untenable, we must evaluate our beliefs according to a mix of criteria relying on various kinds of values.

The suggestion – though this is not made quite explicit in *Reason, Truth, and History* and I return to it below – is that, from within the internalist view, the absurdity of the model-theoretic conclusion does not arise: from within our theory of the world and from within our language, we can say that 'cat' refers to cats and not to cherries, because we use 'cat' in sentences like 'cats rule the internet.' In the rest of *Reason, Truth, and History*, Putnam extends his discussion beyond reference and truth to a wide range of philosophical problems.

The next few sections of this chapter consider how various aspects of Putnam's argument look from the point of view of some strands of contemporary naturalism. Several factors prompt such an investigation. Some contemporary naturalists take up themes closely related to Putnam's, even while arriving at different conclusions. For example, with respect to commonalities, naturalists often share Putnam's doubts about metaphysics, single true descriptions, and a God's eye point of view on the world. Penelope Maddy's (2007) *Second Philosophy* emphasizes the bottom-up nature of inquiry, endorsing the use of scientific methods from a range of disciplines to make headway on philosophical problems. Mark Wilson (2006) emphasizes the multiplicity and complexity of scientific descriptions, pointing out that general conclusions about language, concepts, and correspondences to reality are never simple and straightforward; he and Maddy both point out there may be multiple equally good ways of describing the world (see e.g. Maddy 2007: 106). John Burgess (2004) rejects Realism-with-a-capital-R, which he associates with Ultimate Metaphysical Reality and "what God was saying to Himself when He was creating the universe" in favor of what he calls "anti-anti-realism"; Maddy, too, proposes distinguishing "Thin Realism" from "Robust Realism" in the context of mathematical truth (Maddy 2005, 2011a).

Of course, these naturalists also diverge from Putnam in important ways. Maddy takes pains to show that meaningful talk about how words refer to things does not require the kind of unifying "theories" of reference or truth that Putnam is concerned about (Maddy 2007: part II). Wilson explains that the multiplicity and complexity of scientific descriptions do not, and should not, prevent us from analyzing how our language and concepts do and do not connect up with the world (Wilson 2006; see also 2000). Burgess suggests that the form of "realism" we ought to adopt "amounts to little more than a willingness to repeat in one's philosophical moments what one says in one's scientific moments, not taking it back, explaining it away, or otherwise apologizing for it" (Burgess 2004: 19) – a realism that privileges science, not the rationality associated with human flourishing. And Maddy wholeheartedly rejects the association of justification with idealized rational acceptability, partly on the familiar ground that "a theory's being true is different from its being reasonable for us to believe it" (Maddy 2007:100).

To keep this investigation manageable, in this chapter I will focus on Maddy's *Second Philosophy* – comparing its approach and conclusions to those of Putnam, exploring relations to some of Putnam's later work, diagnosing differences and discussing them. As an approach, *Second Philosophy* is focused on epistemological and methodological questions; though conclusions about existence may follow, it is not, in first instance, a doctrine about ontology or the nature of reality. Second Philosophy does not look to philosophy to provide epistemological support for scientific methods, but rather begins inquiry from within the scientific methods we already use and trust. As Maddy (2011b: 121) puts it:

> The Second Philosopher is actually a quite mundane and familiar figure. She begins her investigations of the world with perception and common sense, gradually refines her observations, devises experiments, formulates and tests theories, always striving to improve her beliefs and her methods as she goes along; at some points in her investigation of the world, she addresses (her versions of) traditional philosophical questions; and the result is Second Philosophy.

Whether encountering questions about traditional philosophical problems, questions about scientific practice, or questions about other areas of inquiry, the Second Philosopher adopts the same approach: attempting to discern whether there is good evidence for the claims in question.

12.2 Reference and truth

First I consider truth and reference. As is well known, some of the immediate responses to Putnam's arguments centered on the possibility of appeal to causation – and causal theories of reference – as a way of pinning down the relationship between words and the things they refer to. Roughly speaking, in a causal theory of reference, 'cat' refers to cats because there is a causal chain, of some appropriate type, linking our use of the word 'cat' to actual cats. If this is right, it would allow us to explain why 'cat' refers always and only to cats and never to cherries. One of Putnam's responses to this line of thought was to claim that this strategy cannot achieve its ends, because appeal to a causal theory must be articulated in words, which are themselves subject to reinterpretation: when we try to articulate the idea that there is an appropriate causal chain, we must make use of the word 'cause'; but according to Putnam's arguments, this word can be multiply interpreted: in particular, we may interpret 'cause' as referring to cause*, where 'cat' is linked by a causal* chain to cherries and not cats (Lewis 1984; see also Devitt 1983; Douven 1999a; Devitt 1997).

David Lewis and others challenged Putnam on grounds that this this response misinterpreted the causal theorists' proposal: the idea was not to say that 'cat' and cats were linked by the referent of our word 'cause'; rather the idea was that they are linked by actual causes – whether we know about these and are able to articulate the connection or not (Lewis 1984). Michael Devitt, endorsing this line of thought, points out that the causal theorist's response to further questions about how causation is fixed should always appeal back to causation itself, "until the cows come home" (Devitt 1997: 114). Putnam has suggested this is begging the question in favor of metaphysical realism, since the response appeals to actual causes as distinguished from the referent of the word 'cause.' At least one commenter has described the situation as "an impasse" (Sosa 1993: 606).

But one of the most striking developments in philosophical thinking since the writing of *Reason, Truth, and History* has been the rise of the disquotational views of truth and reference, and the relative waning of interest in causal theories. Such a move is common among self-professed naturalists including Quine, Maddy, Burgess, and Hartry Field. This prompts us to ask to what extent and how naturalistic forms of disquotationalism diverge from or challenge Putnam's own understanding of reference and truth. As an entry into this question, let's take a look first at how the Second Philosopher understands truth and reference. In *Second Philosophy*, Maddy shows that the Second Philosopher will, like Putnam, eschew anything like a magical theory. For her, the question of reference and truth is not focused on the metaphysical realist project of attaching words systematically to things to find One True Description of the World; instead, the Second Philosopher approaches questions of reference and truth just as she approaches any other question: by examining evidence and assessing what set of beliefs best explains the phenomena.

In one attempt at this project, Maddy argues that a disquotational theory of reference and truth, in which truth and reference are characterized by T- and R-sentences ("'snow is white' is true iff snow is white" etc., and "'cat' refers to cats" etc.) represents an apt default position: from this default, we would investigate whether richer theories, such as causal theories, are needed to explain our practices. In an investigation of this latter issue, Maddy argues that although the T- and R-sentences are indeed all that is needed to characterize truth and reference, this is compatible with local investigations into particular terms and the worldly connections to which they refer. For example, while "'phlogiston' refers to phlogiston" follows immediately from the T- and R-sentences, a naturalistic inquiry would reveal that, in the past, some uses of the term "phlogiston" correlated with certain worldly conditions – for example, a belief that "this air is dephlogisticated" would correlate with the air being rich in oxygen (Maddy 2007: 155–6). The worldly conditions involved in these correlations are called "indication relations"; investigations into indication relations are necessary to explain important phenomena, for example why dephlogisticated air was useful for those with difficulty breathing. Explanations of successful reasoning can reveal information about indication relations and how they function.

As Field says about indication relations, "It is a fact about me that I am a pretty good barometer of whether there is rain falling on my head at that moment: when there is rain falling on my head, I tend to believe 'There is rain falling on my head'; conversely, when I do believe this sentence, usually there is rain falling on my head. This is simply a correlation, there to be observed; and a [disquotationalist] is as free to take note of it as is anyone else, and as free as anyone else to deem it an ingredient of what he calls content" (Field 1994a: 254).

From this point of view, we don't need metaphysical theories of reference and truth, or unified theories such as "causal theories," in order to meaningfully investigate the relationships that certain bits of language bear to certain bits of the world. Instead, truth and reference are taken care of by the disquotation schemas, and we use ordinary tools of observation and reasoning to give reasons for beliefs that language is functioning as it is in certain contexts.[1] Of course, nothing in this approach suggests there would be One True Description; as Maddy emphasizes, there are often multiple apt ways of describing the same thing (2007: 106). Neither is a unified "theory" of reference and truth proposed; instead, semantic relationships are analyzed in a local piecemeal way (see also Wilson 2006).

Let's investigate what happens if we try to apply this Second Philosophical approach to disquotationalism to some specifics of the MTA. We conclude first that 'cat' refers to cats and 'cherry' to cherries simply follows from the T- and R-schemas, and then see that there is a very high degree of correlation between our sentences involving 'cat' and states of affairs involving cats and 'cherry' and states of affairs involving cherries. These correlations will allow us to draw inferences about the indication relations of these sentences; these inferences can be drawn from explanations of facts like "There are fewer rats

---

[1] Though he expresses the results in less deflationary terms Mark Wilson also stresses the importance of investigating the way words connect up to the world. To explain the success of our methods, he says, we must take up the "correlational point of view," asking when, and in what ways, our theories connect up with the world. He imagines bad guys from the "land of gavagai" who, weary of MTV and the Home Shopping Channel, decide to shoot down our communications satellites. Their success in doing so prompts us to ask about their methods: "how do these linguistic moves *correspond* to the worldly conditions against which the calculations proceed?" (Wilson 2000: 373).

in the barn" and "The sailors didn't get scurvy," where 'rat' denotes rats, 'scurvy' denotes scurvy, and so on.

Putnam does discuss something like disquotationalism: he describes the "equivalence principle" associated with the T-schema as "philosophically neutral," adding that "On *any* theory of truth, 'snow is white' is equivalent to '"snow is white" is true'" (Putnam 1981a: 129). Contemporary disquotationalists are likely to agree: indeed, the modesty Putnam refers to is part of what motivates the Second Philosopher's idea that it is an appropriate default, from which we ask whether it fails to explain things we need to explain. But if that is so, we may wonder: why isn't the right response to the model-theoretic argument simply to point out that of course 'cat' refers to cats – this is part of what reference is?

It might seem that the answer to this question is that, in context, the response is a non-starter, since the metaphysical realist cannot endorse this answer. But this is not at all obvious. Why couldn't a metaphysical realist insist that reference and truth are given by the schemas, and then give separate analyses of metaphysics, belief, etc. that buttress metaphysical realism? The real answer to why the T- and R-schemas are of no use here is, I believe, more subtle, and has to do with assumptions about what the aims of a theory of reference and truth are. Such an answer is hinted at in Putnam's claim that the "neutrality" of the equivalence principle is the very difficulty, since "the problem is not that we don't understand 'snow is white,' the problem is that we don't understand what it is to understand 'snow is white.' This is the philosophical problem. About this [the T-schema] says nothing" (Putnam 1981a: 129).

This remark suggests that when Putnam aims for an analysis of reference and truth, he is understanding the scope of the problem in a particular way: that the answers to questions about truth and reference must illuminate, in some way, broader epistemological issues. This suggestion is borne out in Putnam's response to Field's remarks on *Reason, Truth, and History* at the time. Putnam says that the idea that "a realist can also be a disquotationalist" is "the most substantive – but also the most amazing – idea in Field's paper" – on grounds that "the problem of truth reappears when we ask what it is for an assertion to be correct and what it is for it to be incorrect" (Putnam 1982: 575–6). Putnam understands questions of reference and truth to be intimately connected to questions of justification and assertibility – so intimately connected, indeed, that an account of reference and truth that is silent on these matters conveys, in its very silence, a form of skepticism about them. But many contemporary disquotationalists do not understand the scope this way, taking pains to separate out analysis of truth and reference from analysis of broader epistemological issues – just as the Second Philosopher separates out truth and reference relations from indication relations and other matters.[2]

Disagreements about the nature of truth and reference that are partly disagreements about the way concepts of truth and reference are related to other concepts are not uncommon: elsewhere I have used the idea of the "scope" of reference and truth to diagnose these disagreements more specifically (Marino 2006, 2010). As I interpret him, when Putnam inquires into an analysis of the reference of words like 'cat,' the reason the disquotational "'cat' refers to cats" is not a solution to his problem is that he wants not merely any explanation of the relationship between the thing and the word, but also an explanation that would shed light on epistemological questions having to do with assertibility and justification, particularly those questions bearing on the matter of whether, and how, certain words and sentences manage to *represent* things in the world. I've used the term "scope" disquotationalism to indicate the view that disquotationalism does not entail any particular conclusions about such epistemological questions precisely because they are epistemological problems. For scope disquotationalists, the R- and T-schemas tell us all we need to know about reference and truth, and questions about understanding, assertibility, and justifications are part of another area of inquiry. Likewise, as we saw in the discussion of indication relations above, analysis of how words and sentences connect up to things in the real world is possible and fruitful: it just doesn't tell us about reference or truth *per se*.[3] For the scope deflationist, of course disquotationalism is compatible with realism: reference and truth are disquotational, while realism is a doctrine in epistemology and metaphysics.

One reason appreciation of this difference matters is that when we encounter the model-theoretic argument, we'd like to know more about the kinds of realism it is a *reductio* of. Putnam's definition of metaphysical realism incorporates a few elements that make it a very narrow definition, inviting straw-man charges: surely many who would style themselves "realists" would nonetheless shy away from claims about One True Description and a God's eye view of the world. If what I have said about scope is correct, we cannot adjudicate any difference in view between an internalist and any other –ist with respect to any substantive issues, including issues concerning

---

[2] Leeds (2007) also argues a disquotationalist can be a realist.
[3] Maddy (2007: 138) puts it this way: "Word–world connections aren't eliminated, their description just isn't to be found under the heading of truth or reference; we might say they turn up in the local epistemology."

representation and its relation to realism, by looking narrowly at what they say about truth and reference themselves: a broad investigation into epistemological matters is essential.

This applies as well, of course, to any analysis of the difference between internalism and Second Philosophy. To understand their differences with respect to the questions of representation, we should look not just at their claims about reference and truth but more generally at how they analyze the relations between language and the world. We've seen already some of the Second Philosopher's views on such things, which involve using and refining the empirical methods we have, doing local and piecemeal analysis, and using the concept of "indication relations" to explicate word-world connections that go beyond the R- and T-schamas. How does the internalist understand the proper analysis of relations between language and the world?

It is striking that *Reason, Truth, and History* has so little direct discussion of these matters. In more recent writings, Putnam has tried to address them, describing in a 1993 paper on Quine and ontological relativity how *he* thinks the absurd conclusion of the model-theoretic argument is properly avoided. Though Putnam's broader views between the time of writing *Reason, Truth, and History* and 1993 changed from "internalism" to "direct realism," he glosses his discussion of reference in 1993 as a refinement of his ideas in *Reason, Truth, and History*. In that later paper, he appeals to the idea that "meaning is use," distinguishing two versions of this. The first is associated with what he calls "socio-functionalism": the idea is that the use of a word, together with facts about the brain and facts about the environment, would enable drawing conclusions about what a word means. The second, "naive" interpretation, is associated with Wittengstein, Strawson, Austin, and James; here we simply acknowledge that "the use of words in a language game cannot, in general, be described without employing the vocabulary of that very game" (Putnam 1993: 182). From within our language, we state facts about the relations between words and things in a way that avoids the semantic indeterminacy of the model-theoretic argument.

Putnam describes himself as having been somewhat in the grip of the socio-functionalist view when writing *Reason, Truth, and History*, but says in this paper that it's the naive view we want. The difficulty, he thinks, is making the naive view plausible, given recent work in brain science and cognitive science: in one way our focus on these has disrupted our ability to simply use our language as if we were not puzzled by the way it works. But once we get over the desire for distance from our language, and resign ourselves to simply using it, the answer becomes clear: "The answer to Quine's [ontological relativity] argument," Putnam says, "seems to me ... to be as simple as this: when we use the word 'Tabitha', we can refer to Tabitha and not to the whole cosmos minus Tabitha, because, after all, we can see the cat, and pet her, and many other things, and we can hardly see or pet the whole cosmos minus Tabitha" (Putnam 1993: 183).

Setting aside the scope differences, and focusing on the substantive issue of how the name can connect up with the actual cat, we see certain similarities between this explanation and that of the Second Philosopher. The latter explanation begins with "'Tabitha' refers to Tabitha," goes on to explore the high degree of correlations between sentences involving "Tabitha" and the cat herself, noting along with Putnam that ordinary observable facts will bear on the matter. The Second Philosopher agrees that we can and ought to carry out, using our own language, further investigation into how our language functions; indeed, the metaphor of regaining the naivete of Austin is characteristic of Maddy's more recent work (e.g. 2011b).

However, there are substantive differences. Notice that the kinds of ordinary facts that seem most relevant are different: Putnam emphasizes "seeing" and "petting," while the Second Philosopher's inquiry into indication relations emphasizes the explanation of successful bits of reasoning from which we draw inferences. Furthermore, Putnam presents the naive view as one we'll struggle to regain; the Second Philosopher treats the fact that she must use her own language and tools in inquiry as obvious and unproblematic. Perception, for the Second Philosopher, plays no special *a priori* role in our explanations of successful reasoning; instead, we can explain why and when perception works by appeal to biological facts about our senses, evolution, and so on. To understand these differences, we'll need a broader investigation into the relations between internalism and naturalism; I pursue this in the next section.

12.3 Internalism and naturalism

Here I pursue the relations between internalism and naturalism through consideration of three topics. Going beyond reference and truth, how does the model-theoretic argument look from the point of view of the Second Philosopher? How do the internalist and Second Philosophical analyses differ when applied to the examples of mathematical objects? How do the internalist and Second Philosophical analyses differ when applied to an example from Putnam's text, of the brain-in-a-vat true believers, convinced by the Guru of Sydney?

First, let's address the question of how the model-theoretic argument itself looks from the point of view of the Second Philosopher. As Maddy explains, the Second Philosopher is unimpressed by the argument itself because she was never attracted to metaphysical realism in the first place. Of course we cannot completely step outside our own conceptualizations to compare how our thoughts, sentences, etc. compare with a raw, unconceptualized world.[4] The internalist's project of analyzing, from within our ways of knowing, how thoughts and language function to represent the world is a project she shares. Their disagreement is over whether there is anything useful to say, from a different epistemic level, to support and justify those ways of knowing. Putnam's "higher purpose," Maddy writes, "is fairly clear: for all the attractions of a lower-level empirical account, he wants a theory of truth that isn't restricted to the confines of our current science" (Maddy 2007: 100). The Second Philosopher does not feel the motivation of this project. Of this other form of inquiry, Maddy says "If the Second Philosopher were pushed this far, she might well ask on what grounds Putnam draws any conclusions in this higher context, where all her ordinary methods have been set aside, but she will not be pushed this far" (Maddy 2007: 102). I take this to mean the rejection of metaphysical realism seems significant to Putman only because of his desire for an account that will, from outside the use of our methods, support and justify those methods – a desire the Second Philosopher does not share.

Of course, it is notable that the Second Philosopher mentions "the confines of our current science." In my view, the most substantive difference between the positive views of the internalist and the Second Philosopher is this: though they both believe in working within our theories and using our methods, they disagree about what "our" theories and methods are: the Second Philosopher takes our best ways of understanding the world to be scientific methods, while the internalist appeals to "flourishing."

In interpreting this, it is essential to remember that the Second Philosopher is a native to the scientific worldview: it's not that we demarcate "science" and "non-science" and appeal to the former; it's simply that when we consider our best methods, they turn out to be broadly scientific. For example: when asked about the reasons to believe that atoms exist, the Second Philosopher does not answer "because science says so," but rather "because of 'the range of evidence provided by the likes of Einstein and Perrin'" (Maddy 2007: 397).

---

[4] I've called this the "Comparison Problem;" it is raised often in discussions about truth and realism. As Maddy (2007) says, the Second Philosopher does not aim to step outside our own conceptualizations, so the difficulty does not arise. See Marino (2006).

We're still appealing to "our" methods, it's just that we have some consensus that our methods are most trustworthy when they're based on evidence, and as natives to the scientific context, that's where we look for evidence. The internalist appeal to "flourishing" represents a different approach: we take up all our ways of knowing, broadly conceived, refine those methods as best we can, and use them.

Let me try to illuminate this difference by considering examples. First, consider inquiry into the status of mathematical statements. With an aim to illuminating issues in ethics, Putnam (1981a) suggests that an internalist will take the statements of mathematics to be true despite the fact that mathematical objects are not material objects. Of fundamental assumptions, such as proposed new axioms of set theory, Putnam says "[these] may be adopted partly because of [their] agreement with the 'intuition' of expert mathematicians and partly for [their] yield" (1981a: 146) – that is, for what they allow us to prove. But intuition is not some mysterious faculty: "mathematical intuition is good when it enables us to see mathematical facts 'as they are' – that is, as they are in the mathematical world which is constructed by human mathematical practice (including the application of mathematics to other subject matters)" (146).

Now let's look at the Second Philosopher's approach. Maddy considers three possibilities for mathematical objects. Roughly described, these are "Robust Realism," in which mathematical objects are abstract, eternal, objectively existing things; "Thin Realism," in which mathematical objects, like "posits," are things whose features are revealed by the proper practices of set theory, including definitions, axioms, and means–ends arguments for and against new axioms; and "Arealism," in which we look to exactly the same aspects of mathematical practice to understand mathematics, but refrain from saying the objects in question exist (Maddy 2005, 2011a). Rejecting Robust Realism, she argues that Thin Realism (TR) and Arealism (AR) are ultimately not very different, with the choice hinging partly on how we understand the word "exists." But what is most relevant here is the reason mathematics comes out as trustworthy at all, and for TR and AR alike, this has to do with its role in scientific practice: it is essential to science, and thus accorded special standing not appropriate for just any area of inquiry. Astrology is a practice, but we have no reason to regard it as trustworthy. Mathematics, because of its role in science, is different.[5]

---

[5] Maddy notes, however, that "This is not a reversion to a Quinean indispensability argument, because the conclusion is only that mathematics is different from pure astrology, not that mathematics is confirmed" (Maddy 2007: 346).

A full comparison isn't possible here, but it's noteworthy that, as realisms, Thin Realism and internalism about mathematics bear some similarities, each taking mathematical objects to have the properties accorded them by mathematical theories and each emphasizing the way mathematical assumptions are evaluated for both their fit with other mathematical facts and for their usefulness in proving certain theorems. The bigger difference isn't over what, but over why: the difference concerns *why* a person would adopt such an –ism for this particular area of inquiry: for the Second Philosopher the role mathematics plays in science gives it a special status; for the internalist this role is not directly relevant.

This difference comes out more starkly in consideration of the internalist and naturalist approaches to a problem like that of the Sydney Guru. In this imaginary situation presented in Putnam (1981a), the thesis that we are all brains in a vat is believed by "virtually all the people in some large country, say Australia," who have been convinced of this by the "Guru of Sydney" who "just knows" that it is true – and who is very convincing. These believers can do ordinary science in the normal way – their airplanes fly, and their bridges stay up, and they agree with us about all worldly empirical matters – they just also believe we are brains in a vat. Putnam says these Australians are "crazy" in the sense of having "sick minds" (1981a: 132). We should, he says, try to convince them of the error of their ways, and the best way to do this is to appeal to the way their views do not exhibit the virtues associated with an appropriate representation of the world – one that is instrumentally efficacious but also "coherent, comprehensive, and functionally simple" (134). Putnam says "having this sort of representation system is *part of our idea of human cognitive flourishing*, and hence part of our idea of total human flourishing, of Eudaimonia" (134).

What would a Second Philosopher make of this thought experiment? Based on Maddy's discussions of astrology and creationism in *Second Philosophy*, I propose a multi-part answer to this question. First, she would emphatically agree with Putnam that an examination and refinement of our methods using our methods is always appropriate: we examine our scientific practices by subjecting them to all kinds of analysis, and this analysis is often important when we defend our theories against rival views.

But second, from the point of view of the Second Philosopher, this suggests that as long as they have no explanation of what makes the Guru so trustworthy, there is one straightforward sense in which the Australians are forming their beliefs in a peculiar way: their own methods are adopted for no good reason, even by their own lights. It would seem simple to set up tests for the Guru to show that in ordinary matters he does not have extraordinary ways of knowing; if the believers have not done so this is a simple evidence failure, not a complex one requiring appeal to values and human flourishing.

Third, if the believers respond to the idea of a test by insisting that there is no possible relationship between the facts about our world and the facts about the vat-world, because there is no way, even in principle, for us to perceive or know about objects in the vat-domain, then for the Second Philosopher these vat-beliefs cannot be investigated for truth at all. Considering systems of belief concerning angels in a realm entirely disconnected from ours, Maddy says "as human activities, [these] would be apt subjects for the Second Philosopher's sociological or anthropological study" (2007: 346), but they would not be beliefs about the world and so they would not be of interest otherwise – that is, they are not assessable for whether they are true. The brain-in-a-vat scenario is not quite the same, since there is a degree of causal overlap – something is causing our collective hallucinations – but presents a similar challenge, since it is a case in which, by hypothesis, our methods cannot work. For the Second Philosopher, we cannot assess such beliefs for craziness or sickness, because we cannot evaluate them at all.

Finally, the Second Philosopher may question Putnam's claim that it is essential that we be able to explain what is "sick" about the believer's views. If these people truly agree with us about every single thing related to this world and our life in it, if we can cooperate with them, live alongside them, and carry out successful projects with them, what difference does it make that they have peculiar views about matters we have no evidence to adjudicate? As we've seen, the Second Philosopher will want to understand the Australians' beliefs – from the psychological, anthropological, and social point of view – but does not need a way of showing that that these beliefs are false and "crazy." Of course, the hypothetical situation in this case is very different from the one we typically encounter in the real world, in which beliefs about gurus typically lead people to infer very worldly particular things. In the hypothetical, there are no such inferences.

What can we learn from these examples? As I mentioned in the introduction, in my view a crucial distinction has to do with what "our" methods are: do the methods we associate with science have special epistemic status? For the Second Philosopher the answer is Yes: "our" methodology is to trust the kind of evidence we find in scientific practice and experiment in a special way. Asked about a practice like astrology, the Second Philosopher points out, along with Richard Feynman, that there are all sorts of ordinary tests that would determine whether astrological predictions work, and none of them show that they do (2007: 108–9). For the internalist, the answer seems to be No: because of the way facts and values are intermingled in our epistemic practices, there is no reason to treat scientific evidence as a special kind of evidence.

12.4 Discussion and implications

Of course, there is not space here for a full discussion of the question of whether scientific methods have – or should have – some kind of special epistemic status. But let me use this section to raise a few considerations.

As we've seen, Putnam's appeal to the very general notion of "flourishing" as an essential part of rationality is based partly on his rejection of the fact–value distinction. Briefly, the connection is as follows: since science requires epistemic values, Putnam says, and since epistemic values can't be separated from other values, reasoning concerning the empirical world and reasoning including normative matters cannot be separated. But there is a difference between saying that some values play some role in science and saying that all kinds of beliefs must be evaluated from the very general point of view of human flourishing.

One striking development in philosophy since the writing of *Reason, Truth, and History* is a set of more nuanced reflections on the particular roles values do and should play in scientific reasoning. For example, Heather Douglas (2009) distinguishes between appropriate and inappropriate uses of values in science. Douglas says that there is no way to rid science of values, and nor should we want to. Values do, and should, play certain roles in science, as when value considerations prompt us to ask one research question rather than another, or when judgments about tolerable risk inform conclusions over questions like "is this drug dangerous for humans?" But there are inappropriate roles for values to play. The most obvious is allowing a scientific conclusion or process to be altered specifically to reach outcomes that fit well with value judgments and interests. In the "internal stages" of science, as when we're characterizing phenomena and interpreting evidence, values should not play any such "direct" role. Preferring a certain outcome, or regarding that outcome as socially beneficial, should not be allowed to influence the methodology of a study so that a particular outcome is more likely to be found.

As I see it, forms of naturalism like that of Second Philosophy should have no problem incorporating and making sense of the appropriate roles that values can play in scientific reasoning – Second Philosophers are, after all, appealing to practice. But I'd like to raise two thoughts about the generalized appeal to flourishing and the role of values in science.

First, appealing to flourishing to understand rationality makes it difficult to explain why values should not play a direct role in the internal stages of science – and thus difficult to explain why political and ethical commitments should inform plans but should not alter our understanding of the facts. To seek out the most coherent and comprehensive view of the world given considerations of all kinds seems to allow the possibility that judgments about ethical and political matters should appropriately influence judgments about the facts, when to allow this would be a mistake. Consider the contemporary debate over climate change. Some climate-change deniers have strong political commitments against government intervention and against regulation. If rationality means forming an overall comprehensive and coherent theory with flourishing as its goal, and science has no particularly special status, then it would seem just as rational – perhaps more so – for this person to change his beliefs about whether climate change is real than to acknowledge that his political opinions do not fit with the scientific facts. Obviously, this would be a terrible error. Naturalism, according science a special status, makes plain and obvious that when it comes to matters like addressing climate change, scientific methods should have a special authority and the focus should be on these forms of evidence.

Of course, it is possible to say that failure to address climate change will not tend toward flourishing. But this is largely because of the facts – facts we must take on the basis of evidence offered. The conceptualization of the point in terms of flourishing obscures this point while naturalism makes it clear.

Even ethical and political commitments that are likely to lead to flourishing should not, simply because they are more coherent with empirical conclusions, make us more likely to believe those empirical conclusions. That great distributive inequality is plausibly antithetical to flourishing is not a reason to believe any particular facts about the causes of inequality. For example, in the middle twentieth century, Simon Kuznets gave an argument that claimed to show that market forces tend toward decreasing inequality in the long run. The reasoning has been criticized on various grounds. But clearly an ethical commitment in favor of reduced inequality should carry no weight with respect to the question of whether the Kuznets claim is true. In fact, it's the opposite; an ethical commitment to equality should make us subject Kuznets's claim to extra-rigorous testing and skepticism, given that its falseness would be so bad for us. This is an appropriate role for values in science, addressed toward such questions as "what are the risks of accepting the claim if it is wrong?" But if rationality is having a coherent, comprehensive set of beliefs and rationality is about human flourishing, it is obscure why the ethical commitment would not count in favor of the empirical one, given how well they fit together.

My second thought has to do with way naturalism makes sense of some of our current practices of disagreement in a way that internalism does not. I'd like to suggest first that it is characteristic of our time, perhaps more than in the 1970s, to recognize the possibility of multiple forms of flourishing, so that relativism in ethics and politics is a real and complex issue in ways that it is not in science.[6] We often respond to others very differently in cases of scientific disagreements than in ethical or political ones.

Consider as an example the ways that responses to the AIDS epidemic in Africa have prompted extraordinary measures to combat the illness. Some of these responses rest on empirical beliefs widely shared, but also rest on controversial ethical considerations, such as how to make trade-offs between the collective good, justice, and respect for individual autonomy. But other responses, like those of the South African president Thabo Mbeki, deny that HIV causes AIDS, thus disagreeing about scientific matters. Though not universal, it is common in our era to sharply distinguish the kinds of differences involved in these forms of disagreement and to respond to them in very different ways. To the claim that HIV causes AIDS we respond with a discussion about empirical evidence, and have no hesitation to adjudicate the matter on those grounds. To the idea that values can be prioritized in different ways our response is much more complex, varied, and nuanced.

Naturalism fits with and explains these different responses in ways the internalist approach cannot. After his discussion of the Guru of Sydney brain-in-a-vat believers, Putnam raises a parallel problem of "super-Benthamites" who always act to maximize "hedonic tone." Putnam emphasizes the parallel between the brain-in-a-vat true believers and the ultra-Benthamite true believers: each group has worldviews that rest on a "sick conception of human flourishing" (1981a: 141). This parallel suggests that our ethical disagreements and our scientific ones are to be understood as deeply similar – a conclusion that is, at the very least, seriously at odds with our current practices.

---

[6] I do not claim there are no issues to do with relativism in science, only that there is a difference.

In this investigation of the views of Putnam (1981a) from the point of view of contemporary naturalism, I've argued (1) that claims about reference and truth cannot be adjudicated except in the context of broader epistemological considerations, (2) that when it comes to the broad issues of internalism versus naturalism, the main difference concerns whether scientific methods have a special epistemic status, and (3) that in certain ways internalism is an ill-fit both with contemporary understandings of the role of values in science and with contemporary practices having to do with disagreement.

13 The model-theoretic argument: from skepticism to a new understanding

Gila Sher

Two well-known arguments by Putnam, the one skeptical (Putnam 1980), the other anti-skeptical (Putnam 1981b), are the "model-theoretic argument" (henceforth, MT) and "brains-in-a-vat argument" (henceforth, BIV).[1] The MT argument shows, according to Putnam, that (i) we cannot theoretically determine the reference of our words, and that, as a result, (ii) we must renounce the correspondence theory of truth and robust realism. The BIV argument shows, Putnam says, that (iii) we cannot truly believe that we are BIVs, and that (iv) Cartesian skepticism is thus undermined.

Three questions naturally arise: (a) Is there a conflict between Putnam's skeptical and anti-skeptical conclusions? In particular: Given that the key to (iii) is Putnam's claim that we, unlike BIVs, have referential access to the world, is there a conflict between his claims about referential access in the two arguments? (b) Is Putnam's skeptical conclusion concerning truth and realism warranted? (c) What is the philosophical significance of the BIV thought experiment?

The answer to the first, more general, part of the first question appears to be negative. If we understand BIV as arguing against an especially extreme form of skepticism, Cartesian or Evil-Demon skepticism, and MT as arguing for a weaker form of skepticism, correspondence-truth skepticism or robust-realism skepticism, there need not be a general conflict between them. However, some ideas developed in recent articles about Putnam's BIV (see e.g. Tymoczko 1989a, b; A. W. Moore 2011) suggest to me that on some level there might be a conflict between the two arguments. The answer to the second, more specific, part of the first question depends on whether the referential access denied by MT is of the same kind as that affirmed by BIV. But the first question is not one I will focus on in this chapter.

---

[1] I will use "MT" and "BIV" as abbreviations of other locutions involving the expressions "model theoretic" and "brains in a vat" as well. It will be clear from the context what I mean.

The questions I will focus on are the second and the third questions. I will offer new challenges to Putnam's skepticism with respect to robust truth and realism, and I will raise a new philosophical question about BIVs (and us).

The chapter is divided into four sections. In Section 13.1 I will challenge Putnam's MT-skepticism on the ground that it is based on a mistaken understanding of Tarskian models. In Section 13.2 I will discuss Putnam's skeptical permutation-argument. In Section 13.3 I will question Putnam's understanding of robust correspondence and realism. And in Section 13.4 I will identify a new BIV challenge, significant for understanding our cognitive access to reality.

Although Putnam's point in his MT and BIV arguments is, on the surface, semantic, I believe his deeper point is epistemic, as my own standpoint in this chapter will be. By characterizing my standpoint as epistemic, however, I do not mean what Putnam means when he talks about "an epistemic approach" to truth or realism, which he contrasts with a "correspondence" approach. On the contrary. For me, to approach truth epistemically is to ask (i) whether genuine knowledge requires something like a correspondence standard of truth, and (ii) whether a correspondence standard of truth sufficient for genuine knowledge is possible. And it is the relevance of semantic considerations to these two questions that interests me here.

In spite of my difference with Putnam on these two questions, I have much in common with him. Like Putnam, my approach to knowledge in general, and to philosophical knowledge in particular, is holistic. This means, among other things, that I do not draw sharp boundaries between epistemology, metaphysics, and the philosophy of language. Thus I see the failure of reference as posing a serious problem to knowledge in a rather straightforward way: if there is no fact of the matter about what our theories say about the world, then they cannot provide us definite knowledge about the world. Other philosophical positions I share with Putnam include rejection of Platonism, rejection of narrow naturalism, rejection of pure apriorism, and rejection of "magic" (i.e. appeal to magical or supernatural forces in philosophical explanation). Like Putnam, too, my starting point is "common-sense realism" (Putnam 1994b: 303), where by this I understand "the idea that thought and language can represent parts of the world which are not parts of thought and language" (299). I also share Putnam's view that "[t]here are many ways of describing things, some better and some worse and some equally good but simply different, but none which is Nature's own way" (302). And I agree with him that *if* we identify "world" with a Kantian "thing in itself" and *if* we identify transcendence with God's eye view, then we must give up the correspondence approach to truth and reject robust realism. But I do not agree that robust correspondence (or realism) requires us to identify world with thing-in-itself and transcendence with God's eye view, and I disagree with his conclusion that we have to renounce the correspondence theory of truth and robust theoretical realism.

13.1 What models are designed and not designed to do – a new challenge to MT

The skeptical MT appeals to certain meta-logical results. The lesson Putnam draws from these results is that it is impossible to determine reference theoretically (as opposed to pragmatically), that is, by means of a theory that says what the referents of our words are. This, according to Putnam, leads to another conclusion, namely, that the correspondence account of truth, and with it, the only acceptable forms of robust realism, fail.

For the sake of clarifying the issues, we may divide Putnam's MT into two arguments, a narrower argument and a broader argument. The narrower argument applies to theories of reference formulated within the framework of standard first-order logic. The broader argument applies to theories of reference formulated within any model-theoretic logical framework. The narrow argument relies on the Löwenheim–Skolem Theorem, the broader argument relies on what I will call the isomorphism theorem.

Before turning to these arguments, however, let me briefly introduce two terminological distinctions: (i) "model for" and "model of," and (ii) "standard" and "non-standard" first-order logic.

(i) Model theory distinguishes between "M is a model for a language L" and "M is a model of a sentence S of L, or of a theory T formulated in L." Any model in which every sentence of L has a truth-value is a model *for* L. Any model for L in which S/T is true is a model *of* S/T. It will always be clear from the context whether by "model" I mean a model for the language or a model of S/T.

(ii) By "standard first-order logic" I mean the kind of logical system described in common textbooks of mathematical logic (e.g. Enderton 2001 [1972]). What makes such a first-order logical system "standard" is that it limits its logical constants to the "standard" ones: a complete set of truth-functional connectives (e.g. ~, &, ∨, ⊃, and ≡), the existential and/or universal quantifier (∃/∀), the identity relation between individuals (=), and any terms defined from these. Non-standard first-order logic includes additional logical constants, such as the quantifier "most."

The narrow MT argument. This argument appeals to a meta-logical theorem called "the Löwenheim–Skolem Theorem" or "LS:"

(LS) Let T be a standard first-order theory. Then, if T has any model, it has a countable model.[2]

It follows from LS, Putnam says, that if you formulate your theory – say, your mathematical theory of sets – within the framework of standard first-order logic, then your theory will not accurately determine the reference of its terms. For example, it will not accurately determine the reference of the first-level predicate "x is uncountable." Why? Because first-order set theory has models in which "x is uncountable" is satisfied by countable sets. In order to determine the reference of terms like "x is uncountable," Putnam says, your theory would have to single out an "intended" model or a class of models, that is, those in which "x is uncountable" has its *intended reference* or extension. But although ("uncountable" being a mathematical predicate) this only requires that your theory determine an intended model up to isomorphism, even this it cannot do: a countable model of set theory is not isomorphic to an uncountable model of set theory, but first-order set theory cannot distinguish between the two.

Putnam's conclusion is radical: it is impossible in principle to determine the reference of terms theoretically, and this applies both to theories of reference that list the referents of words one by one and to theories that determine their referents by means of general principles, for example by means of a *causal* principle of reference. In the case of theories of the second kind the problem is that they have models in which "x is a causal relation" is satisfied by non-causal relations.

Before evaluating Putnam's conclusion let us be more precise about what follows and does not follow from LS. What follows from LS is that at least some non-logical predicates have unintended denotations in some models of theories in which they appear. What does not follow from LS is, for example, that any logical terms have unintended denotations in any models (see below). We also need to indicate that the reason first-level predicates like "x is a cat" and "x causes y" have unintended denotations is due to a more general

---

[2] A countable model is one whose universe is either finite or denumerable, that is, has the smallest infinite cardinality.

meta-logical result: the isomorphism result. This brings us to the broad MT argument.

The broad MT argument. The broad Putnamian argument appeals to the isomorphism theorem (ISOM):

(ISOM) Let T be a theory/sentence formulated in any logical framework with a Tarskian model-theoretic semantics. Then, if T has any model, M, it has infinitely many distinct models, namely, all the models isomorphic to M. In other words: the notion "X is a model of T/S" is closed under isomorphisms.

Now, the argument says: Take a theory of reference, T, formulated within the framework of any model-theoretic logic.[3] If T has a model in which "cat" refers to cats, then it also has models in which "cat" refers to dogs, trees, numbers, and so on. Similarly, if T explains the reference of words in terms of causal relations between words and objects in the world, then T has models in which "cause" refers to things other than causes: for example, to certain mathematical relations between numbers. Therefore, no theoretical (as opposed to pragmatic) account of reference is adequate.

Is Putnam's radical conclusion justified? Is it impossible to account for reference by means of a theory that states either the specific referents of words or general principles of reference? I believe the answer to this question is negative. To understand why it is negative, let us turn to "theories."

Theories. For Putnam, to determine reference theoretically (as opposed to pragmatically) is to formulate a standard first-order axiomatic theory of reference and use its intended model to determine what it says. Is this the right way – or an acceptable, reasonable, fruitful way – to think of a theoretical account of reference? A number of philosophers, for example Plantinga (1982), give a negative answer to this question.[4] But most do not provide a precise explanation of why the answer is negative. Plantinga, for example, raises the rhetorical question "So what?": "[I]ndeed number theory does have models of . . . different sorts, but so what?", concluding that "the process of formalization is severely limited in a certain dimension" (Plantinga 1982: 59–60).

---

[3] By "model-theoretic logic" I mean, in this chapter, simply a logical system that has a Tarskian model-theoretic semantics and is subject to ISOM.

[4] Such negative answers are aligned with claims by philosophers of science that it is unfruitful to think about scientific theories as theories formulated within the framework of some model-theoretic logic or think about scientific models as models in the model-theoretic sense. (For discussion, see Frigg and Hartman (2012 [2006]) and references there.)

I think we can go further and pinpoint the reason models and logical frameworks are not appropriate tools for determining reference. The key question is: "What are models and logical frameworks designed to do and what, as a result, are they incapable of doing?"

Models and logical frameworks.[5] If we turn to the paper in which Tarski explained his motivation for constructing a model-theoretic semantics (Tarski 1936), we see that the designated task of this semantics was to identify *logical consequences* correctly. One way to identify logical consequences correctly, Tarski realized, was to formulate the language whose logical consequences we wish to identify within a *logical* framework and construct an apparatus of models that *takes into account the reference of the logical terms of this language while disregarding the reference of its non-logical terms*. That is how model-theoretic semantics is built.[6] Logical terms are semantically "pre-fixed," while non-logical terms are "highly variable" (Sher 1991: chapter 3).[7] To determine whether an arbitrary sentence S_2 is a logical consequence of an arbitrary sentence S_1 we have to overlook the full truth conditions of S_1 and S_2 and in particular the "intended" reference of their non-logical terms. And we must focus on their logical form and its significant constituents – the logical constants. It is paramount that model-theoretic semantics get the reference of the logical constants of a given language right (in every Tarskian model "=" must denote the identity relation, "∃" the second-level property of non-emptiness, "∀" the property of universality, the logical connectives must denote certain Boolean operators, and the same holds for other logical constants, if there are any). But it is also paramount that the semantics abstract from the particular reference of the non-logical vocabulary. For that reason it is misguided to think of model-theoretic semantics as a general theory of reference, or as a tool for identifying non-logical reference.

Consider, once again, the uncountability predicate. If we build the uncountability predicate, or the membership relation in terms of which it can be defined, as a *logical constant* of a first-order logical framework of set theory (i.e. as a logical quantifier denoting a second-level cardinality property in the case of uncountability, and as a relational quantifier whose first argument is an individual and whose second argument is a property or a set in the case of the membership predicate), then first-order model-theoretic

---

[5] For an earlier discussion of some of the points in this subsection see Sher (2000).
[6] Although models were used in logic before 1936 (e.g. by Skolem), the capacities and limits of model-theoretic semantics are best understood, in my view, by reference to Tarski's 1936 principles.
[7] For other aspects of the model-theoretic apparatus and an explanation of how it identifies logical consequences and why it is suitable for this task, see Sher (1991, 2013a).

semantics would get its reference conditions right. In Tarski's words: "[I]f we treat ∈ like a logical symbol ... interpreted as signifying membership, we will, in general, not have a denumerable [hence, countable] model" (cited in Skolem 1958: 638).[8] That is, we will not have a countable model of "There are uncountably many things" or "There is an uncountable set." If, however, we build the uncountability predicate as a non-logical constant, then it is incumbent on model-theoretic semantics to abstract from its reference, hence assign it "unintended" referents in some models. And, given the role of models in determining logical consequences, it is essential that model-theoretic semantics treat all models on a par, that is, not distinguish "intended" from unintended "models." The question is, then, why would anyone use a tool designed to overlook non-logical reference to identify (determine, specify, account for) this very kind of reference?[9]

Turning back to LS and ISOM, I think that a reasonable conclusion to draw is that model-theoretic semantics is not a suitable tool for determining reference and that therefore we should not think of a general theory of reference as a theory that determines the reference of our terms by identifying an "intended" model or a set of such models. Thinking of a general theory of reference in this way is counter-productive.

Putnam, however, presented a version of his skeptical argument that does not appeal to model-theory at all, the so-called *permutation argument*. Let us now turn to this argument.

13.2 The significance of invariance under permutation

The permutation argument appeals to a variant of the isomorphism thesis. We may call it the "permutation thesis" (PERM):

(PERM)   Let T be a theory, and let A be the ontology of T. Then, if there is one determination of reference for all terms of our language under which all the sentences of T are true, there are many such determinations of reference, obtained from the original determination by permutations of the given ontology. We may say that T is closed under permutations.

---

[8] A denumerable model is one which is infinite yet countable. The translation of Tarski's sentence (from French) is mine.
[9] It is true that sometimes we can use a tool to do something it was not specifically designed to do. But in the case of Tarskian models and determination of non-logical reference this is especially problematic.

The skeptical argument can now be stated as follows: Let T be an adequate theory of reference for our language. Then, presumably, T assigns to "x is a cat" and to "x is a causal relation" a set of cats and a set of causal relations, respectively, as their referents/extensions. But the truth of T is preserved under permutations. So T remains true under some reference-determinations which assign to "cat" a set of non-cats and to "causal relation" a set of non-causal relations. This renders T an inadequate theory of reference. Contradiction. Conclusion: Determining the reference of our words theoretically, that is, by a theory T, is impossible.

In response to this argument let me make two comments:

1. Permutation does not change the reference of *all* words in our vocabulary. Take, for example, the second-level predicate "non-empty" (the existential quantifier of first-order logic), understood as "X is a non-empty property of individuals," or "X is a non-empty set of individuals." Now, the (correct) extension of "non-empty" is the set of all non-empty sets of individuals in the world. Let us call this set "NE." It is easy to see that the image of NE under any permutation of the individuals in the world ("universe of discourse" of our language) is NE itself. That is, the reference of the second-level predicate of non-emptiness does not change under permutations. The same holds for the first-level relations of identity and non-identity, the second-level predicates "is universal," "has cardinality α" (for any cardinal α), "is symmetric" (i.e. "is a symmetric relation"), and so on. Elsewhere (e.g. Sher 2013a) I suggested that we characterize all the predicates that are preserved under all isomorphisms – hence, all permutations – as *formal*.[10] Under this characterization, the reference of formal terms, unlike the reference of terms like "cat" and "is a causal relation," which are not formal, is preserved under all permutations. So the claim that PERM undermines the possibility of a theoretical account of reference is at most partially correct, that is, correct for that part of the theory of reference that deals with non-formal terms.

2. PERM does not undermine the possibility of a theoretical account of reference for non-logical terms as well. PERM shows that if by a theory you understand just a pattern of truth-values assigned to sentences of our language (those assigned "true" belong to the theory, those assigned "false" do not), then a theory in this sense cannot account for reference. It also shows that if by a theory you understand a set of uninterpreted sentences considered as axioms and closed under the relation of logical consequence,

---

[10] All logical terms are formal in this sense.

then again, a theory in this sense cannot account for reference. A mere pattern of truth values is something formal, hence invariant under permutations. And by paying attention only to patterns of truth values what we get is a theory of truth-functional operators, not of reference. An uninterpreted axiomatic theory, too, cannot convey non-formal content. But these are not the only ways to think of a theory of reference. A theory of reference is itself an interpreted theory, and its basic terms (e.g. "is a causal relation") must all be interpreted.

Someone might complain that such a theory cannot determine the reference of its interpreted terms. For example, the reference of "causal relation" must be determined outside the theory. This is true in some sense, but not in a sense that is problematic for me, or that should be problematic for Putnam, since we both share a holistic outlook on theories. As a holist, I believe that, for a theory to be significant, at least some of its words must come with a prefixed meaning. We cannot get something from nothing, and even our theories of meaning/reference must assume some meanings/references. But I also believe that we do not have to hold the same meanings/references fixed in all our theories or at all times. To develop a general theory of reference we may take the term "cause" from other theories, where this term was defined, explained, characterized, and its satisfaction conditions were at least partly determined. Then, using the theory of reference we have just developed with the help of this term, we might revisit the theories we used to fix its reference in the first place, reexamine their use of this term in light of what our newly developed theory of reference (which has other resources besides the prefixed meaning/reference of "cause") teaches us about reference, in light of what other theories teach us about causes and things related to causes, and so on. And based on this we decide whether to leave the reference of this term as it is or revise it.[11] We may even account for the reference of "cause" within the theory of reference by holding other terms fixed (relying on other theories, other discoveries, other contacts with the world, and so on). There is nothing skeptical in this conclusion: A theory of reference is an ongoing project just like any other human project.

Putnam, however, claims that in the case of the correspondence theory of truth, in the (closely related) case of robust realism, and in the case of the

---

[11] Other possibilities are discarding the term or replacing it by another, which will then lead to revisions in our theory of reference.

theory of reference they require, we are doomed to failure. Here, the only way to proceed is to appeal to magic (supernatural cognitive powers). Let us now turn to this claim.

13.3 Do correspondence and robust realism require magic?

The key to evaluating Putnam's claim is understanding what he means by "the correspondence theory of truth" and "robust realism." Let us begin by seeing what adjectives he uses to describe the realism he rejects. They include "*moderate*" (Putnam 1980: 464), "**metaphysical**" (Putnam 1981a: 49), "*externalist*" (49), "modern" (51), "**hard-line**" (Putnam 1983b: viii), "causal" (xi), "naive" (xi), and "classical metaphysical" (xviii)[12]

Next, let us look at some of the ways Putnam characterizes this realism. This realism, according to Putnam, "seeks to preserve the centrality of the classical notions of truth and reference ***without postulating non-natural mental powers***" (Putnam 1980: 464). "[I]ts **favorite point of view is a God's Eye point of view**" (Putnam 1981a: 49). It is a realism which holds that "the truth of a theory ... consist[s] ... in its **corresponding to the world as it is in itself**" (50). It adheres to "*the notion that our words 'correspond' to determinate objects (where the notion of an 'object' is thought to have a determinate reference which is independent of conceptual scheme)*" (Putnam 1983b: viii). It is a realism that **requires "an absolute**[13] **relation to the world**" (xi). It assumes "that we can think and talk about things as they are, independently of our minds" (Putnam 1983a: 205). This realism "claims that **there is**[14] a 'transcendental' reality in Kant's sense, one absolutely independent of our minds**, that the regulative ideal of knowledge *is* to copy it or put our thoughts in 'correspondence' with it, *but ... **we need no intellektuelle Anschauung***[15] *to do this: the 'scientific method' will do the job for us.* 'Metaphysics **within the bounds of science alone** might be its slogan" (226). **It involves** the "idea of a coherent **theory of the noumena**; consistent, systematic, and ***arrived at by 'the scientific method'***" (226).

Now, a careful look at these characterizations shows that Putnam sometimes views the realism he rejects as an *enlightened* realism, one held by

---

[12] Here and below I use bold in citations to direct the reader's attention to things I will focus on later. Because I would like to point a potential tension in Putnam's view of the realism he rejects, I will use two styles of bold: regular and italics. In the above citations, "moderate" is already italicized in the original text, though for a different purpose.
[13] In the original text, "absolute" is italicized for emphasis.
[14] In the original text, "is" is italicized for emphasis.
[15] In the original text, too, "*intellektuelle Anschauung*" is italicized, but not for emphasis.

enlightened philosophers – enlightened in the sense of being moderate and rejecting supernatural powers. (See italicized bold expressions.) At other times Putnam views this realism as an *unenlightened* realism, in the sense of being extreme and assuming a radical, outdated conception of reality and a radical, outdated standpoint: *thing-in-itself* and *God's eye view*. (See regular bold expressions.)[16]

So, is the realism Putnam criticizes an enlightened realism, in which case his criticism might be very significant for the viability of robust realism and the correspondence theory of truth, or is it an unenlightened realism, in which case his criticism would be less significant? One clue to understanding Putnam's conception of this realism is his statement that "it is, unfortunately, the **moderate** realist position which is put into deep trouble by the Löwenheim–Skolem theorem and related model-theoretic results" (Putnam 1977: 2). This suggests that Putnam thinks that robust realists who support science and reject magic believe they are enlightened, but in fact they are not, since their realism is committed to *noumenal reality* and a *God's eye view*.

Putting aside the question of what kind of robust realism scientifically-minded contemporary philosophers actually support, the question I would like to raise here is whether an enlightened robust realism, one that does not appeal either to things-in-themselves or to a God's eye view, is possible. If the answer to this question is positive, this, together with my earlier challenges to Putnam's meta-logical arguments, would challenge his entire skeptical argument.

I believe that the answer to the above question is, indeed, positive. To show why it is positive, I will briefly delineate a philosophical methodology that renders robust correspondence and realism possible without rendering commitment to thing-in-itself, a Godly standpoint, or magic, possible. The discussion below is based on Sher (1999, 2004, 2010, 2013a, b, and 2015).

The methodology I have in mind was already introduced earlier in this chapter. It is the *holistic* methodology, or rather a specific version of holism, which in Sher (2013a) I call "foundational holism." My claim is that if we realize holism's potential, we can develop an enlightened yet robust correspondence theory of truth, one that requires substantive correspondences

---

[16] Of course, it is an open question whether in every place identified here as indicating an unenlightened conception of realism this accurately captures Putnam's intention in this particular place. But what is important for the purpose of the present chapter is that (i) in order for Putnam's criticism of robust realism to make sense he must attribute to robust realists views of realism involving noumena (things-in-themselves) and a God's eye view, and that (ii) there are many places in his writings in which he either attributes these views to them explicitly or uses expressions that, given his criticism, are naturally interpreted as representing these views.

between truths and reality yet eschews the problematic commitments feared by Putnam. My discussion will be divided into three parts: (a) foundational-holistic approach to knowledge; (b) reality and correspondence without things-in-themselves; and (c) transcendence and correspondence without God's eye view.

(a) *Foundational-holistic approach to knowledge.* Following Quine (1951), many contemporary philosophers classify themselves as holists, though different philosophers understand different things by holism. Here I am not interested in the historical roots of holism, its current sub-classifications (e.g. meaning holism versus confirmation holism), or who supports (objects to) what kind of holism. Rather, I would like to briefly delineate a conception of holism that is pertinent to the question at hand and that, I believe, opens up more options in developing a correspondence theory of truth, a realistic epistemology, and a theory of reference. The holism I have in mind, *foundational holism*, may best be understood by comparison with *foundationalism*. Foundational holism shares with traditional foundationalism the view that a substantive grounding of knowledge in reality is both required and possible, and it goes further than most versions of foundationalism in making this requirements truly universal, that is, applicable to highly abstract disciplines like logic as much as to largely empirical disciplines like biology. Unlike foundationalism, however, it does not impose a rigid ordering on our system of knowledge (collection of disciplines and subdisciplines) according to "basicness," and it does not require that in grounding a given discipline (subdiscipline) in reality we limit ourselves to resources produced by more basic disciplines (subdisciplines). The grounding process, like knowledge itself, is an ongoing process, involving back and forth motion, change and revision, and setting demanding, yet not impossible, requirements on both the construction and the grounding of theories.

(b) *Reality and correspondence without things-in-themselves.* The foundationalist methodology, as I understand it here, aims at an absolute foundation for knowledge, a grounding of knowledge in absolute reality, an account of how terms of our language refer to absolute objects, and how sentences correspond to absolute facts or states of affairs. In short, the foundationalist thinks of reality as *noumenal* reality or *thing-in-itself* in Putnam's sense, something which is absolutely and completely independent of the way the human mind conceives reality or cognitively accesses it. In contrast, the foundational holist thinks of reality in non-absolutist terms. When I say that my standard of truth for "Snow is white" is a correspondence standard I mean that for this sentence to be true it has to be the case that the worldly, non-noumenal, stuff snow has, in the world, the worldly, non-noumenal, property of being white. This kind of standard is a robust correspondence standard,[17] but it has nothing to do with noumenal reality. Similarly, when I say that my standard of truth for first-order arithmetic sentences is a correspondence standard, I mean that such sentences have to be systematically connected to certain facets of reality in order to be true, but not that they have to be systematically connected to noumenal reality or even to Platonic reality. This point is worth elaborating on.

From a holistic point of view there is considerable flexibility concerning the form correspondence takes, namely, what pattern the connection between true sentences and reality takes in different fields. In particular, there is no need to insist that the correspondence relation is a copy or an isomorphism relation, or that it is a direct relation or the same relation in all fields. This is especially important in developing a correspondence account of mathematical truth, since the traditional way of thinking about mathematical correspondence involves the requirement that there are mathematical individuals in the world and the mathematical vocabulary refers to these individuals, a requirement that has turned out to be highly problematic (see e.g. Benacerraf 1965, 1973).

From a holistic perspective, it is an open question how our words, including our abstract words, are connected to reality. The key to answering this question is Wittgenstein's injunction: "Look and see!"[18] Don't decide in advance how words are related to objects, but look and see, search, find out. The fact that humans use 0-level expressions like "one" to state the laws of finite cardinalities, for example, does not automatically mean that for their statements to be true – correspondence true, true about the world – the term "one" must be connected to a numerical individual in the world, let alone directly connected to such an individual. Perhaps there are no numerical individuals in the world, but there is something else in the world that "one" is connected to and in virtue of

---

[17] I can make my standard of truth for this sentence still stronger by setting precise scientific conditions on something to be snow and equating the condition of being white with some non-trivial physical condition in terms of wavelength.

[18] Wittgenstein (1953: §66), where it is written "*look and see.*" Unlike Wittgenstein, however, I do not contrast looking and thinking. On the contrary I see some forms of thinking as falling under "looking."

which mathematical statements are true or false about the world, true or false in a correspondence sense.

Thus, consider the observation that objects and properties in the world have properties of many kinds, and these include formal properties like cardinalities. Suppose there are no numerical individuals in the world, but properties of individuals in the world have cardinality properties. For example, the first-level property *is-a-moon-of-Earth* has, in the world, the second-level property of having cardinality ONE. Suppose, further, that for some reason having to do with our cognitive capacities we prefer to construct first-order theories of cardinalities rather than second-order theories. Suppose, for example, that we, humans, get confused when we deal with higher-level properties and their relations, but see our way clearly into these relations when we translate them into relations between individuals. That might result in our having a language with a 0-level term, "one," which *refers* to the second-level cardinality property ONE. How would it do that, and how would first-order arithmetic statements be true of second-order cardinality properties? Well, we, humans, might exercise our "epistemic freedom" and create a 0-level model of second-level cardinalities. Our word "one" would be systematically connected to our 0-level "posit" one, which, in turn, would be systematically connected to the second-level cardinality property ONE. In this way first-order arithmetic statements could be true, in a "composite" correspondence sense, of certain formal facets of reality, namely those involving second-level finite cardinalities. (For more details, including how this account can be extended to theories of infinite cardinalities, see Sher (2013b; 2015).) Mathematics, then, even higher mathematics, would be true of our world, true about some abstract facets of our world, without requiring any noumenal or Platonic world to be true of.

(c) *Transcendence and correspondence without a God's eye view.* A correspondence standard of truth requires a three-level setting: Level W (world), level L (language), and level T (transcendence). On level L there is a theory, statement, or thought S. S says something about the world (where "world" is broadly understood). In the simplest case, S attributes a property to an object in the world, that is, S attributes a property of level W to an object of level W. Now, to apply a correspondence standard of truth to S we must transcend L to a level T from which we can see both S and that portion of the world that S has to be systematically connected to in order to be true. That is, our correspondence standard for S lies in T, a level that has both L and W in view. A paradigmatic example of level T is that of a Tarskian meta-language.

Considering a pair of levels <W, L>, where objects of level L refer, or attribute properties, to objects of level W, and characterizing level L as a *human level of thought*, we can in principle distinguish two types of transcendence (cognitive movement) from level L to a level transcendent to it, T. We may call these *Human–Human (HH)* and *Human–God (HG)* transcendence:

HH-transcendence: We transcend a human level of thought to a different human level of thought.

HG-transcendence: We transcend a human level of thought to a different, non-human or Godly level of thought.

Now, according to Putnam, a correspondence standard of truth requires HG-transcendence. But from a holistic perspective, a correspondence standard of truth requires only HH-transcendence. According to Putnam, a Tarskian meta-language is a Godly language; according to us, it is a human language. It is not surprising that for Putnam level T of thought is a Godly level: if level W is the level of thing-in-itself or noumenon, and if level T is a level from which we can access both level W and level L, then level T must be a Godly level. Only a God is capable of seeing which things-in-themselves have which properties-in-themselves. But if level W is the level of *regular* reality, the reality studied by *humans* (by our physical, biological, psychological, and mathematical theories), then level T is a level of *regular* cognition, that is, *human* cognition. It is a more powerful level of cognition than level L, as we have learned from Tarski. We can see things from level T that we cannot see from level L. But level T is just as human as level L. To set a standard of truth for human theories (statements, thoughts) there is no need to be God. This is something that humans do, can do, and have always done. It is also something that we can do better or worse, something that it takes quite a lot of work to be better at (figuring out ways to access physical aspects of the world that are not accessible to us at the moment, replacing common-sense methods of accessing the world by rigorous methods, creating sophisticated meta-languages, and so on). But it does not require either being Gods or using supernatural resources.

I can sum up my challenge to Putnam by saying: Putnam believes that robust realists and correspondence theorists must renounce their positions because (i) they cannot give an account of reference of the kind required by their positions, and because (ii) their positions unavoidably carry problematic commitments. But the meta-logical considerations that lead Putnam to conclude (i) are irrelevant to a robust realist/correspondence account of reference. And the considerations that lead Putnam to conclude (ii) are incorrect:

there are ways to be robust realists and correspondence theorists, including ways that are friendly to many aspects of Putnam's philosophical outlook, that do not involve the problematic commitments rejected by Putnam.

I have said earlier that Putnam is a holist rather than a foundationalist. How does Putnam's holism differ from foundational holism? A full answer to this question is not possible in this chapter. But one significant difference is a difference in the *balance of pragmatic and veridical considerations.* Both from the point of view of Putnam's holism and from the point of view of foundational holism, pragmatic considerations are integral to the project of knowledge in all fields, including philosophy and, within it, epistemology and semantics. But while Putnam gives more weight to pragmatic goals, considerations, and methods than to veridical ones, especially in philosophy, foundational holism gives more weight to veridical methods, goals, and considerations. This explains why, for foundational holism, a correspondence standard of truth, which focuses on veridicality requirements, is crucial for knowledge in all fields, while for Putnam a pragmatic standard, like acceptance of theories at "the ideal limit," is sufficient.

This is connected to the "foundational" aspect of foundational holism. While holism is usually viewed as an *antidote* to foundational interests, foundational holism is holism put *in the service of* just such interests. Foundational holism says that the holistic rather than the foundationalist method is the preferred method for foundational investigations, including those aiming at understanding the relations between mind and world, theories and their targets, words and the objects they refer to.

Another distinctive characteristic of foundational holism is its approach to humans' cognitive resources. One resource, in particular, is viewed very differently by the foundational holist and by other epistemologists, holists as well as foundationalists: intellect. This brings me back to Putnam's BIV argument, which focuses on such resources.

13.4 Intellect and the BIV challenge

BIV skepticism is a modern version of Cartesian, Evil-Demon skepticism, and Putnam's anti-skeptical argument is a modern counterpart of Descartes's anti-skeptical argument. But the two differ in substantial ways. In particular, while Descartes's argument is a rationalist argument, Putnam's argument is to a large extent an empiricist argument. This difference is crucial to the success of Putnam's argument. While Descartes's argument does not distinguish between creatures that share the same intellectual capacities but not the same sensory capacities, Putnam's argument does. It is the fact that we stand in direct causal relations to the physical world, mediated through our sensory organs, that distinguishes us from BIVs, according to Putnam. And it is this difference that makes it impossible for us to entertain the skeptical possibility that rather than humans with cognitive access to the world we are BIVs controlled by a computer run by a (possibly malevolent) scientist or by an indifferent nature.

Now, one feature of this anti-skeptical argument is that it neglects to examine the possibility that, under certain conditions, intellect, as a *natural* resource, is also capable of forging significant cognitive routes to the world. What I am talking about is *not* the specific possibility of purely *a priori* knowledge which, as a holist, I tend to be skeptical of. What I have in mind is the more general possibility that intellect plays a significant role in our cognitive access to the world, either in isolation from our other cognitive resources or in cooperation with these resources. I think that exploring this possibility is an important task for contemporary holists who, like Putnam and myself, reject both radical empiricism and radical rationalism.

Furthermore, one way to orient ourselves toward this investigation is to pose a *new* BIV question. Not "Could I truly believe (or seriously entertain the possibility) that I am a BIV?" but: "Given that it is possible that BIVs exist, is it possible that under certain conditions *they* will have some genuine knowledge of the world, and if so, what kind of knowledge and under what conditions?" Although this question does not directly concern our own cognitive access to the world, it could potentially teach us something about our own cognitive access, and, in particular, about the possible role of human intellect (which, by construction, is the same as BIV intellect) in this access.

One source of inspiration for this question is Kant's observation that while there is "no doubt that all our knowledge [cognition] begins with experience[,] . . . it does not follow that it all arises out of experience" (Kant 1787 [1781]: B1). Kant himself went on to ask whether there was purely *a priori* knowledge, but the possibility that human knowledge arises partly out of intellect does not require *a priori* knowledge. Nor does it require intellectual intuition akin to perception. A more suitable paradigm of intellect's ability to access reality is "figuring out," where this might be a lengthy process, involve use of background knowledge, and so on. Figuring out is a natural activity, one found in animals as well as in humans, and in humans it occurs in all ages and in all contexts, from everyday practical endeavors to the most abstract mathematical endeavors. This is how I would formulate the "new" BIV question: "Could BIVs figure out some things about the world? What kind of things? Under what conditions?" Could *we* figure out some things about the world in a similar way?

Another source of inspiration comes from real-life examples of humans who overcame severe sensory limitations, such as Helen Keller. BIVs are severely limited in their physical ability to access the world. But they have some physical contact with the world – their brains are physically connected to a physical object, a computer, which, at least under some conditions, is connected to a person who herself might have sensory contacts with the world. Under what conditions are such contacts sufficient (necessary, instrumental) for BIVs obtaining indirect knowledge of the world?

A third source of inspiration is Plato's parable of the cave. Is it possible that one of the BIVs will suddenly, or not so suddenly, "awaken from it slumbers," "stand up," "walk out" (cognitively speaking) and "see" the light? Not Platonic forms, but regular things, the kind of things we want our own theories to teach us about? Is it possible that a BIV will outsmart its handler? Could it cooperate with its handler? Could it see through attempts to deceive it? Could it find ways to exploit the computer "controlling" it? Quine said that science has taught us that our contact with the world is *purely* sensory. But has it? Has science given us a full and conclusive account of our cognitive access to the world, our ability to figure out things about the world, the role of intellect in accessing the world? These questions call for "looking and seeing," and "figuring out" is part of it. The question of what BIVs could and could not do and under what conditions calls for the same. And if there are conditions under which BIVs could figure out some things about the world, are we as different from them as Putnam thinks we are? Is it absolutely irrational to entertain the possibility that we are them, that we are at least a little bit like them?

14 Eligibility and ideology in the vat

Tim Sundell

Introduction

Lewis's *reference magnetism* is meant to address worries raised by Putnam's anti-realist *model-theoretic argument* (MTA). I won't try to determine whether it succeeds in that regard. But suppose – as many contemporary metaphysicians do – that it does succeed. Putnam's got another argument. Putnam's *brain-in-a-vat argument* (BVA) is not just another attempt to respond to Cartesian skepticism. It is *also*, like the MTA, an attack on realism. And because the brain-in-a-vat argument proceeds on the basis of different – and more conservative – assumptions about the nature of reference, a solution to the MTA does not automatically extend to the BVA. So: if we suppose that reference magnetism succeeds in addressing the worries raised by the MTA, what should we think of its prospects for mounting a response to the BVA? I argue that the metaphysical realist does have a response to the BVA. That response, however, is importantly different from what the realist might have thought going in. I argue that the realist should insist on a distinction between a theory's *truth* and its *overall epistemic success*. In turn, the realist can maintain that there *are* genuinely radical yet non-self-refuting skeptical hypotheses, but that such hypotheses concern not the truth of a theory but a different aspect of epistemic success, namely the fundamentality of its ideology. Such a response is consistent with the conclusion of the BVA. Nevertheless, it deprives that argument of its anti-realist force. The view I suggest thus makes theoretical space for the semantic considerations Putnam brings to bear while preserving the spirit of the metaphysical picture he attacks.

Sincere thanks for helpful discussion and comments to Mahrad Almotahari, Clare Batty, Gunnar Björnsson, Josh Brown, Andy Egan, Tim Fitzjohn, Sandy Goldberg, Jennifer Hudgens, James Lincoln, Rebecca Mason, Adam Patterson, David Plunkett, and Meg Wallace. I owe a special debt to Tim Button, without whose work and patient correspondence this essay could not have been written. Any mistakes are my own.

14.1 Magnets and model theory

Reference magnetism is the view that part of what determines the meanings of our terms is the objective metaphysical naturalness of the properties and relations to which we refer. Lewis introduces the view (though not under that name) in the context of arguing that there is a great deal of philosophical work to be done by such a notion of naturalness – by the notion that the world contains metaphysical joints the location and nature of which are independent of us and our theorizing (Lewis 1983b). The world can be carved up in all kinds of ways. But Lewis argues that some ways of carving the world are objectively, metaphysically, more natural than others. He argues for this claim by demonstrating some of the philosophical work it can do, and an important bit of that work concerns the determination of the contents of our language and thought. While there are many possible interpretations of my language – many possible mappings from my predicates to various properties and relations – only some of those interpretations will ascribe reference to properties and relations that are metaphysically natural, as opposed to properties and relations that are gerrymandered and perverse. Of course we could refer to gerrymandered categories if we tried. And a full development of the view will acknowledge that many of our everyday concepts pick out categories that are far from metaphysically fundamental (see Sider 2011: 37–9). But those horribly, hopelessly gerrymandered categories – the grues, the quuses, the coins-in-my-pocket-plus-Eiffel-towers, the cow-or-electrons – those simply aren't eligible to be the kinds of things to which we refer with our ordinary terms. Not when alternative interpretive schemes are available that are simpler and more charitable.

Lewis introduces this view in an attempt to defend the metaphysical realist from an anti-realist attack by Putnam. In particular, he's responding to Putnam's model-theoretic argument (MTA). That argument, very roughly, goes like this. Consider an ideal theory T.[1] By "ideal," I'll just mean that T is fully predictively adequate and that it has all of the members of your favorite list of theoretical virtues. As Putnam puts it, T is "operationally ideal." If T is ideal, then it's consistent. If T is consistent, then there is a model – an interpretation – on which it is true.[2] Pick one such model and call it M. Now

---

[1] It's not crucial to this part of the argument that T be ideal – it just needs to be consistent – but it matters later.
[2] See Putnam (1980: 473; 1977: 485). Williams (2007) discusses the difference between "model existence" arguments like the one I gesture at here and "permutation arguments," in which the correspondence between the terms of a theory and the entities in some domain is scrambled to preserve truth. As that work shows, there are important differences between the two types of

take the domain of M and map the objects in that domain one-to-one to objects in the world. Now reinterpret the predicates of T, grouping objects in the world not by how those objects seem to us to go together, but instead mechanically, in ways mirroring their correspondents' grouping on M. This procedure yields a second interpretation, N, on which T is not just true, but true of the world. Without ever having looked at what the world is *actually like*, we've constructed an interpretation on which theory T is not just operationally ideal, but true. In other words, for any (consistent) theory and any (big enough) world,[3] there is some word–world relation (indeed, many) on which that theory is true of that world.

The argument goes on. Suppose you object that N is not the intended interpretation of T. Yes, it makes T true of the world, but since it's not the *right* interpretation of T, that's neither here nor there. How is such a response to be defended? How are we to demonstrate that N is not the intended interpretation? Proposing further constraints on reference won't help. Anything we suggest or stipulate will itself be part of our own theorizing and thus open to the same referential rejiggering that gave us N in the first place. The rejiggered interpretation of our new, augmented theory will satisfy the proposed constraint on reference – whatever it may be – along with everything else. It also won't help to say instead that there are intrinsic relations – independent of our theorizing – between our words and their referents. That kind of view is tantamount to belief in the supernatural, to the antiquated thought that symbols are magically connected to the things they represent or that the world gives things their names. For Putnam, "we interpret our languages or nothing does" (Putnam 1980: 482). But we can't rule out interpretation N. So nothing can.

The MTA is an argument for semantic indeterminacy, an argument about language and thought and reference. But why should we think of it as an *anti-realist* argument? The kind of realism Putnam attacks in "Models and Reality" and *Reason, Truth, and History* – what he calls *metaphysical realism* – is a view on which truth is "radically non-epistemic." (For convenience, I'll simply use *realist* to pick out the type of metaphysical realist who is the target of the MTA.) For the realist, what the world is like is a matter independent of us and our concepts and our theorizing. There is an objective way that the world is, complete with objects and properties and relations, and the question is simply how close our theories come to

argument, but since I set aside the MTA below to address the BVA, the differences will not matter to me here.

[3] The argument can go wrong if the world is too small. I set this wrinkle aside here.

describing it accurately. For Putnam, the most important consequence of such a view is that even an operationally ideal theory could turn out to be hopelessly, radically mistaken. (After all, "we might all be 'brains in a vat,' the metaphysical realist tells us" (Putnam 1977: 485).) Since, for the realist, there is no constitutive relation between ideal theory and truth – which is just to say that truth is non-epistemic – the two must be able in principle to come apart. Call this – the possibility of radical error in ideal theory – *pervasive error*.[4]

The dialectical position for the realist on this understanding is admittedly odd. It's hardly the case that all metaphysical realists are skeptics after all. But the point is not that the realist must accept skepticism itself. The claim is not that the realist must accept, when all is said and done, that she could not know her own best theory to be true. The point is just that she can *make sense* of the possibility that it is not, that "the theory that is 'ideal' from the point of view of operational utility, inner beauty and elegance, 'plausibility', simplicity, 'conservatism', etc., *might be false*" (Putnam 1977: 485, original italics). Whatever the realist's favorite anti-skeptical maneuver, the skeptical scenario itself is a coherent possibility, one to be taken seriously and addressed with care. Since the skeptical scenario is coherent, so is pervasive error. And since pervasive error is coherent, the realist can maintain her radically non-epistemic view of truth.

The problem is that if the MTA is successful, then pervasive error is not a coherent possibility. For an ideal theory to be false, it must be the case that the theory fails to correspond to what the world is like *on the correct interpretation of that theory*. But the MTA shows that there is no way to privilege such an interpretation as correct. The theory is guaranteed to be true on some interpretation, and nothing from inside or outside of the theory can show that that interpretation is the wrong one. (Everything *inside* of it is "just more theory," and nothing *outside* of it is the kind of thing that can interpret our theories. Only we get to do that.) The best thing to say is that it was a misguided project to think of truth as independent of ideal theory in the first place. That's what required us to drive a wedge between the two. If we simply define truth in terms of ideal theory – if we adopt an epistemic notion of truth – then the problem doesn't arise. But of course, if we define truth in terms of ideal theory, then the thought that such a theory

---

[4] Button (2013) gives to this possibility – or rather, to worry about the possibility's obtaining – the excellent label *Cartesian angst*. Lewis (1984: 235) refers to Putnam's target simply as *massive error*. For reasons that will become clear below, I prefer a label closer to Lewis's, but I think there is not a deep philosophical difference here.

could be false is incoherent. Thus, and not to put too fine a point on it: if metaphysical realism is true, then pervasive error is a coherent possibility. But pervasive error is not a coherent possibility. So metaphysical realism is false.

Lewis's response gets around Putnam's argument – if it does – by avoiding what Lewis calls the "just more theory trap" (Lewis 1984: 228). Lewis rejects Putnam's declaration that we interpret our language or nothing does. We have a role to play, of course, but there are other factors. If we look to the referents, in addition to the referrers, then we shall see that "reference consists in part of what we do in language or thought when we refer, but in part it consists in eligibility of the referent. And this eligibility to be referred to is a matter of natural properties" (Lewis 1983b: 371). The correct interpretation of a language is the one that assigns eligible referents – properties and relations that are reasonably metaphysically natural – to the predicates of that language. This is not the claim that "eligibility-theory is to be satisfied somehow," or that "the referents of 'cat' etc. are to be included among the referents of 'eligible'" (Lewis 1984: 228). That type of view is clearly vulnerable to the "just more theory" objection. But Lewis's suggestion is meant to be different. It's not our theorizing about the joints in nature that determines which referents are most eligible. It's the joints themselves. To accuse Lewis of simply doing more theory is to misunderstand the view.

Of course, if Lewis does evade the "just more theory trap," then he may still remain open to the accusation of magical thinking. Lewis quotes Putnam calling the view "spooky" and "medieval sounding" and asks

> [W]hat's wrong with sounding medieval? If the medievals recognized objective joints in the world – as I take it they did, realists and nominalists alike – more power to them. But I don't suppose that inegalitarianism of classifications is an especially medieval notion – rather, egalitarianism is a peculiarity of our own century. (Lewis 1984: 229)

More recent defenders have gone further, arguing that in fact the substance of the eligibility view follows quite naturally from nothing more exotic than Lewis's commitment to simplicity as a theoretical virtue.[5]

---

[5] Sider (2011: chapter 3) draws on Williams (2007) to make this argument. Williams argues that, for Lewis, simplicity of a theory is measured by the number and syntactic complexity of the axioms required to state it. But to avoid triviality for such comparisons, what must be measured is the number and syntactic complexity of the axioms when stated in a language the primitives of which

If the view works, and if it thus makes sense to talk of a privileged interpretation after all, then it makes sense to ask, even of an ideal theory, whether it gets the world right or hopelessly, radically wrong.

> When we limit ourselves to the eligible interpretations, the ones that respect the objective joints in nature, there is no longer any guarantee that (almost) any world can satisfy (almost) any theory. It becomes once again a worthy goal to discover a theory that will come true on an eligible interpretation, and it becomes a daring and risky hope that we are well on the way toward accomplishing this. (Lewis 1984: 227)

This hope – and the corresponding possibility of the hope's being dashed – is what saves realism from Putnam's attack. Interpretations that, like N, are constructed mechanically to guarantee truth will inevitably make reference to properties and relations that are highly non-natural, and thus ineligible to be the referents of our words. The truth of N really is neither here nor there. We want to know whether the theory is true on an *eligible* interpretation.

My topic here is not whether reference magnetism succeeds as a response to the MTA.[6] Whether Lewis's view avoids the "just more theory trap," and whether, if it does, it also avoids the accusation of magical thinking is not a settled matter. But many contemporary metaphysicians work in a realist vein and do not take the MTA to be a decisive consideration against doing so. Indeed, arguably many of those metaphysicians proceed in this way in part on the basis of their endorsement of reference magnetism. If the view is plausible enough for them, then it's plausible enough to take as a supposition in addressing related arguments downstream. The question of whether the realist has the resources to respond to Putnam's *other* anti-realist argument therefore has independent philosophical interest, even if we ask it under the potentially controversial supposition that the MTA has been successfully addressed.

---

pick out fundamental properties. A gruesome theory might at first appear equally syntactically simple as a non-gruesome theory. But when both are stated in primitive terms corresponding to metaphysically fundamental properties, the gruesome theory will require more, and more complex, axioms. The eligibility constraint for theories of interpretation in particular follows from this. Williams goes on to make trouble for the eligibility constraint, however, arguing that the constraint successfully addresses permutation arguments, but not model-existence arguments for indeterminacy. As noted above, that issue is outside the scope of this chapter, in which I set aside the MTA in order to address the BVA.

[6] See Williams (2007), Sider (2011: chapter 3), and Button (2013: chapters 3–4) for some recent discussion.

14.2 Reference in the vat

A great deal of work has been devoted to reconstructing the best version of Putnam's BVA, but a recent and especially pointed reconstruction, due to Tim Button, will serve my purposes. Putnam (1981b) begins by asking that we consider a very particular kind of skeptical scenario. We are brains in vats. We have always been brains in vats. Our brains are hooked up to computers and also to each other. (So when we take ourselves to have a conversation, we are in fact communicating.) But there is nothing in the universe other than the brains and the vats and the computers. In particular, there is no programmer. Let's say that by quantum fluke the universe came to consist of the brains and the vats and the computers and nothing else. This is what I'll call the BIV scenario.

Putnam famously asks us to reflect on what a brain in such a scenario refers to with its words. Consider, for example, the brain's word "cat." Very weak semantically externalist assumptions suggest that the brain's word "cat" doesn't refer to cats. After all, the brain has never encountered a cat in its life. It's never met anyone else who has either. It hasn't encountered the kinds of things a cat is made out of, and cats play no role in the causal processes surrounding the brain's use of its word. What, then, does the brain refer to with its word "cat"? Perhaps the brain refers to nothing; perhaps its predicament is so dire as to prevent it altogether from making claims or having thoughts with content. We don't have to think that though. There is something that the brain tracks with uses of its word "cat." It's just that the something isn't cats. What is it? Opinions vary, but I'll simply call it cats-in-the-software.

The brain has encountered cats-in-the-software many times, and its encounters with cats-in-the-software are systematically linked to the brain's tokening of its word "cat." When the brain says something using its word "cat," it's thus reasonable to think that what it's talking about is actually cats-in-the-software. When a brain B says "there's a cat in front of me," what it expresses, on this view, is a proposition like this: There's a cat-in-the-software standing in the in-front-of-in-the-software relation to B. And that proposition might very well be true. Over the course of the brain's life there have been plenty of cats-in-the-software that have stood in the in-front-of-in-the-software relation to it. Supposing this is one of those occasions, and given the contents of what it has actually said, the brain isn't wrong after all. Indeed, as we apply the argument more generally, we find that the brain is deceived about much, much less than we originally thought it was.

So far we've seen that the brain in a vat might not be as bad off, epistemically, as we thought. But that isn't the BVA. Or at least it isn't yet. The conclusion of the BVA is "I am not a brain in a vat" and that conclusion has not yet been reached. So how do we get to the strong conclusion from the considerations just described? Button (2013) offers the following reconstruction.[7] What goes for cats goes for brains,[8] so:

(1) A BIV's word "brain" does not refer to brains.
(2) My word "brain" refers to brains.
(3) I am not a BIV.

Not everyone will agree that the brain's word "brain" succeeds in referring to brains-in-the-software. But to accept premise (1), you just need to think that it fails to refer to brains. The only thing required to sign on for that is a commitment to some reasonable version of a causal constraint on reference. Putnam doesn't think such a constraint can reach outside of our theories to refute the MTA. But he certainly thinks such a constraint is in fact an internal part of our best theory of reference. Most people do. If you think reference has to do with and is in some way constrained by your environment – if, say, you think that residents of Twin Earth don't refer to H_2O with their use of the word "water," or if you think that Putnam's ant has failed to create an actual representation of Churchill with its random tracings (Putnam 1981b: 1) – then you should probably be willing to grant premise (1).

The only other thing the argument needs is disquotation.[9] Disquotation is not always entirely innocent as an argumentative move of course.[10] But the skeptic is hardly in a position to raise a fuss about its application in premise (2). After all, "even to understand or talk about about the BIV scenario at all, we need to rely on disquotation. Otherwise, the BIV scenario does not confront us with the worry *that* we are brains in vats" (Button 2013: 125). [11]

---

[7] See Button (2013: chapter 12), and this volume, Chapter 9. In giving this version of the argument, Button gives credit to Tymoczko (1989a), Brueckner (1992a), Ebbs (1992a), Wright (1992), Putnam (1992), Warfield (1998), and DeRose (2000).
[8] There are no cats in the brain's universe, while there are brains. But, pretty uncontroversially, the brain's causal contact with itself is not the right kind of causal contact to underwrite reference.
[9] Putnam (1992: 369): "The premises of the Brain in a Vat argument are (1) the disquotation scheme for reference ... and (2) that reference to common objects like vats, and their physical properties ... is only possible if one has information carrying causal interactions with those objects and properties, or objects and properties in terms of which they can be described."
[10] Wright (1992) argues that even if semantic externalism denies us certain kinds of semantic self knowledge, the knowledge it denies us is not what's needed for disquotation of the kind in premise (2).
[11] Button attributes this argument to Tymoczko (1989a).

In other words, the skeptic herself requires that our word "brain" refers to brains. If she challenges premise (2), then she calls into question whether she has succeeded in presenting us with the skeptical scenario.

The BVA, especially when formulated in this way, is a pretty good argument. Still, it is no more obvious than it was with the MTA why, *prima facie*, we should take it as an *anti-realist* argument. Shouldn't the realist be happy? Putnam insists that the realist must treat pervasive error as a genuine problem. That means she needs a solution – and now she has one. In fact, though, the anti-realist application of the BVA is the same as the anti-realist application of the MTA. Both arguments attack the coherence of pervasive error. The MTA concludes that pervasive error is incoherent by showing that nothing could force us to interpret an ideal theory in such a way as to make it false. The BVA concludes that pervasive error is incoherent by going directly after the realist's method for demonstrating its coherence.

The realist demonstrates the coherence of pervasive error by observing that we might be brains in vats. The BVA – in contrast to the MTA – raises no questions about whether there could be a determinate interpretation of the brain's language. But it asks us to observe that very conservative constraints on reference show that such an interpretation simply *isn't* one on which the brain's theory is massively mistaken. That's the point about how a brain isn't as bad off, epistemically, as we might have thought. More importantly, the BVA demonstrates that the brain in a vat *lacks the representational resources to describe its own predicament*. The brain in a vat, in other words, cannot contemplate the BIV scenario. That means that if I can contemplate the BIV scenario, then I'm not in it. The possibility that the realist mobilizes to demonstrate the coherence of pervasive error is such that simply to contemplate it is to know that it doesn't obtain.[12] Once again, if metaphysical realism is true, then pervasive error is a coherent possibility. But pervasive error is not a coherent possibility. So metaphysical realism is false.

14.3 Eligibility in the vat

What exactly should the realist say in response to the BVA? Lewis himself does address the vat argument (Lewis 1984). But he treats the argument as an

---

[12] It is notoriously difficult to state with precision what is wrong with the BIV scenario according to the BVA. It is in some sense "self-undermining," a sense that I won't attempt to make more precise. For me it will be enough to focus on the observation that the brain lacks the representational resources to describe its own predicament, and to ask whether the same holds for various other skeptical hypotheses.

attempt at "exonerating" the brain of error (Lewis 1984: 234–6). In other words, he takes the conclusion to be that the brain is less bad off, epistemically, than we might have thought. Lewis argues in response that Putnam overestimates just how far the argument generalizes, and that therefore the brain may have a great many false beliefs after all. Setting aside issues of Putnam interpretation, however, this kind of response won't work against the reconstruction I discuss here. Again, the conclusion of what I've called the BVA is not "being a brain in a vat wouldn't be so epistemically bad after all." Rather, the conclusion is "I'm not a brain in a vat." And this version of the BVA doesn't require that the argument generalize at all. That the brain's word "brain" doesn't refer to brains is enough to do the trick.[13]

So does the realist have available another form of response? It's important at this point to recall that there are two arguments at work here. There is the BVA itself, which concludes that I am not a brain in a vat. And then there is the anti-realist *modus tollens*, which concludes that metaphysical realism is false. The connection of course is that the *modus tollens* gets support for its second premise – "pervasive error is not a coherent possibility" – from the BVA. The realist could thus mount a defense either by addressing the BVA itself or by taking on the anti-realist *modus tollens*. I consider the latter option below, but first I consider how the realist might address the BVA itself. That is to say, how the realist could defend the claim that I might, after all, be a brain in a vat. The prospects for a realist response of this type will of course depend greatly on what, specifically, the realist has to say about the brain and about the reference of its terms.

The first thing to note in this regard is that – *prima facie* at least – the realist's acceptance of reference magnetism provides nothing in the way of special or surprising results. Reference magnetism was brought in to address radical indeterminacy of semantic content. It allows the realist to reject perverse interpretations of our language. But the BVA never raised

---

[13] Chalmers (2005) offers a take on the brain in a vat that, though it differs in emphasis, bears similarities to Lewis's response. Chalmers suggests that the brain can be exonerated quite extensively of error, but that a number of its more fundamental metaphysical beliefs are false. The brain believes, for example, that it lives in a universe in which fundamental physical particles are not themselves constituted by a yet more fundamental layer of computational processes. But, since the things the brain calls "tables" are made out of bits of software, that belief is false. The skeptical scenario is thus, for Chalmers, a collection of metaphysical views rather than a distinctively nightmarish epistemic predicament. Chalmers's view, like Lewis's, combines agreement with Putnam that the brain's beliefs are true when it comes to ordinary objects with the contention that the argument will at some crucial point fail to generalize. (In that essay, Chalmers also employs an "exemplification" response to Putnam's argument. See Section 14.5 below for discussion of that strategy.)

the possibility of radical indeterminacy of semantic content. All it asked us to accept was some kind of causal constraint on reference. And it never raised the specter of perverse interpretations either. Indeed, the interpretation that is tentatively proposed in the course of presenting the argument – cats-in-the-software, in my version – is not just determinate but highly charitable. Lots of people who reject the set-up for the MTA – "we interpret our language or nothing does," in particular – are going to accept a causal constraint on reference. That puts the realist in pretty much the same boat as everyone else.[14]

So what should the realist say about the brain's words?[15] If the realist concludes that the brain fails to refer, then the BVA will immediately go forward: if the brain's word "cat" doesn't refer to anything, then it doesn't refer to cats. And that, plus disquotation, is all that's required. So the realist will have to argue that the brain does succeed in referring. What specifically do the brain's words refer to? Well if the brain's word "cat" refers to cats-in-the-software, then the BVA *still* goes through. (Since referring to cats-in-the-software is one way of not referring to cats.) So: if the realist is to defend the possibility that we might be brains in vats, she will have to argue (1) that the brain's word "cat" succeeds in referring and (2) that in particular it succeeds in referring to cats.

At this point in the argument, it might be tempting to lean – heavily – on the eligibility constraint. The property of being a cat is more natural than the property of being a cat-in-the-software. To see this, just consider that, as strange as the BIV scenario is, it takes place in a universe composed of the same fundamental parts, governed by the same fundamental laws, as our own. There *are* ordinary physical objects in the BIV scenario. (Brains, vats, computers, wires, etc.) It just so happens that the brain never interacts with them as we do. A complete scientific account of the BIV's universe will thus, at the fundamental level, look much like an account of our own. And a fundamental

---

[14] Sider (2011: chapter 3) points out that Lewis's eligibility constraint can be combined with a variety of other views about reference. You could use it to augment a kind of global descriptivism, as Lewis does for the sake of argument in presenting the view. But you could just as easily combine it with other meta-semantic views. But, whether you hold to global descriptivism, or the causal historical theory, or Millikan's metasemantics, or conceptual role semantics, or whatever, you're still likely to think that residents of Twin Earth do not have H_2O in the extension of their word "water." And if you think that, then you're unlikely to object to the semantic assumptions at work in the BVA.

[15] It is no longer important for the argument that we talk about the brain's word "brain" in particular, and doing so renders the discussion unnecessarily baroque. I switch the example back to "cat" now, simply so that I don't have to use the word "brain" so much. Everything I say should apply to brains and to "brain" as well.

theory of our own universe is going to take a long time before it gets around to describing the contents of computer programs. It will have to tell us what a computer is first, for one thing, which means it will already have worked its way up to medium-sized dry goods. Once it's done that, it will already be able to tell us about cats. Consider also that, as Fodor famously observes, *content itself* is unlikely to appear in the "complete catalogue ... of the ultimate and irreducible properties of things" (Fodor 1987: 97).[16] So before the theory can tell us about the contents of software, cats-in-the-software included, it will first have to explain intensionality. And to do that, again, it will have to have worked its way up to ordinary objects and organisms – like brains and computers – since electrons and quarks are not the kind of things that are capable of referring. If the theory has reached a point where it is working in terms of categories like *brain* and *computer* and *aboutness*, then it will long since have reached a stage where it can make sense of a category like *cat*.

Reference magnetism is precisely the view that an interpretation mapping more natural properties to our terms is to be preferred over an interpretation mapping less natural properties to our terms. As we've just seen, the property of being a cat is more natural than the property of being a cat-in-the-software. So perhaps the realist could declare cats-in-the-software *ineligible* as a referent, and cats – even though they don't happen to exist in the brain's world – *eligible*. Thus, the brain's utterance of "there's a cat in front of me" would mean that there is a *cat* in front of it, which is false. Precisely what the realist wants to be able to say.

This maneuver is actually in keeping with other uses to which reference magnetism has been put. Weatherson (2003) puts the view like this:

> [F]or any predicate t and property F, we want F to meet two requirements before we say it is the meaning of t. We want this meaning assignment to validate many of our pre-theoretic intuitions ... and we want F to be reasonably natural ... In hard cases, these requirements pull in opposite directions; *the* meaning of t is the property which on balance does best.[17] (Weatherson 2003: 9, original italics)

[16] The complete quote is: "I suppose that sooner or later the physicists will complete the catalogue they've been compiling of the ultimate and irreducible properties of things. When they do, the likes of spin, charm, and charge will perhaps appear upon their list. But aboutness surely won't; intentionality simply doesn't go that deep."
[17] Those philosophers who combine the eligibility constraint with different meta-semantic theories may object to Weatherson's suggestion for this other requirement. But analogous considerations apply. For example, if eligibility is combined with Millikan's metasemantics rather than Weatherson's pre-theoretic intuitions constraint, we shall see that one interpretation but not the other assigns to the brain's word "cat" an extension that neither it nor any of its ancestors has ever

Weatherson's point is that reference magnetism allows us to maintain some distance between pre-theoretic intuitions and meaning. Here's one of his examples of how that could work: for eighteenth-century speakers who used their word "fish" to describe whales, an interpretation on which that word really meant *fish-plus-whales* would vindicate more of their intuitions. But an interpretation on which their word "fish" simply meant *fish* would still respect *most* of their intuitions, and it would *also* respect the facts about naturalness. It is sensitive to speaker usage and intuition, but still allows us to say that an eighteenth-century utterance of "whales are fish" expresses the false proposition that whales are fish, rather than the true proposition that whales are fish-or-whales. The first interpretation hews too closely to speaker usage, and doesn't allow us to make sense of the fact that the speakers, however consistent their usage of the term "fish," were in error about whales. The second interpretation thus represents the better balance of the two constraints.

In the case of the BIV, as in the case of Weatherson's eighteenth-century mariners, we are trying to make sense of systematic error. The brain's case, however, is simply too extreme for this kind of application of the eligibility view. As the passage from Weatherson makes clear, the eligibility constraint is meant to be one consideration among others in choosing an interpretation. Cat-hood is indeed a more natural property than cat-in-the-softwarehood, just as being a fish is a more natural property than being a fish-or-whale. But an interpretation on which a BIV's word "cat" refers to cats respects *none* of the brain's pre-theoretic intuitions. It correctly describes none of the patterns in the brain's usage of that word, and accurately characterizes none of the brain's linguistic dispositions.

Moreover, cat-in-the-software is not itself an entirely unnatural property. It's more natural, for example, than cat-or-Eiffel-tower-in-the-software or cwat-in-the-software. (We'll let cwats-in-the-software be a property possessed by cats-in-the-software along with lamps-in-the-software if it's a Thursday-in-the-software.) The categories needed to explain the brain's linguistic behaviour, and pre-theoretical intuitions will have a role to play in a theory of the brain's world. Cat-in-the-software is one such category. Cwat-in-the-software is not. So cat-in-the-software is a less natural category than cat, but (a) it is still reasonably natural and (b) an interpretation assigning it to the brain's word does a much better job of meeting other constraints on reference than

> successfully *tracked*, in Millikan's sense; see Millikan (1987). That makes the property of being a cat a terrible interpretation of the brain's word "cat," and it does so for reasons analogous to those described above in terms of Weatherson's suggestion.

one assigning cats. However great the difference in naturalness, eligibility is to be balanced against some degree of charity or sensitivity to usage.[18] Using the eligibility constraint to force a *cat*, rather than *cat-in-the-software*, interpretation privileges naturalness to the thorough exclusion of any of the other factors that play a role in the determination of reference. No plausible version of reference magnetism could get – or would want to get – that result.

The point here is that, at the level of first-order semantics, the realist and Putnam will have largely the same kinds of things to say about the semantic values of various speakers' terms. As emphasized above, most advocates of reference magnetism are going to accept some kind of causal constraint on reference. And – in stark contrast to the MTA – some kind of causal constraint is really all that's needed for the BVA to have bite. As Weatherson argues, the eligibility constraint can be used to pull questions about meaning apart from questions about dispositions or first-order intuitions. It does help us explain how we could get things consistently wrong. But while that may be a plausible analysis for errors like thinking mistakenly that whales are fish, it's far less plausible for more radical and wide-ranging forms of error. As long as the eligibility constraint is to be balanced against other factors – causal contact, dispositions, intuitions, tracking, etc. – it can't be strong enough to wrestle the brain's reference all the way out of the vat and onto the uninstantiated property of cathood. Such a view would count as magical, even by the lights of the realist. So what should the realist say about the brain's word "cat"? Pretty much the same thing everybody else should. It refers to cats-in-the-software, if anything.

14.4 Variations on the vat

I've argued that the realist should concede that the brain's word "cat" does not refer to cats. And that claim, along with disquotation, is all that's needed for the BVA to be sound. The upshot of the argument so far is therefore this: the best strategy for the realist is not to attack the BVA itself. The BVA's assumptions about reference are too conservative for a plausible form of reference magnetism to reject them. That means that the realist must instead attack the anti-realist *modus tollens* that draws its support from the BVA. The relevant premise of that *modus tollens* was this: "Pervasive error is not a coherent possibility." The best course for the realist is to *accept* the BVA – to accept that the BIV scenario is self-undermining and thus to give up on the

---

[18] Or attention to the properties actually being tracked, or to conceptual role, etc.

possibility that she is a brain in a vat – but to break the link between that conclusion and the incoherence of pervasive error. Before presenting what I think is the best strategy for accomplishing this, I consider one that may spring more quickly to mind.

The skeptical hypothesis Putnam asks us to consider is extremely specific. But there are a lot of skeptical hypotheses. I might be dreaming. I might be deceived by an Evil Demon. The world might have come into existence five minutes ago. I could even be a brain, but under circumstances different from those Putnam describes. There could be a programmer, or I could be recently envatted, or recently devatted, etc. Yet while Putnam's skeptical scenario is highly specific, the conclusion his BVA is meant to support – that pervasive error is incoherent – is extremely general. To show that radical falsehood of ideal theory is incoherent, it's not enough to show that *one specific* skeptical hypothesis is self-undermining. You would need to show that *all* skeptical hypotheses radical enough to do the trick are self-undermining. Why couldn't the realist simply concede the point about Putnam's BIV scenario, and then cheerfully point to any of the other skeptical hypotheses in the neighborhood to drive her wedge between ideal theory and truth?

I'm not entirely sure that some version of this response won't work. But if it does, it won't work nearly as easily as this description makes it sound.[19] Skeptical hypotheses vary from one another in many different respects. But one way in which they differ is in degree of radicalness. So consider an example of the type of skeptical hypothesis the realist might point to as an alternative to Putnam's BIV scenario: the hypothesis of recent envattment. Last night my brain was scooped from my head and I am now, undetectably, living in a simulation of the world I previously inhabited. If that scenario obtained, my word "vat" *would* refer to vats and my word "brain" *would* refer to brains. There's good reason therefore to think that a BVA-style argument would not apply to this skeptical hypothesis, and that we therefore cannot dismiss it as self-undermining.

As bizarre as the scenario is, however, I submit that it is also significantly less radical a skeptical hypothesis than the BIV scenario (see Wright 1992: 87–8). After all, if I was envatted last night (and nothing else is stipulated to differ from the actual world), then most of my beliefs are still true! I believe that I live in a world filled with medium-sized dry goods like vats and computers and bottles. I believe that Lexington is in Kentucky, that whales

---

[19] This section owes a great deal to Button (2013: chapter 15). My presentation differs in certain respects however, and my goals in making the argument are different.

are mammals, and that most persons are not envatted brains. All of those beliefs succeed in representing the world outside of the vat – that's how this scenario avoids a BVA-type argument, if it does – but they are also *true* beliefs.

Of course, some of my beliefs about my immediate environment are false on this hypothesis. I believe that I am sitting in front of a computer, in an office, using my two hands to type, and that my brain was not recently removed from my body and put in a vat. I'm wrong about all of those things, despite my seeming-evidence to the contrary. The scenario is plenty radical enough to be of interest to an epistemologist. But it's not at all obvious that this pattern of deception is radical enough to satisfy the metaphysical realist. Here's what that would sound like: "Because truth is non-epistemic, even our very best theory could turn out to be hopelessly, radically mistaken. After all, I might be a recently envatted brain with largely true beliefs about the world in general but lots of mistaken beliefs about what happened last night and what's going on in my immediate vicinity!" It doesn't sound quite as convincing.

The worry about the "alternative skeptical hypothesis" strategy is this: think of the complete set of skeptical scenarios as partially ordered along a scale of *radicalness*. How to generate such a ranking would of course be a difficult question in itself. It might simply involve the number of our beliefs rendered false, were the hypothesis in question to obtain. More plausibly, it might privilege some of our beliefs as more central than others, and scenarios that target beliefs central to our overall theories as more radical than scenarios that target more peripheral beliefs.[20] For my purposes, fortunately, a rough and ready understanding of the scale will do. At the high end of the scale are scenarios where we're deceived about everything or almost everything. At the low end of the scale are scenarios where we're deceived about only a very limited set of facts. Inhabitants of scenarios at the low end of the scale interact with the same kinds of things that we do, and can thus use their words to refer to the same things we do. Therefore we can't rule out, by virtue of describing those scenarios, that we are those speakers. Skeptical hypotheses at the low end of the scale really do evade the BVA. But of course they are also less skeptical.

Skeptical hypotheses at the high end of the scale are truly radical. Deception of the kind described in these hypotheses represents genuinely pervasive error. But of course these are also the scenarios where BVA-style arguments will most naturally apply. Speakers in scenarios like these – Putnam's BIV scenario, Descartes's Evil Demon scenario, Russell's five-minute hypothesis

---

[20] Thanks to Mahrad Almotahari for helpful discussion on this point.

(Russell 1921) – are so thoroughly deceived about their environment as to lack the capacity to describe it. So, in describing it, we demonstrate that we are not those speakers. The more radical a skeptical scenario is, the more likely that Putnam's argument will attach, and the more likely we can dismiss the scenario as self-undermining and stop worrying about it.

Somewhere in the middle, as you move up the scale, is the place where hypotheses change from coherent to self-undermining. Knowing where that threshold lies would tell us just how radically it is possible to be deceived, and thus just how false an ideal theory could be. Is the threshold far enough along the spectrum for the corresponding amount of error to count as *pervasive*? It's anything but clear. Button (2013: chapter 15) argues that it is simply impossible to identify the point at which skeptical hypotheses become susceptible to the BVA. But even if we could locate the threshold, it would not be enough. We would also have to know whether that threshold is high *enough* for the realist. That is, we would have to say precisely how much potential for falsehood there must be for the realist to be satisfied that truth really is non-epistemic.

These tasks represent a tremendous amount of careful and difficult (and possibly – if Button is right – futile) philosophical work, jointly constituting a project as far as could be from simply shrugging one's shoulders and picking out another skeptical hypothesis. Perhaps, *pace* Button, the threshold for radicalness could be identified with precision and, *pace* my own hunch, some form of metaphysical realism deserving of the name could demonstrate itself to be content with skeptical scenarios lower in radicalness than that threshold. But conceding the point about Putnam's BIV scenario starts us on a slippery slope. And the general applicability and conservative nature of the BVA's premises make it hard to see how the brakes could be applied while the deception is still reasonably thorough. It's easy to imagine getting argued far enough down the scale as to render this strategy pretty deeply unsatisfying to a serious realist.

14.5 Ideology in the vat

I submit that the realist should take a very different approach. Having signed up for the idea of objective metaphysical joints in nature, the realist is in a position to draw a distinction that matters greatly in this context. The distinction is between a theory's *truth* and its *overall epistemic success*. What the realist should insist, I maintain, is that it is not enough that a theory's claims be true. The theory should also employ concepts that cut the world close to the metaphysical joints. Two theories might both be made up entirely of true claims, but if theory A employs concepts that are metaphysically natural and theory B employs concepts that are gerrymandered and gruesome, then A is *better* than B. Crucially, it is not "better" in some instrumental sense. In virtue of employing concepts that cut the world closer to the natural joints, A is *epistemically* better: it more accurately characterizes what the world is like.

On the first page of his book-length defense of a Lewisian notion of structure, Sider asks us to imagine a world composed only of fluid, red on one side and blue on the other. The inhabitants of this world pay no mind to the plane dividing red from blue, however, but rather describe the world in terms of a different divide running diagonally across the fluid, each side incorporating a bit of red and a bit of blue. The inhabitants employ predicates corresponding to this diagonal plane, and they use those predicates – "bred" and "rue" – in making claims about various regions of their world. Sider's comment on the situation is worth quoting in full:

> It is almost irresistible to describe these people as making a mistake. But they're not making a mistake about where the red and blue regions are, since they make no claims about red or blue. And they make no mistakes when they apply their own concepts. The regions that they call "bred" are indeed bred, and the regions they call "rue" are indeed rue. The problem is that they've got the wrong concepts. They're carving the world up incorrectly. By failing to think in terms of the red/blue dividing plane, they are missing something. Although their beliefs are true, those beliefs do not match the world's structure. (Sider 2011: 1)

Sider adopts from Quine the term *ideology* to denote the conceptual toolkit from which a theory is constructed. The people Sider describes have a theory that is epistemically unsuccessful. But it is not epistemically unsuccessful in virtue of being false. It is epistemically unsuccessful in virtue of employing a metaphysically non-natural ideology.

It's important at this point to be clear about the options available to the proponent of reference magnetism. Someone like Weatherson – and indeed many advocates of reference magnetism – might say that if the inhabitants of this world get *close enough* to the red/blue divide with their applications of "bred" and "rue," then the plane dividing red from blue will exert the "magnetism" of the view's title, "attracting" the reference to the natural joint and making it the case that the speakers' terms pick out red and blue after all. Thus, when such a speaker points to a blue region of fluid and calls it "bred" – a term that on this view turns out to mean red – we can say that they are speaking falsely. We can thus describe the sense in which their theory is unsuccessful in the traditional way. The speakers make false claims about their world.[21]

Sider's remark makes it clear, however, that he thinks not all cases should be described in this way. As we saw in Section 14.3, the eligibility constraint is to be balanced against the other factors that play a role in reference determination. Whatever one's other views in metasemantics, it should be uncontroversial that speakers' usage of their terms is one crucial form of evidence about the meanings of those terms.[22] That evidence can be outweighed by other factors – evidence that certain patterns of usage should be explained pragmatically rather than semantically, for example, or a philosophically well-motivated application of some form of semantic externalism. But there is no reason to think that any of those factors need apply in Sider's example. If the inhabitants of Sider's world are systematic enough in their dispositions to apply "bred" and "rue," if they do not tend to retract their claims when the red/blue divide is demonstrated to them, if the more charitable interpretation does a better job of playing an explanatory role in our overall theory of the speakers' thought and talk, then the right thing to say really is the more charitable thing: that "bred" picks out the bred region of their world and "rue" picks out the rue region.

Sider's point in the quoted passage is that to go this route is not to concede that these strange speakers have gotten their world *right*. For a theory to *succeed* epistemically, it must both (a) be true and (b) employ an ideology that cuts close to the joints. A theory can therefore *fail* epistemically in two independent respects. It can be false, or it can employ an ideology that does not cut close to the joints. Nothing prevents the realist from describing these speakers' true theory as an epistemic failure.[23]

---

[21] Note that the motivation for this kind of application of reference magnetism really has nothing to do with the model-theoretic argument. If the MTA's perverse interpretations were still on the table, we could not even make sense of the notion of speakers' "getting close" to a natural joint, since to imagine that their usage has gotten them in the neighborhood of a joint is already to suppose that some interpretations are privileged over others. Whether this downstream application of the eligibility constraint can find independent motivation is, I think, an open question, given the considerations raised in this section. (See Sundell (2011) for discussion. In that essay, I rashly took myself to be objecting to reference magnetism in general. It would have been better to accept the view's application in addressing the MTA, to argue for the independence of the two types of applications, and to focus explicitly on cases where the view is used to motivate a choice among non-perverse interpretations, as it is in the whale/fish case.)

[22] See Plunkett and Sundell (2013: esp. 16–17 and section 6.1).

[23] Burgess and Plunkett (2013a, b) give the label *conceptual ethics* to normative and evaluative questions about thought and talk. Evaluating scientific concepts with respect to their degree of naturalness is a perfect example of an issue in conceptual ethics. But metaphysical naturalness is not

Think then what a realist who has internalized this observation might say about Putnam's brain in a vat. Given highly plausible assumptions about reference, there is no way around the fact that the brain's best theory of its world is largely true. But as to whether the brain's theory is an epistemic success, that question remains open. And it turns out that the brain's largely true theory fails in crucial respects. For example, the brain lives in a world made up of electrons and quarks and brains and vats. But it has no words for any of these things. It lacks the conceptual resources to describe the world at the fundamental level of electrons or quarks, or even at the less fundamental level of ordinary physical objects. And the theory that it does have – the theory made up largely of true claims about bits of software – is constructed out of categories like electron-in-the-software and quark-in-the-software and cat-in-the-software. Those categories, while not irredeemably gruesome – you and I might make reference to them in a theory of the brain's mental states – do not come close to describing the world at the fundamental level. And yet, in the case of electron- and quark-in-the-software, they represent the brain's very best attempt at doing just that. Concede as much as you like about the truth of the brain's theory. The brain *is* radically deceived.

Now this observation by itself is no response to the BVA. As we saw in Section 14.2, the conclusion of the BVA is not "Being a BIV wouldn't be so epistemically bad after all." The conclusion of the BVA is "I am not a brain in a vat." So pointing out one more way in which it would be bad, epistemically, to be a brain in a vat does nothing by itself to combat the argument. What it does accomplish, however, is to make salient the resources that the realist can draw on in mounting a response. The problem with Putnam's BIV scenario came down to this: the BIV lacks the representational resources to describe its own predicament. So what the realist needs is a skeptical scenario that, unlike the BIV scenario, could be represented by someone unfortunate enough to be in it.

So consider the following simple worry: "I could be in a situation preventing even my best theory from describing the world at the fundamental level." A few things to note about such a worry. First, the worry is *not* that I am not in fact sitting at a table, in an office, using my two hands to type a paper. In entertaining this worry I do not call into question the truth of any of those things. Second, please don't ask me to get more specific about the nature of

---

the only measure by which we might judge a concept. In other domains, we ask different things of our concepts, and even in science there may be a role for concepts that are held to standards other than naturalness.

the situation in question. What I've described is precisely the worry that I lack the representational resources necessary to characterize the world at a level fundamental enough to give such a description. Finally, and most importantly, observe that it is entirely possible for someone unfortunate enough to be in this predicament to nevertheless have the representational resources to entertain it.

To see this, consider again Putnam's BIV. Now, we know that *we're* not brains in a vat. If the above worry obtains for us, the relevant situation will have nothing to do with brains or with vats. Brains and vats are ordinary objects to which we successfully refer and about which we make largely true claims. If we are in such a predicament, it will have to do with objects and circumstances that are beyond our representational capacities, just as brains and vats are beyond the BIV's. But that point can be set aside. We can look to the BIV as an example of the relevant type of unfortunate soul and ask about the kinds of worry it can entertain. The brain lacks the representational resources to describe its world at a fundamental level. So: can it wonder whether that's true? What are the representational resources necessary to have this worry? Well, you would need to be able to refer to *theories*. And you would need to be able to think about *ideology*. You would need to have thoughts about *situations* and *descriptions*. And, crucially, you would need a notion of *relative fundamentality* and the ability to worry that even your best theory is doomed to employ an ideology *less* fundamental than a *maximally fundamental*, fully epistemically successful theory would employ.

There is, I submit, no good reason to think that the BIV lacks any of these things. There's not even *prima facie* reason to doubt that the brain could refer to *theories*, *situations*, and the like. The harder question is whether it can share with us a notion of *relative* and of *maximal fundamentality*. It can. After all, the brain can contrast its word "green" and its word "grue." It can categorize objects by whether they are "cats" or "cwats." It can represent and contrast the plus function and the quus function. That the brain's word "green" doesn't pick out the color green, but rather green-in-the-software is irrelevant. That the more natural property of being a cat-in-the-software is not, all things considered, terribly natural is irrelevant. You don't need to represent properties across the complete spectrum of naturalness in order to have a notion of *relative* naturalness. And a notion of relative naturalness is enough to conceive of something's being maximally natural. Compare: you don't need to have come in contact with absolute zero in order to formulate questions about its nature or existence. And you certainly don't need to have had contact with the full range of temperatures in order to categorize the weather around here in terms of relative coldness.[24] When we use the phrase "colder than," we pick out the same relation as speakers in a world where everything is closer to absolute zero than anything you or I will ever experience. Unlike truth and falsity, naturalness is a matter of degree. Being *somewhere* on the spectrum is enough to provide the conceptual resources necessary to wonder just how far you are from the end point.

This response is similar in some ways to responses in Smith (1984), Wright (1992), Forbes (1995), and Chalmers (2005). Those authors each advance some version of an "exemplification" response to the BVA, wherein we concede to Putnam that we are not in Putnam's BIV scenario, but maintain that we might nevertheless be in some more schematically characterized situation "relevantly similar" to Putnam's BIV. Davies (1997) argues forcefully that such responses cannot work. Responding to Smith's formulation, Davies considers the suggestion that the BIV stands in the "delusive relation" to its world, and that while we cannot worry that we are BIVs, we can worry that we stand in that same delusive relation to ours. For that to work, however, it must be the case that the BIV's phrase "delusive relation" refers to the same relation as our phrase "delusive relation." Otherwise, again, the resident of the "delusive scenario" would be incapable of representing its own predicament, and so, likewise, our phrase "delusive relation" would pick out a relation that we could not stand in to our own world.

Using Putnam's convention of capitalized "WORLD" to denote the objective world posited by the metaphysical realist, Davies notes that

> a BIV's ability to use the label 'the delusive relation' to refer to a specific real-WORLD relation between real brains and other things in THE WORLD seems no less problematic than its ability to use the word 'brain' to refer to real brains. And, to the extent that we are envisaging the possibility that our own epistemic situation is analogous to that of a BIV, we should not ascribe to ourselves the sorts of referential capacities that a BIV would lack. (Davies 1997: 53)

What does the BIV's phrase "delusive relation" refer to? The BIV gives that phrase meaning by pointing to instances in its own experience. But those instances – brains-in-the-software "in" vats-in-the-software, for example – exemplify a relation, not between real brains and an external world, but between various images or bits of software. That's nothing like the actual relation the BIV stands in to the world outside its vat. Similarly, our phrase

---

[24] Thanks to Josh Brown for helpful discussion on this point.

"delusive relation" – exemplified by pointing to brains in vats – does no better a job of representing a predicament we might actually be in than our phrase "brain in a vat."

Despite its similarities to other exemplification responses, however, the response I have described is not subject to this objection. The relation between a BIV-in-the-software and the "world" outside the vat-in-the-software is nothing like the relation between the BIV itself and the world outside its vat. That's why we and the BIV mean different things by "delusive relation." However, in drawing comparisons not between epistemic situations but rather between concepts, there is no parallel reason for worry. The relation between the BIV's less natural concepts and its more natural concepts is the same relation that stands between our own less natural concepts and our own more natural concepts. The concepts CATS-IN-THE-SOFTWARE and CWATS-IN-THE-SOFTWARE are both farther down the naturalness scale than the concepts CATS and CWATS. But the *difference* between the respective members of each pair is the same. It is a difference in fundamentality.[25] The phrase "stands in the delusive relation to" may indeed pick out different relations depending on whether it is a phrase in English or vat-English. But there is no analogous reason to think that we and the BIV do not mean the same thing by "is less natural than."

So, the brain in a vat is in a situation preventing it from carving its world at the joints. And the brain in a vat – while it cannot worry that it is a brain in a vat – *can* worry that it is in a situation preventing it from carving its world at the joints. And since naturalness of ideology is one component of epistemic success, this worry is very much a *skeptical* worry. The hypothesis that our concepts – though we may deploy them correctly – are massively more gruesome than we'd hoped or thought is a skeptical hypothesis every bit as nightmarish as the brain in a vat or the Evil Demon or the Young World or any of the others. Indeed, it's worse than any of them, because it describes a pervasive form of deception that sidesteps entirely the fine-grained analysis required to determine whether it is sufficiently *non-radical* to evade the BVA. The most radical of the traditional skeptical hypotheses can be dismissed as self-undermining. The less radical, while they cannot be dismissed – and thus raise interesting epistemological questions of their own – have little to teach us about the prospects for realism. The worry about the nature of our concepts suffers from neither of those problems.

[25] If the fact that both cats-in-the-software and cwats-in-the-software are bits of software makes you nervous, the comparison of "plus" and "quus" – which pick out the same pair of functions inside and outside of the vat – suffices to make this point.

So where exactly is the mistake in the BVA-powered anti-realist *modus tollens*? The mistake is in focusing exclusively on truth. For a certain type of non-realist, it might well be that truth is all there is to epistemic success. If you don't believe in joints, then you won't go in for the idea of evaluating concepts by how close they get to them. It thus might come to appear as if the realist must drive a wedge between ideal theory and *truth*, in particular, if she is to demonstrate that the fundamental nature of the world is independent of our thought and our inquiry. But what Putnam is in a position to demand, and what the realist needs, is not a wedge between ideal theory and truth. What the realist needs is a wedge between ideal theory and *epistemic success*. For the realist – supposing she adopts the strategy I advocate – a theory of the natural world aims to succeed along two dimensions, and thus it risks failure along both of those dimensions. Both of those dimensions are epistemic, and thus failure along either dimension counts as *error* in any relevant sense. Plausible constraints on meaning and reference may demonstrate that an ideal theory is guaranteed to be largely true.[26] Even so, an ideal theory could be hopelessly, radically mistaken. It could be constructed out of a hopelessly, radically non-fundamental ideology. In other words, the BVA may demonstrate that pervasive *falsehood* is incoherent, but that is simply too specific to refute metaphysical realism. What would refute metaphysical realism is the incoherence of pervasive *error*, and sadly enough, there is nothing self-undermining about that.

14.6 Conclusion

Perhaps the strategy I have described will still strike a realist as overly concessive. Although I claim to have cut off the anti-realist *modus tollens*, I've suggested that the realist concede both the soundness and the wide applicability of the BVA, and thus concede that ideal theory is in fact guaranteed to be largely true. But doesn't that just amount to a concession that truth itself is epistemic? Not at all. Consider the question of *why*, given the considerations raised above, an ideal theory is guaranteed to be largely true. Whether the claims we make are true depends on what it is we've claimed. What it is we've claimed depends on what our words mean. What our words mean may not depend *entirely* on us. Under the supposition that reference magnetism is true, for example, there are other factors involved. But what

---

[26] They do not guarantee even an ideal theory to be *entirely* true. The less radical, BVA-resistant skeptical scenarios are enough to show that.

our words mean depends *largely* on us. A semantic theory that paid no mind to speakers' usage, intuitions, dispositions, or surroundings would not be a plausible theory of language. Precisely how close a semantic theory must hew to speakers' usage or first-order intuitions is up for debate. But the fact that a semantic theory must display some sensitivity to our usage, dispositions, surroundings, causal relationships, and so on is not up for debate, as a fan of the BVA will be the first to admit.

That sensitivity by itself is enough to guarantee the truth of much of what we say. But note that to this point we've made no mention at all of the theory's being *ideal*. The considerations raised above demonstrate that *any* theory of ours, ideal or not, is guaranteed to be largely true, simply in virtue of comprising statements in our language. The lesson of the BVA is not that truth is epistemic. The lesson is simply this: *truth is semantic*. The fact that any theory of ours is guaranteed to be largely true is a function of the relationship between truth and meaning, and between meaning and use. By itself such a guarantee has none of the striking metaphysical consequences it might at first appear to. Of course, if truth were all there was to epistemic success, then the guaranteed truth of our theories would indeed be difficult to integrate with a metaphysical picture on which the nature of the world is fully independent of us and our inquiry. It would be hard to see how, given such a guarantee, we could get things seriously wrong. But truth is not all there is to epistemic success. We don't just have to figure out what to say – we also have to select the words and concepts with which we say it. And in our choices about which words and concepts we should be using in inquiry, there are no guarantees of success. We have to hope for the best and keep inquiring.

Bibliography

Achourioti, Theodora, Galinon, Henry, Martinez-Fernández, José, and Fujimoto, Kentaro (eds.) 2015. *Unifying the Philosophy of Truth*. Dordrecht: Springer.
Alston, William 1989a. *Epistemic Justification: Essays in the Theory of Knowledge*. Ithaca: Cornell University Press.
Alston, William 1989b. "Internalism and Externalism in Epistemology," in Alston (1989a), pp. 185–226.
Alston, William 1989c. "Epistemic Circularity," in Alston (1989a), pp. 338–55.
Alston, William 1996. *A Realist Conception of Truth*. Ithaca: Cornell University Press.
Anderson, D. 1993. "What is the Model-Theoretic Argument?" *Journal of Philosophy* 90: 311–22.
Austin, John 1962. *Sense and Sensibilia*. Oxford: Oxford University Press.
Bach, Kent 1985. "A Rationale for Reliabilism," *Monist* 68: 246–63.
Bach, Kent 1997. "Do Belief Reports report Beliefs?" *Pacific Philosophical Quarterly* 78: 215–41.
Ball, D. 2007. "Twin-Earth Externalism and Concept Possession," *Australasian Journal of Philosophy* 85: 457–72.
Bays, Timothy 2001. "On Putnam and His Models," *Journal of Philosophy* 98:. 331–50.
Bays, Timothy 2007. "More on Putnam's Models: A Reply to Bellotti," *Erkenntnis* 67: 119–35.
Bays, Timothy 2009. "Skolem's Paradox," in *Stanford Encyclopedia of Philosophy*, ed. E. N. Zalta. http://plato.stanford.edu/entries/paradox-skolem/.
Beal, J. C. (ed.) 2007. *Revenge of the Liar*. Oxford: Oxford University Press.
Becker, Kelly 2006. "Is Counterfactual Reliabilism Compatible with Higher-Level Knowledge?" *Dialectica* 60: 79–84.
Becker, Kelly 2012. "Methods and How to Individuate Them," in Becker and Black (2012), pp. 81–97.
Becker, Kelly and Black, Tim (eds.) 2012: *The Sensitivity Principle in Epistemology*. Cambridge: Cambridge University Press.
Benacerraf, Paul 1965. "What Numbers Could Not Be," *Philosophical Review* 74: 47–73.
Benacerraf, Paul 1973. "Mathematical Truth," *Journal of Philosophy* 70: 661–79.
Bergman, Michael and Coppenger, Brett (eds.) Forthcoming. *Traditional Epistemic Internalism*. Oxford: Oxford University Press.
Bernecker, Sven 1996. "Externalism and the Attitudinal Component of Self-Knowledge," *Noûs* 30: 262–75.

Bernecker, Sven 1998. "Self-Knowledge and Closure," in Ludlow and Martin (1998), pp. 333–49.
Bernecker, Sven 2000. "Knowing the World by Knowing One's Mind," *Synthese* 123: 1–34.
Bernecker, Sven 2004. "Believing that you Know and Knowing that you Believe," in Schantz (2004), pp. 369–76.
Bernecker, Sven 2014. "How to Understand the Extended Mind," *Philosophical Issues* 24(1): 1–23.
Bernecker, Sven and Pritchard, Duncan (eds.) 2011. *Routledge Companion to Epistemology*. New York: Routledge.
Boghossian, Paul 1989. "Content and Self-Knowledge," *Philosophical Topics* 17: 5–26.
Boghossian, Paul 1997. "What the Externalist Can Know *A Priori*," *Proceedings of the Aristotelian Society* 97: 161–75.
BonJour, Laurence 1985. *The Structure of Empirical Knowledge*. Cambridge, MA: Harvard University Press.
BonJour, Laurence 2010. *Epistemology: Classic Problems and Contemporary Responses*. Lanham, MD: Rowan & Littlefield.
Bourget, David and Chalmers, David 2014. "What Do Philosophers Believe?" *Philosophical Studies*, 170(3): 465–500.
Boyd, Richard 1991. "Constructivism, Realism, and Philosophical Method," in Earman (1991), pp. 131–98.
Brown, Jessica 1995. "The Incompatibility of Anti-Individualism and Privileged Access," *Analysis* 55: 149–56.
Brown, Jessica 2001. "Anti-Individualism and Agnosticism," *Analysis* 61: 213–24.
Brown, Jessica 2004. *Anti-Individualism and Knowledge*. Cambridge, MA: MIT Press.
Brueckner, Anthony 1986. "Brains in a Vat," *Journal of Philosophy* 83: 148–67.
Brueckner, Anthony 1992a. "If I Am a Brain in a Vat, Then I Am Not a Brain in a Vat," *Mind* 101: 123–8.
Brueckner, Anthony 1992b. "Semantic Answers to Skepticism," *Pacific Philosophical Quarterly* 73: 200–19.
Brueckner, Anthony 1995. "Scepticism and the Causal Theory of Reference," *Philosophical Quarterly* 45: 199–201.
Brueckner, Anthony 1996. "Modest Transcendental Arguments," *Philosophical Perspectives* 10: 265–80.
Brueckner, Anthony 1999. "Transcendental Arguments from Content Externalism," in Stern (1999), pp. 229–50.
Brueckner, Anthony 2003. "Trees, Computer Program Features, and Skeptical Hypotheses," in Luper (2003), pp. 217–26.
Brueckner, Anthony 2005. "Cartesian Skepticism, Content Externalism, and Self-Knowledge," *Veritas* 50: 53–64.
Brueckner, Anthony 2010. *Essays on Skepticism*. Oxford: Oxford University Press.
Brueckner, Anthony 2011. "Skepticism and Semantic Externalism," in Bernecker and Pritchard (2011), pp. 500–10.

Brueckner, Anthony 2012. "Skepticism and Content Externalism," in *Stanford Encyclopedia of Philosophy*, ed. E. N. Zalta: http://plato.stanford.edu/archives/spr2012/entries/skepticism-content-externalism/.

Brueckner, Anthony and Altschul, Jon 2010. "Terms of Envatment," in Anthony Brueckner, *Essays on Skepticism*, Oxford: Oxford University Press, pp. 174–6.

Buckwalter, Wesley and Sytsma, Justin (eds.) 2015. *The Blackwell Companion to Experimental Philosophy*. Oxford: Blackwell.

Burge, Tyler 1979: "Individualism and the Mental," *Midwest Studies in Philosophy* 4: 73–121.

Burge, Tyler 1982. "Other Bodies," in Woodfield (1982), pp. 98–120.

Burge, Tyler 1988. "Individualism and Self-Knowledge," *Journal of Philosophy* 85: 649–63.

Burge, Tyler 2007. *Foundations of Mind*. Oxford: Oxford University Press.

Burge, Tyler 2010. *Origins of Objectivity*. Oxford: Oxford University Press.

Burgess, Alexis and Plunkett, David 2013. "Conceptual Ethics I," *Philosophy Compass* 8: 1091–101.

Burgess, Alexis and Plunkett, David 2013. "Conceptual Ethics II," *Philosophy Compass* 8: 1102–10.

Burgess, John 2004. "Mathematics and Bleak House," *Philosophia Mathematica* 12: 18–36.

Burri, Alex (ed.) 1997. *Language and Thought*. New York: Walter de Gruyter.

Button, Tim 2011. "The Metamathematics of Putnam's Model-Theoretic Arguments," *Erkenntnis* 74: 321–49.

Button, Tim 2013. *The Limits of Realism*. Oxford: Oxford University Press.

Button, Tim and Walsh, Sean MS. "Ideas and Results in Model Theory: Reference, Realism, Structure and Categoricity." http://arxiv.org/abs/1501.00472.

Chalmers, David 2005. "The Matrix as Metaphysics," in Grau (2005), pp. 132–77.

Clark, Andy 2008. *Supersizing the Mind: Embodiment, Action and Cognitive Extension*. Oxford: Oxford University Press.

Clark, Andy 2009. "Spreading the Joy? Why the Machinery of Consciousness is (Probably) Still in the Head," *Mind* 118: 963–93.

Clark, Andy 2010. "Memento's Revenge: The Extended Mind," in Menary (2010), pp. 43–66.

Clark, Andy and Chalmers, David 1998. "The Extended Mind," *Analysis* 58: 7–19.

Clark, Peter and Hale, Bob (eds.) 1994. *Reading Putnam*. Cambridge, MA and Oxford: Blackwell.

Cohen, Stewart 1984: "Justification and Truth," *Philosophical Studies* 46: 279–95.

Conant, James (ed.) 1994. *Words and Life*. Cambridge, MA: Harvard University Press.

Cook, Roy 2013. *Paradoxes*. Malden, MA: Polity Press.

Cosmelli, D. and Thompson, E. 2010. "Embodiment or Envatment? Reflections on the Bodily Basis of Consciousness," in Stewart and Di Paolo (2010), pp. 361–85.

Cottingham, John, Stoothoff, Robert, and Murdoch, Dugald (eds.) 1984. *The Philosophical Writings of Descartes. Volume II*. Cambridge: Cambridge University Press.

Damasio, Antonio 1994. *Descartes's Error: Emotion, Reason, and the Human Brain.* New York: Avon Books.
David, Marian 1991. "Neither Mentioning 'Brains in a Vat' nor Mentioning Brains in a Vat Will Prove that We Are Not Brains in a Vat," *Philosophy and Phenomenological Research* 51: 891–6.
Davidson, Donald 1983: "A Coherence Theory of Truth and Knowledge," in Dieter Henrich (ed.), *Kant oder Hegel?* Stuttgart: Klett-Cotta, pp. 423–38.
Davidson, Donald 1984. *Inquiries into Truth and Interpretation.* Oxford: Oxford University Press.
Davidson, Donald 1990. "Afterthoughts, 1987," in Malichowski (1990), pp. 136–68.
Davidson, Donald 1996. "The Folly of Trying to Define Truth," *Journal of Philosophy* 93: 263–78.
Davidson, Donald 1999. "Reply to Barry Stroud," in Hahn (1999), pp. 162–6.
Davidson, Donald 2001. "Knowing One's Own Mind," in *Subjective, Intersubjective, Objective.* Oxford: Oxford University Press, pp. 15–38.
Davies, David 1995. "Putnam's Brain Teaser," *Canadian Journal of Philosophy* 25: 203–28.
Davies, David 1997. "Why One Shouldn't Make an Example of a Brain in a Vat," *Analysis* 57: 51–9.
Davies, Martin 1998. "Externalism, Architecturalism, and Epistemic Warrant," in MacDonald, Smith, and Wright (1998), pp. 321–61.
Dell'Utri, Massimo 1990. "Choosing Conceptions of Realism: The Case of the Brains in a Vat," *Mind* 99: 79–90.
DeRose, Keith 1999. "Introduction: Responding to Skepticism," in DeRose and Warfield (1999), pp. 1–26.
DeRose, Keith 2000. "How Can We Know That We're Not Brains in Vats?" *Southern Journal of Philosophy* 38: 121–48.
DeRose, Keith and Warfield, Ted (eds.) 1999. *Skepticism: A Contemporary Reader.* Oxford: Oxford University Press.
Descartes, René 1984. "Meditations on First Philosophy," in Cottingham, Stoothoff, and Murdoch (1984), pp. 1–62.
Devitt, Michael 1981. *Designation.* New York: Columbia University Press.
Devitt, Michael 1983. "Realism and the Renegade Putnam," *Noûs* 17: 291–301.
Devitt, Michael 1984. *Realism and Truth.* Princeton, NJ: Princeton University Press.
Devitt. Michael 1996. *Coming to Our Senses.* Cambridge: Cambridge University Press.
Devitt, Michael 1997. "On Determining Reference," in Burri (1997), pp. 112–21.
Devitt, Michael and Sterelny, Kim 1987. *Language and Reality.* Oxford: Blackwell.
Devitt, Michael and Sterelny, Kim 1999. *Language and Reality,* 2nd edn. Oxford: Blackwell.
Douglas, Heather 2009. *Science Policy and the Value-Free Ideal.* Pittsburgh, PA: Pittsburgh University Press.
Douven, Igor 1998. "Truly Empiricist Semantics," *Dialectica* 52: 127–51.
Douven, Igor 1999a. "Putnam's Model-Theoretic Argument Reconstructed," *Journal of Philosophy* 96: 479–90.

Douven, Igor 1999b. "A Note on Global Descriptivism and Putnam's Model-Theoretic Argument," *Australasian Journal of Philosophy* 77: 342–8.

Douven, Igor 2013. "The Epistemology of Conditionals," *Oxford Studies in Epistemology* 4: 3–33.

Douven, Igor 2015. "Experimental Approaches to Conditionals," in Buckwalter and Sytsma (2015).

Douven, Igor, Horsten, Leon, and Romeijn, Jan-Willem 2010. "Probabilist Antirealism," *Pacific Philosophical Quarterly* 91: 38–63.

Dretske, Fred 1970. "Epistemic Operators," *Journal of Philosophy* 67: 1007–23.

Dretske, Fred 1971. "Conclusive Reasons," *Australasian Journal of Philosophy* 49(1): 1–22.

Earman, John (ed.) 1991. *Inference, Explanation, and Other Frustrations*. Berkeley, CA: University of California Press.

Ebbs, Gary 1992a. "Realism and Rational Inquiry," *Philosophical Topics* 20: 1–34.

Ebbs, Gary 1992b. "Skepticism, Objectivity, and Brains in Vats," *Pacific Philosophical Quarterly* 73: 239–66.

Ebbs, Gary 1996. "Can We Take Our Words at Face Value?" *Philosophy and Phenomenological Research* 56: 499–530.

Einheuser, Iris 2010. "The Model-Theoretic Argument against Quantifying over Everything," *Dialectica* 64: 237–46.

Enderton, Herbert 2001 [1972]. *A Mathematical Introduction to Logic*. San Diego, CA: Hardcourt.

Engel, Mylan 1992. "Personal and Doxastic Justification in Epistemology," *Philosophical Studies* 67: 133–50.

Falvey, Kevin and Owens, John 1994. "Externalism, Self-Knowledge, and Skepticism," *Philosophical Review* 103: 107–37.

Feldman, Richard and Conee, Earl 2004. *Evidentialism: Essays in Epistemology*. Oxford: Clarendon Press.

Field, Hartry 1994a. "Deflationist Views of Meaning and Content," *Mind* 103: 249–85.

Field, Hartry 1994b. "Are Our Logical and Mathematical Concepts Highly Indeterminate?" *Midwest Studies in Philosophy* 19: 391–429.

Field, Hartry 2008. *Saving Truth from Paradox*. Oxford: Oxford University Press.

Fischer, Martin 2008. *Davidsons semantisches Programm und deflationäre Wahrheitskonzeptionen*. Frankfurt am Main: Ontos Verlag.

Fischer, Martin 2012. Review of Horsten (2011), *Bulletin of Symbolic Logic* 18: 403–5.

Fodor, Jerry 1987. *Psychosemantics*. Cambridge, MA: MIT Press.

Foley, Richard 1985: "What's Wrong with Reliabilism," *The Monist* 68: 188–201.

Forbes, Graeme 1995. "Realism and Skepticism: Brains in a Vat Revisited," *Journal of Philosophy* 92: 205–22.

Fost, Joshua 2013. "The Extended Self, Functional Constancy, and Personal Identity," *Linguistic and Philosophical Investigations* 12: 47–66.

Frigg, Roman and Hartmann, Stephan 2012 [2006]. "Models in Science," in *Stanford Encyclopedia of Philosophy*, ed. E. N. Zalta: http://plato.stanford.edu/entries/models-science/.

Gärdenfors, Peter 2000. *Conceptual Spaces*. Cambridge, MA: MIT Press.

Gärdenfors, Peter 2014. *The Geometry of Meaning*. Cambridge, MA: MIT Press.
Giere, Ronald 1988. *Explaining Science*. Chicago, IL: University of Chicago Press.
Glock, Hanjo (ed.) 2003. *Kant and Strawson*. Oxford: Oxford University Press.
Glymour, Clark 1982. "Conceptual Scheming, or Confessions of a Metaphysical Realist," *Synthese* 51: 169–80.
Goldberg, Sanford 2006a. "Brown on Self-Knowledge and Discriminability," *Pacific Philosophical Quarterly* 87: 301–14.
Goldberg, Sanford 2006b. "An Anti-Individualistic Semantics for 'Empty' Natural Kind Terms," *Grazer Philosophische Studien* 70: 55–76.
Goldman, Alvin 1976. "Discrimination and Perceptual Knowledge," *Journal of Philosophy* 73: 771–91.
Grau, Christopher (ed.) 2005. *Philosophers Explore the Matrix*. New York: Oxford University Press.
Grundmann, Thomas 2002. "Die Struktur des skeptischen Traumarguments," *Grazer Philosophische Studien* 64: 57–81.
Grundmann, Thomas 2003. *Der Wahrheit auf der Spur: Eine Verteidigung des erkenntnistheoretischen Externalismus*. Paderborn: mentis.
Grundmann, Thomas 2007. "The Nature of Rational Intuitions and a Fresh Look at the Explanationist Objection," *Grazer Philosophische Studien* 74: 69–87.
Grundmann, Thomas 2010. "Some Hope for Intuitions: A Reply to Weinberg," *Philosophical Psychology* 23: 481–509.
Grundmann, Thomas 2011. "Defeasibility Theory," in Bernecker and Pritchard (2011), pp. 156–66.
Grundmann, Thomas and Misselhorn, Catrin 2003. "Transcendental Arguments and Realism," in Glock (2003), pp. 205–18.
Haddock, Adrian and Macpherson, Fiona (eds.) 2008. *Disjunctivism: Perception, Action, Knowledge*. Oxford: Oxford University Press.
Hahn, Lewis (ed.) 1999. *The Philosophy of Donald Davidson*. Chicago, IL: Open Court.
Halbach, Voker 2011. *Axiomatic Theories of Truth*. Cambridge: Cambridge University Press.
Hale, Bob and Wright, Crispin (eds.) 1997a. *A Companion to the Philosophy of Language*. Oxford: Blackwell.
Hale, Bob and Wright, Crispin 1997b. "Putnam's Model-Theoretic Argument against Metaphysical Realism," in Hale and Wright (1997a), pp. 427–457.
Hanna, Robert 2011. "Minding the Body," *Philosophical Topics* 39: 15–40.
Hawking, Stephen 1993. *Black Holes and Baby Universes and Other Essays*. London: Bantam Books.
Heil, John and Mele, Al (eds.) 1993. *Mental Causation*. Oxford: Oxford University Press.
Heylighen, Frances 2012. "A Brain in a Vat Cannot Break Out: Why the Singularity Must Be Extended, Embedded and Embodied," *Journal of Consciousness Studies* 19: 126–42.
Hickey, Lance 2005. "The Brain in a Vat Argument," in *Internet Encyclopedia of Philosophy*, ed. J. Feiser and B. Dowden: http://www.iep.utm.edu/brainvat/.

Hofweber, Thomas 2007. "Validity, Paradox and the Ideal of Deductive Logic," in Beal (2007), pp. 145–58.
Hookway, Christopher 2010. "Pragmatism," in *Stanford Encyclopedia of Philosophy*, ed. E. N. Zalta: http://plato.stanford.edu/archives/spr2010/entries/pragmatism/.
Horgan, Terry and Kriegel, Uriah 2008. "Phenomenal Intentionality Meets the Extended Mind," *Monist* 91: 347–73.
Horsten, Leon 2011. *The Tarskian Turn*. Cambridge MA: MIT Press.
Horwich, Paul 1990. *Truth*. Oxford: Oxford University Press.
Jackson, Frank 1998. "Reference and Description Revisited," *Philosophical Perspectives* 12: 201–18.
Jackson, Frank 2003. "Narrow Content and Representation – Or Twin Earth Revisited," *Proceedings and Addresses of the American Philosophical Association* 77: 55–70.
Jackson, Frank and Pettit, Philip 1993. "Some Content is Narrow," in Heil and Mele (1993), 259–82.
Kallestrup, Jesper 2011a. "Actually-Rigidified Descriptivism Revisited," *Dialectica* 66: 5–21.
Kallestrup, Jesper 2011b. *Semantic Externalism*. London: Routledge.
Kant, Immanuel 1787 [1781]. *Critique of Pure Reason*, trans. N. Kemp Smith. London: Macmillan.
Keim-Campbell, Joseph, O'Rourke, Michael, and Silverstein, Harry (eds.) 2010. *Knowledge and Skepticism*. Topics in Contemporary Philosophy 5. Cambridge, MA: MIT Press.
Khlentzos, Drew 2011. "Challenges to Metaphysical Realism," in *Stanford Encyclopedia of Philosophy*, ed. E.N. Zalta: http://plato.stanford.edu/archives/spr2011/entries/realism-sem-challenge/.
Klenk, Virginia 1976. "Intended Models and the Löwenheim–Skolem Theorem," *Journal of Philosophical Logic* 5: 475–89.
Korman, Dan 2006. "What Externalists Should Say About Dry Earth," *Journal of Philosophy* 103: 503–20.
Kornblith, Hilary 2002. *Knowledge and Its Place in Nature*. Oxford: Oxford University Press.
Kripke, Saul 1980. *Naming and Necessity*. Cambridge, MA: Harvard University Press.
Kripke, Saul 2011. "Nozick on Knowledge," *Philosophical Troubles: Collected Papers I*. Oxford: Oxford University Press, pp. 162–224.
Kroon, Frederick 1987. "Causal Descriptivism," *Australasian Journal of Philosophy* 65: 1–17.
Langacker, Ronald 2008. *Cognitive Grammar*. Oxford: Oxford University Press.
Leeds, Stephen 2007. "Correspondence Truth and Scientific Realism," *Synthese* 159: 1–21.
LePore, Ernest and Ludwig, Kirk (eds.) 2004. *Blackwell Companion to Donald Davidson*. Oxford: Blackwell.
Lewis, David 1979. "Attitudes De Dicto and De Se," *Philosophical Review* 88: 513–43.
Lewis, David 1983a. *Philosophical Papers, Vol. I*. Oxford: Oxford University Press.

Lewis, David 1983b. "New Work for a Theory of Universals," *Australasian Journal of Philosophy* 61: 343–77.

Lewis, David 1984. "Putnam's Paradox," *Australasian Journal of Philosophy* 62: 221–36.

Loar, Brian 1996. "Social Content and Psychological Content," in Pessin and Goldberg (1996), pp. 180–91.

Ludlow, Peter 1995. "Externalism, Self-Knowledge, and the Prevalence of Slow-Switching," *Analysis* 55(1): 45–9.

Ludlow, Peter and Martin, Norah (eds.) 1998. *Externalism and Self-Knowledge*. Stanford, CA: CSLI Press.

Ludwig, Kirk 1992. "Brains in a Vat, Subjectivity, and the Causal Theory of Reference," *Journal of Philosophical Research* 17: 313–45.

Luper, Steven (ed.) 2003. *The Skeptics: Contemporary Essays*. Aldershot: Ashgate.

Luper-Foy, Steven (ed.) 1987a. *The Possibility of Knowledge: Nozick and His Critics*. Totowa, NJ: Rowman & Littlefield.

Luper-Foy, Steven 1987b. "The Possibility of Skepticism," in Luper-Foy (1987a), pp. 219–41.

Lyons, Jack 2013. "Should Reliabilists be Worried about Demon Worlds?" *Philosophy and Phenomenological Research* 86: 1–40.

MacDonald, Cynthia, Smith, Barry, and Wright, Crispin (eds.) 1998. *Knowing Our Own Minds*. Oxford: Oxford University Press.

Machuca, Diego, and Reed, Baron (eds.) Forthcoming. *Skepticism: From Antiquity to the Present*. London: Continuum.

Madden, Rory 2013. "Could a Brain in a Vat Self-Refer?" *European Journal of Philosophy* 21: 74–93.

Maddy, Penelope 2005. "Mathematical Existence," *The Bulletin of Symbolic Logic* 11: 351–76.

Maddy, Penelope 2007. *Second Philosophy: A Naturalistic Method*. Oxford: Oxford University Press.

Maddy, Penelope 2011a. *Defending the Axioms*. Oxford: Oxford University Press.

Maddy, Penelope 2011b. "Naturalism, Transcendentalism, and Therapy," in Smith and Sullivan (2011), pp. 120–56.

Malichowski, Alan (ed.) 1990. *Reading Rorty*. Oxford: Blackwell.

Margalit, Avishai (ed.) 1979. *Meaning and Use*. Dordrecht: Springer.

Marino, Patricia 2006. "What Should a Correspondence Theory Be and Do?" *Philosophical Studies* 127: 415–57.

Marino, Patricia 2010. "Modest Correspondence versus Representation-Friendly Deflationism," in Wright and Pederson (2010), pp. 218–31.

McGinn, Colin 2004. *Mindsight*. Cambridge, MA: Harvard University Press.

McKinsey, Michael 1991. "Anti-Individualism and Privileged Access," *Analysis* 51: 9–16.

McLaughlin, Brian. and Tye, Michael 1998a. "Externalism, Twin Earth, and Self-Knowledge," in MacDonald, Smith, and Wright (1998), pp. 285–320.

McLaughlin, Brian and Tye, Michael 1998b. "Is Content-Externalism Compatible with Privileged Access?" *Philosophical Review* 107: 349–80.

Menary, Richard 2007. *Cognitive Integration: Mind and Cognition Unbounded*. Basingstoke: Palgrave Macmillan.
Menary, Richard (ed.) 2010. *The Extended Mind*. Cambridge, MA: MIT Press.
Millikan, Ruth 1987. *Language, Thought, and Other Biological Categories*. Cambridge, MA: MIT Press.
Moore, A. W. 2001. *The Infinite*, 2nd edn. London: Routledge.
Moore, A. W. 2011. "Vats, Sets, and Tits," in Sullivan and Smith (2011), pp. 42–54.
Moore, G. E. 1939. "Proof of an External World," *Proceedings of the British Academy* 25.
Moore, G. E. 1959. "Certainty," in *Philosophical Papers*, London: Allen and Unwin, pp. 227–51.
Mostowski, Andrjez 1969. *Constructible Sets with Applications*. Amsterdam: North Holland.
Nagel, Thomas 1986. *The View from Nowhere*. Cambridge: Cambridge University Press.
Nozick, Robert 1981. *Philosophical Explanations*. Cambridge, MA: Harvard University Press.
Nuccetelli, Susanna (ed.) 2003. *New Essays on Semantic Externalism and Self-Knowledge*. Cambridge, MA: MIT Press.
Parent, Ted 2013. "Externalism and Self-Knowledge," in *Stanford Encyclopedia of Philosophy*, ed. E. N. Zalta: http://plato.stanford.edu/archives/sum2013/entries/self-knowledge-externalism/.
Pedersen, Nikolaj and Wright, Cory (eds.) 2013. *Truth and Pluralism: Current Debates*. Oxford: Oxford University Press.
Pessin, Andrew and Goldberg, Sanford (eds.) 1996. *The Twin Earth Chronicles*. New York: M. E. Sharpe.
Pfeifer, Niki and Douven, Igor 2014. "Formal Epistemology and the New Paradigm Psychology of Reasoning," *Review of Philosophy and Psychology* 5: 199–221.
Plantinga, Alvin 1982. "How to be an Anti-Realist," *Proceeding and Addresses of the APA* 56: 47–70.
Plato 1992. *The Republic*. Indianapolis: Hackett.
Plunkett, David and Sundell, Tim 2013. "Disagreement and the Semantics of Normative and Evaluative Terms," *Philosopher's Imprint* 13: 1–37.
Pritchard, Duncan 2002a. "McKinsey Paradoxes, Radical Scepticism, and the Transmission of Knowledge across Known Entailments," *Synthese* 130: 279–302.
Pritchard, Duncan 2002b. "Recent Work on Radical Skepticism," *American Philosophical Quarterly* 39: 215–57.
Pritchard, Duncan 2002c. "Resurrecting the Moorean Response to the Sceptic," *International Journal of Philosophical Studies* 10: 283–307.
Pritchard, Duncan 2005. *Epistemic Luck*. Oxford: Oxford University Press.
Pritchard, Duncan 2008. "McDowellian Neo-Mooreanism," in Haddock and Macpherson (2008), pp. 283–310.
Pritchard, Duncan 2012. *Epistemological Disjunctivism*. Oxford: Oxford University Press.
Pritchard, Duncan. 2013. "Davidson on Radical Skepticism," in LePore and Ludwig (2013), pp. 521–33.
Pritchard, Duncan and Ranalli, Chris 2013. "Rorty, Williams and Davidson: Skepticism and Metaepistemology," *Humanities* 2: 351–68.

Pritchard, Duncan and Ranalli, Chris Forthcoming a. "On Metaepistemological Scepticism," in Bergman and Coppenger (eds.).
Pritchard, Duncan and Ranalli, Chris Forthcoming b. "Scepticism and Disjunctivism," in Machuca and Reed (eds.).
Pryor, Jim 2000. "The Sceptic and the Dogmatist," *Nous* 34: 517–49.
Putnam, Hilary 1975. "The Meaning of 'Meaning,'" in Hilary Putnam (1979), *Mind, Language, and Reality: Philosophical Papers, Vol. 2*. Cambridge: Cambridge University Press, pp. 215–71.
Putnam, Hilary 1977. "Realism and Reason," *Proceedings and Addresses of the American Philosophical Association* 50: 483–98.
Putnam, Hilary 1978. *Meaning and the Moral Sciences*. London: Routledge.
Putnam, Hilary 1979. "Reference and Understanding," in Margalit (1979), pp. 199–271.
Putnam, Hilary 1980. "Models and Reality," *Journal of Symbolic Logic* 45: 464–82.
Putnam, Hilary 1981a. *Reason, Truth, and History*. Cambridge: Cambridge University Press.
Putnam, Hilary 1981b: "Brains in a Vat," in Putnam (1981a), pp. 1–21.
Putnam, Hilary 1981c. "Two Philosophical Perspectives," in Putnam (1981a), pp. 49–74.
Putnam, Hilary 1982. "Reply to Two Realists," *Journal of Philosophy* 79: 575–7.
Putnam, Hilary 1983a. *Realism and Reason: Philosophical Papers, Vol. 3*. Cambridge: Cambridge University Press.
Putnam, Hilary 1983b. "Introduction: An Overview of the Problem," in Putnam (1983a), pp. vii–xviii.
Putnam, Hilary 1983c. "Why There Isn't a Ready-Made World," in Putnam (1983a), pp. 205–28.
Putnam, Hilary 1990a. *Realism with a Human Face*. Cambridge, MA: Harvard University Press.
Putnam, Hilary 1990b. "Is Water Necessarily H_2O?" in Putnam (1990a), pp. 54–79.
Putnam, Hilary 1992. "Replies," *Philosophical Topics* 20: 347–408.
Putnam, Hilary 1993. "Realism Without Absolutes," *International Journal of Philosophical Studies* 1: 179–92.
Putnam, Hilary 1994a. "Comments and Replies," in Clark and Hale (1994), pp. 242–95.
Putnam, Hilary 1994b. "The Question of Realism," in Conant (1994), pp. 295–312.
Putnam, Hilary 1996. "Introduction," in Pessin and Goldberg (1996), pp. xv–xxii.
Putnam, Hilary 2000. "Das modelltheoretische Argument und die Suche nach dem Realismus des Common sense," in Willaschek (2000), pp. 125–42.
Quine, Willard 1951. "Two Dogmas of Empiricism," in Quine (1980), pp. 20–46.
Quine, Willard 1980. *From a Logical Point of View*, 2nd edn. Cambridge, MA: Harvard University Press.
Regier, Terry 1996. *The Human Semantic Potential*. Cambridge MA: MIT Press.
Russell, Bertrand 1921. *The Analysis of Mind*. London: George Allen & Unwin Ltd.
Salerno, Joe 2010. "Truth-tracking and the Problem of Reflective Knowledge," in Keim-Campbell, O'Rourke, and Silverstein (2010), pp. 73–84.
Salmon, Nathan 1979. "How Not to Derive Essentialism from the Theory of Reference," *Journal of Philosophy* 76: 703–25.

Sawyer, Sarah 1999. "An Externalist Account of Introspective Knowledge," *Pacific Philosophical Quarterly* 80: 358–78.
Sawyer, Sarah 2001. "The Epistemic Divide," *Southern Journal of Philosophy* 39: 385–401.
Schantz, Richard (ed.) 2004. *The Externalist Challenge*. Berlin: de Gruyter.
Shapiro, Larry 2004. *The Mind Incarnate*. Cambridge, MA: MIT Press.
Shapiro, Larry 2011. *Embodied Cognition*. London: Routledge.
Sher, Gila 1991. *The Bounds of Logic: A Generalized Viewpoint*. Cambridge, MA: MIT Press.
Sher, Gila 1999. "On the Possibility of a Substantive Theory of Truth," *Synthese* 117: 133–72.
Sher, Gila 2000. "The Logical Roots of Indeterminacy," in Sher and Tieszen (2000), pp. 100–23.
Sher, Gila 2004. "In Search of a Substantive Theory of Truth," *Journal of Philosophy* 101: 5–36.
Sher, Gila 2010. "Epistemic Friction: Reflections on Knowledge, Truth, and Logic," *Erkenntnis* 72: 151–76.
Sher, Gila 2013a. "The Foundational Problem of Logic," *The Bulletin of Symbolic Logic* 19: 145–98.
Sher, Gila 2013b. "Forms of Correspondence: The Intricate Route from Thought to Reality," in Pedersen and Wright (2013), pp. 157–79.
Sher, Gila 2015. "Truth as Composite Correspondence," in Achourioti *et al.* (2015), pp. 191–210.
Sher, Gila and Tieszen, Richard (eds.) 2000. *Between Logic and Intuition: Essays in Honor of Charles Parsons*. Cambridge: Cambridge University Press.
Sider, Theodore 2011. *Writing the Book of the World*. Oxford: Oxford University Press.
Skolem, Thoralf 1929. "Über einige Grundlagenfragen der Mathematik," in Skolem (1970), pp. 227–73.
Skolem, Thoralf 1941. "Sur la Porté du Théorème Löwenheim-Skolem," in Skolem (1970), pp. 455–82.
Skolem, Thoralf 1958. "Une Relativisation des Notions Mathématiques Fondamentales," in Skolem (1970), pp. 633–8.
Skolem, Thoralf (1970). *Selected Works in Logic*, ed. E. J. Fenstad. Oslo: Universitetsforlaget.
Smart, J. J. C. 1995. "A Form of Metaphysical Realism," *Philosophical Quarterly* 45: 301–15.
Smith, Joel and Sullivan, Peter (eds.) 2011. *Transcendental Philosophy and Naturalism*. Oxford: Oxford University Press.
Smith, Peter 1984. "Could We Be Brains in a Vat?" *Canadian Journal of Philosophy* 14: 115–23.
Soames, Scott 2005. *Reference and Description: The Case Against Two-Dimensionalism*. Princeton, NJ: Princeton University Press.
Sosa, Ernest 1993. "Putnam's Pragmatic Realism," *Journal of Philosophy* 90: 605–26.
Sosa, Ernest 1999. "How to Defeat Opposition to Moore," *Philosophical Perspectives* 13: 141–53.

Sosa, Ernest 2007a. *A Virtue Epistemology*. Oxford: Oxford University Press.
Sosa, Ernest 2007b. "Dreams and Philosophy," in Sosa (2007a), pp. 1–21.
Stalnaker, Robert 1989. "On What's in the Head," *Philosophical Perspectives* 3: 287–319.
Stalnaker, Robert 1997. "Reference and Necessity," in Hale and Wright (1997), pp. 534–54.
Steinitz, Yuval 1994. "Brains in a Vat: Different Perspectives," *Philosophical Quarterly* 44: 213–22.
Stern, Robert (ed.) 1999. *Transcendental Arguments: Problems and Prospects*. Oxford: Clarendon Press.
Stern, Robert 2007. "Transcendental Arguments: A Plea for Modesty," *Grazer Philosophische Studien* 74: 143–61.
Stewart, John, Gapenne, Oliver, and Di Paolo, Ezikiel (eds.) 2010. *Enaction: Towards a New Paradigm for Cognitive Science*. Cambridge, MA: MIT Press.
Stroud, Barry 1968. "Transcendental Arguments," *Journal of Philosophy* 65: 241–56.
Stroud, Barry 1984. *The Significance of Philosophical Skepticism*. New York: Oxford University Press.
Sundell, Timothy 2011. "Disagreement, Error, and an Alternative to Reference Magnetism," *Australasian Journal of Philosophy* 90: 743–59.
Tarski, Alfred 1936. "On the Concept of Logical Consequence," in Tarski (1983 [1956]), pp. 409–20.
Tarski, Alfred 1983 [1956]. *Logic, Semantics, Metamathematics*. Indianapolis: Hackett.
Thompson, Evan and Cosmelli, Diego 2011. "Brain in a Vat or Body in a World? Brainbound versus Enactive Views of Experience," *Philosophical Perspectives* 39: 163–80.
Thompson, Evan and Stapleton, Mog 2009. "Making Sense of Sense-Making: Reflections on Enactive and Extended Mind Theories," *Topoi* 28: 23–30.
Tichý, Pavel 1986. "Putnam on Brains in a Vat," *Philosophia* 16: 137–46.
Tollefsen, Deborah 2006. "From Extended Mind to Collective Mind," *Cognitive Systems Research* 7: 140–50.
Tomasello, Michael 2003. *Constructing a Language: A Usage-Based Theory of Language Acquisition*. Cambridge, MA: Harvard University Press.
Tomasello, Michael 2008. *Origins of Human Communication*. Cambridge, MA: MIT Press.
Tymoczko, Tom 1989a. "In Defense of Putnam's Brains," *Philosophical Studies* 57: 281–97.
Tymoczko, Tom 1989b. "Mathematical Skepticism: Are We Brains in a Countable Vat?" *Philosophica* 43: 31–47.
van Fraassen, Bas. 1989. *Laws and Symmetry*. Oxford: Oxford University Press.
van Fraassen, Bas 1992. "From Vicious Circle to Infinite Regress, and Back Again," *PSA: Proceedings of the Biennial Meeting of the Philosophy of Science Association* 2: 6–29.
Velleman, Daniel 1998. "Review of Levin's 'Putnam on reference and constructible sets'," *Mathematical Reviews* 98c: 1364.

Vogel, Jonathan 1987. "Tracking, Closure, and Inductive Knowledge," in Luper-Foy (1987a), pp. 197–215.
Vogel, Jonathan 2000. "Reliabilism Leveled," *Journal of Philosophy* 97: 602–23.
Vogel, Jonathan 2012. "The Enduring Trouble with Tracking," in Becker and Black (2012), pp. 122–51.
Warfield, Ted 1992. "Privileged Self-Knowledge and Externalism are Compatible," *Analysis*, 52: 232–7.
Warfield, Ted 1995. "Knowing the World and Knowing Our Own Minds," *Philosophy and Phenomenological Research* 55: 525–45.
Warfield, Ted 1998. "A Priori Knowledge of the World: Knowing the World by Knowing our Minds," *Philosophical Studies* 92: 127–47.
Warfield, Ted 1999. "A Priori Knowledge of the World: Knowing the World by Knowing Our Minds," in DeRose and Warfield (1999), pp. 76–92.
Warfield, Ted 2000. "How Can We Know That We're Not Brains in Vats?" *Southern Journal of Philosophy* 38: 121–48.
Weatherson, Brian 2003. "What Good Are Counterexamples?" *Philosophical Studies* 115: 1–31.
Weatherson, Brian 2008. "Deontology and Descartes' Demon," *Journal of Philosophy* 105: 540–69.
Weinberg, Jonathan, Nichols, Shaun, and Stich, Stephen 2001. "Normativity and Epistemic Intuitions," *Philosophical Topics* 29: 429–60.
Willaschek, Marcus (ed.) 2000. *Realismus*. Paderbon: Ferdinand Schöningh Verlag.
Williams, J. Robert 2007. "Eligibility and Inscrutability," *Philosophical Review* 116: 361–99.
Williamson, Timothy 2000. *Knowledge and its Limits*. Oxford: Oxford University Press.
Wilson, Mark 2000. "Inference and Correlational Truth," in André Chapuis and Anil Gupta (eds.) *Circularity, Definition, and Truth*. New Delhi: Indian Council of Philosophical Research / Munshiram Manoharlal.
Wilson, Mark 2006. *Wandering Significance: An Essay on Conceptual Behavior*. Oxford: Oxford University Press.
Wilson, N L 1959. "Substances without Substrata," *Review of Metaphysics* 12: 521–39.
Wittgenstein, Ludwig 1953. *Philosophical Investigations*. Oxford: Basil Blackwell.
Woodfield, Andrew (ed.) 1982. *Thought and Object*. Oxford: Clarendon Press.
Wright, Cory and Pedersen, Nikolaj (eds.) 2010. *New Waves in Philosophy: Truth*. New York: Palgrave Macmillan.
Wright, Crispin 1986. "Facts and Certainty," *Proceedings of the British Academy* 71: 429–72.
Wright, Crispin 1991. "Scepticism and Dreaming: Imploding the Demon," *Mind* 100: 87–116.
Wright, Crispin 1992. "On Putnam's Proof that We Are Not Brains in a Vat," *Proceedings of the Aristotelian Society* 92: 67–94.
Wright, Crispin 1994. "On Putnam's Proof that We are Not Brains in a Vat," in B. Hale and P. Clark, *Reading Putnam*. Oxford: Blackwell, pp. 216–41.

Wright, Crispin 2000. "Cogency and Question-Begging: Some Reflections on McKinsey's Paradox, and Putnam's Proof," *Philosophical Topics* 10: 140–63.
Wright, Crispin 2004. "Warrant for Nothing (and Foundations for Free)?" *Proceedings of the Aristotelian Society* 78: 167–212.
Zagzebski, Linda 2009. *On Epistemology*. Belmont, CA: Wadsworth.
Zalabardo, José 2009. "How I Know I'm Not a Brain in a Vat," *Royal Institute of Philosophy Supplement* 64: 65–88.

Index

Alston, William, 22, 99, 179, 180
analytic/synthetic distinction, 29, 33
anti-luck condition, 103
anti-realism, 85, 86, 131, 152, 177, 187, 191, 226, 228, 234, 249
Austin, John, 97, 198, 199

Bach, Kent, 44, 105
Ball, Derek, 72
Bays, Timothy, 141, 180
Becker, Kelly, 10, 111, 125
Benacerraf, Paul, 220
Berkeley, George, 173
Bernecker, Sven, 7, 49, 59, 68, 72, 77–79
Boghossian, Paul, 82, 116, 123, 124
Bonjour, Larry, 91, 97, 105
bootstrapping, 96, 99
Bourget, David, 184
Boyd, Richard, 184
brain-in-a-vat scenario spelled out, 1, 55–56, 134, 232
Brown, Jessica, 115, 118, 119–120
Brueckner, Tony, 5, 8, 28, 29, 36, 40, 45, 46, 49, 59, 83–84, 85, 87, 114, 115, 118, 135, 137, 163, 170, 172, 233
Burge, Tyler, 4, 40, 72, 111, 113, 115, 117, 118, 124
Burgess, Alexis, 244
Burgess, John, 192, 194
Button, Tim, 13, 133, 135, 136, 137, 138, 140, 141, 142, 144, 149, 151, 153, 208, 229, 231, 232, 233, 240, 242

causal constraints on reference, *see* reference, causal constraints on
Chalmers, David, 60–62, 184, 235, 247
Charity, Principle of, 181, 227, 239, 244
circularity, epistemic, 22
Clark, Andy, 60–62, 63, 69, 70
closure, 20, 75, 78, 79, 93, 95
Cohen, Stewart, 8, 91, 105

conceptual role semantics, 60
conditionals, 188
Conee, Earl, 92
content, mental, 26, 44, 48, 54, 59, 60, 68, 101, 114, 183, 237
   wide vs. narrow, *see* externalism, semantic *and* internalism, semantic
content externalism, *see* externalism, semantic
Cook, Roy, 170
correspondence theory (of truth), *See* truth, correspondence theory of
Cosmelli, Diego, 70, 71

Damasio, Antonio, 70
David, Marian, 46
Davies, Martin, 82, 247–248
Davidson, Donald, 66, 87, 108, 185, 186
defeater, 92–93, 101, 102
Dell'Utri, Massimo, 46
DeRose, Keith, 24, 49, 233
Descartes, René, 2, 8, 9, 24, 55, 71, 90, 91, 94, 97, 108, 134, 142, 173, 208; *see also* skepticism, cartesian
descriptivism, 41, 42, 47, 48, 51–52, 53, 181, 236
Devitt, Michael, 40, 132, 180, 184, 185, 186, 187, 188, 193–194
disquotation, 22, 23, 26, 28, 30, 44, 45, 48, 58, 79, 80, 81, 83–84, 136, 148, 194, 195–197, 233–234, 236
division of linguistic labor, 4, 39
Douglas, Heather, 204
Douven, Igor, 14, 179, 180, 181, 186, 188, 193
Dretske, Fred, 75, 111
Dry Earth, 124

Ebbs, Gary, 6, 138, 233
Einheuser, Iris, 143
embedded cognition, 54, 69
empirical adequacy, 174, 175, 176, 177, 178–179

Enderton, Herbert, 210
Engel, Pascal, 105
Evil Demon, 2, 8, 9, 19, 24, 55, 90–103, 156, 208, 223, 240, 241, 248
 new, 9, 91, 103–110
extended mind hypothesis, 7, 54, 59–62, 69–71, 72
externalism
 epistemic, 94, 102, 138–139; *see also* reliabilism
 semantic, 2, 4, 6, 7, 9, 10, 11, 20–22, 26, 30, 37, 48–52, 53, 54, 56, 57, 58, 59–62, 64–69, 76, 77, 82, 87, 88, 108, 111–112, 113, 114, 115–116, 117, 120, 123, 124, 125, 126–127, 138–139, 163–169, 244

fake barns, 120
fallibilism, 91, 118, 175, 177–179
Falvey, Kevin, 45, 59, 115, 122
Feldman, Rich, 92
Feynman, Richard, 203
Field, Hartry, 148, 180, 185, 194, 195, 196
Fischer, Martin, 185,
Fodor, Jerry, 237
Foley, Richard, 91
Folina, Janet, 13
Forbes, Graeme, 114, 247
Fost, Joshua, 66
Frigg, Roman, 212

Gardenfors, Peter, 187,
Giere, Ronald, 181
Glymour, Clark, 180
God's Eye point of view, *see* realism, metaphysical
Goldberg, Sanford, 72, 117–118
Goldman, Alvin, 111, 119, 120
Grundmann, Thomas, 9, 93, 94, 96, 97, 99, 102–103, 106, 108, 109, 110

Halbach, Voker, 185
Hale, Bob, 180
Hanna, Robert, 71
Hartman, Stephann, 212
Hawking, Stephen, 67
Heylighen, Frances, 70
Hickey, Lance, 163
Hobbes, Thomas, 97
Hofweber, Thomas, 162

holism, 216, 218–221, 219, 223, 224
 epistemic, 209, 219
 foundational, 219
 meaning, 219
Hookway, Christopher, 177
Horgan, Terry, 63, 64, 67
Horsten, Leon, 179, 185,
Horwich, Paul, 185

ideology, 243, 244, 246, 248
indeterminacy, 198, 228, 236
indispensability argument, 201
inference, 106–107
intentionality, 5, 188
internal realism, *see* realism, internal
internalism
 epistemic, 9, 92, 101, 102
 semantic, 37, 48, 50–52, 53, 163–169, 183
intuition, 106, 201, 250
Isomorphism Theorem, 15, 210, 212, 214

Jackson, Frank, 41, 44, 50, 51, 52
James, William, 198
JJ-principle, 96, 99
justification, epistemic, 8, 22, 23, 91–110, 157, 171, 172, 178, 197
 see also externalism, epistemic; internalism, epistemic; mentalism; reliabilism

Kallestrup, Jesper, 6, 52
Kant, Immanuel, 217, 224
Keller, Helen, 225
Khlentzos, Drew, 183
Klenk, Virginia, 144
Korman, Dan, 72
Kornblith, Hilary, 110
knowledge, conditions on, 112, 113, 115, 117, 138–139, 209, 219; *see also* self-knowledge; justification, epistemic
Kriegel, Uriah, 63, 64, 67
Kripke, Saul, 40, 111, 158, 164, 168
Kroon, Frederick, 41
Kuznets, Simon, 205

Langaker, Ronald, 187
Leeds, Stephen, 197
Lewis, David, 16, 41, 44, 52, 146, 150, 180, 193–194, 226, 227–228, 229, 230–231, 234–235, 243

liar paradox, 159, 161–162
Loar, Brian, 44,
Locke, John, 97
Löwenheim–Skolem Theorem, *see* Skolem–Löwenheim Theorem
Löwenheim–Skolem–Mostowksi Theorem, 140, 141; *see also* Skolem–Löwenheim Theorem
Ludlow, Peter, 120, 122
Ludwig, Kirk, 46
Luper-Foy, Steven, 125–126
Lyons, Jack, 106, 107

Madden, Rory, 49
Maddy, Penelope, 14, 192–193, 194–196, 197, 199, 200–204
Marino, Patricia, 14, 197, 200
McGinn, Colin, 100, 101,
McKinsey, Michael, 10, 82
McLaughlin, Brian, 72, 123, 125
meaning, 29, 34, 48–49, 51, 57, 59, 67, 82, 158, 160, 163, 164, 165, 167, 168, 185, 186, 187, 188, 198, 216, 227, 237
"Meaning of 'Meaning'", 3, 56, 57
Menary, Richard, 62
mentalism, 91–92, 97, 104
methods, 125–126, 201, 202, 203
Millikan, Ruth, 67, 236, 237
Misselhorn, Catrin, 108
model theory, 4, 12, 13, 15, 147, 152, 174, 190, 210–223, 226, 227–231
model-theoretic argument, *see* model theory
Moore, Adrian, 131, 140, 141, 142, 143, 147, 208
Moore, G. E., 94, 134–135, 137, 142–143, 151
Mostowski, Andrjez, 140

Nagel, Thomas, 8, 88–89, 172, 173
natural kinds, *see* natural kind term
natural kind term, 10, 37, 38, 42, 123, 124, 125, 164, 167, 168, 177, 230
naturalism, 14–15, 190, 209
  semantic, 14, 174–189
new Evil Demon, *see* Evil Demon, new
Nichols, Shaun, 109
Nozick, Robert, 75, 111, 112, 119, 125
Nuccetelli, Susana, 82

ontological relativism, 198,
Owens, Joseph, 45, 59, 115, 122

Parent, Ted, 115
permutation argument, 15, 149–152, 209, 214–217, 227
Pettit, Philip, 50
Pfeifer, Niki, 188
physicalism, 14, 174, 176–177, 184, 186–187, 188, 189
Plantinga, Alvin, 212
Plato, 166, 225
Platonism, 209, 220, 221, 225
Plunkett, David, 244,
Pragmatism, 177, 223
Pritchard, Duncan, 7, 75, 82, 87, 90, 92, 104
private language argument, 160
Pryor, Jim, 91
Putnam, Hilary, 1, 25, 27, 28, 29, 31, 33, 40, 42, 45, 51, 54, 57, 58, 67, 75, 80, 83, 113, 114, 115, 131, 132, 133, 135, 136, 139, 146, 147, 148, 149, 151, 153, 155, 157, 158, 160, 161, 164, 165, 167, 168, 169, 174, 177–178, 179, 183, 190, 191, 196, 198, 199, 202, 208, 217, 227, 228, 229, 233

Quine, Willard, 194, 198, 201, 219, 243

Ranalli, Chris, 7
realism
  external, *see* realism, metaphysical
  internal, 12, 14, 157, 167–169, 170, 171, 173, 177, 178–179
  metaphysical, 2, 4, 11, 12, 13, 14, 15, 16, 114, 131, 139, 151–152, 153, 155–173, 174, 183–189, 190–193, 194, 196, 208, 209–210, 216, 217–223, 228–230, 232–242, 249
  moderate, 147, 151–152, 217, 218
  pragmatic, *see* realism, internal
reference, 2, 3, 5, 14, 15, 16, 20, 26, 29, 34, 44, 47, 48, 49, 51, 57, 159–160, 163–169, 179, 180, 183, 186, 190, 191, 192, 212, 214, 228, 230, 232–242, 249
  causal constraints on, 3, 6, 21, 28, 34, 37–42, 47, 48, 49, 53, 76, 136, 163–169, 182, 236
  causal theory of, 6, 7, 14, 37, 40, 46, 48, 53, 136, 158, 160, 163–169, 171, 180, 184, 193–194, 195
  eligibility for, *see* reference magnetism

reference (cont.)
  magical theory of, 2, 13, 31, 136, 138, 158, 163, 217–223, 239
  reference determination, 40, 88, 165, 180, 182, 208, 210, 211, 215–217, 239, 244
  reference magnetism, 16, 226, 227–250
Regier, Terry, 187
relevant alternatives, 112, 117, 118, 119–122, 126, 127
reliabilism, 9, 90–110, 117, 118, 119
representation, 2, 37, 38–39, 67, 85, 100, 102, 165, 181, 197–198, 202
rigid designators, 167
Romeijn, Jan-Willem, 179
Russell, Bertrand, 241

safety, 43, 103
Salerno, Joe, 111
Salmon, Nathan, 57
Sawyer, Sarah, 117, 118, 121–122
self-knowledge, 9, 11, 35, 59, 68, 82, 111–113, 115–122, 123, 125, 233
self-verifying thought, 117, 118, 119, 121, 122, 123, 126, 127
semantics
  cognitive, 187
  indeterminacy of, *see* indeterminacy
  model-theoretic, 212, 213–214
  science of, 176–177, 179–183
sensitivity, 10, 43, 111–127
Sher, Gila, 15, 213, 218
Sider, Ted, 185, 227, 230, 231, 236, 243–244
skepticism, 7, 9, 11, 13, 16, 31, 37, 43, 55–56, 67, 75–77, 87–89, 93, 94, 132–154, 155–173, 177, 190, 229, 241–242
  cartesian, 21, 149, 155, 156–157, 208, 223–224, 226
  internal, 33, 132, 134–135, 136, 138, 139, 141, 142, 143, 146, 147, 151
  moorean response to, *see* Moore, G. E.
  metaphysical, 142
  permutation, 149
  semantic, 150
  semantic response to, 19–26, 37, 43–45, 53, 59, 64–69, 76–77, 88, 113–116, 131, 135–140, 149–152, 157–173, 190, 208
Skolem, Thoralf, 146, 213, 214

Skolem–Löwenheim Theorem, 12, 15, 131, 210, 211–212, 214, 218
Skolem's Paradox, 13, 131, 140–148
slow switching cases, 115, 118, 120, 122
Smart, J. J. C., 150
Smith, Peter, 247
Soames, Scott, 41
Sosa, Ernie, 111, 194
Stapleton, Meg, 71
Stienitz, Yuval, 46
Sterelny, Kim, 40
Stern, Robert, 49
Stitch, Stephen, 109
Strawson, Peter, 198
Stroud, Barry, 8, 59, 84–87, 94
Sundell, Tim, 16, 244,
Swampman, 66–67

Tarski, Alfred, 15, 209, 213, 214, 221, 222,
Thomson, Evan, 70, 71
Tichy, Pavel, 46
Tollefsen, Deborah, 60
Tomasello, Michael, 188
transcendental argument, 8, 82–87
truth, 2, 14, 89, 157, 163–169, 174, 175, 178, 180, 185, 186, 187, 190, 191, 192, 193–199, 226, 229–230, 240, 241, 250
  correspondence theory of, 11, 15, 16, 167, 174–179, 185, 186, 190, 191, 208, 209, 210, 216, 217–223
  deflationary theory of, 15, 185,
  disquotational theory of, *see* disquotation
  vs. epistemic success, 226, 242–249
Twin Earth, 50, 51, 53, 56, 57, 66, 72, 112, 119, 124, 233, 236
Tye, Michael, 72, 123, 125
Tymoczko, Thomas, 131, 135, 137, 139, 140, 143, 145, 147, 153, 208, 233,

values, 15, 191, 203, 204–205
Van Fraasen, Bas, 181–182
verificationism, *see* anti-realism
Vogel, Jonathan, 111

Walsh, Sean, 140, 144, 149
Warfield, Ted, 24, 44, 46, 116, 233
Weatherson, Brian, 105, 237, 238–239

Weinberg, Jonathan, 109
Williams, Robert, 227, 230, 231
Williamson, Tim, 92, 102–103, 138
Wilson, Mark, 192, 195,
Wilson, N. L., 181
Wittgenstein, Ludwig, 155, 158, 198, 220

Wright, Crispin, 8, 28, 29, 30, 44, 45, 46, 58, 79–82, 93, 94, 96, 97, 135, 136, 138, 172, 180, 233, 240, 247

Zagzebski, Linda, 88
Zalabardo, Jose, 138, 139

For EU product safety concerns, contact us at Calle de José Abascal, 56–1°, 28003 Madrid, Spain or eugpsr@cambridge.org.

www.ingramcontent.com/pod-product-compliance
Ingram Content Group UK Ltd.
Pitfield, Milton Keynes, MK11 3LW, UK
UKHW030759060825
461502UK00007B/66